Your
Chinese
Horoscope
2014

Neil Somerville

What the Year of the Horse holds in store for you

Your
Chinese
Horoscope
2014

HARPER
element

HarperElement
An Imprint of HarperCollins*Publishers*
77–85 Fulham Palace Road,
Hammersmith, London W6 8JB

www.harpercollins.co.uk

and *HarperElement* are trademarks of
HarperCollins*Publishers* Ltd

Published by HarperElement 2013

1 3 5 7 9 10 8 6 4 2

A catalogue record of this book is
available from the British Library

ISBN 978-0-00-747955-9

Printed in the USA

31088100819976

MIX
Paper from
responsible sources
FSC C007454

FSC™ is a non-profit international organisation established to promote
the responsible management of the world's forests. Products carrying the
FSC label are independently certified to assure consumers that they come
from forests that are managed to meet the social, economic and
ecological needs of present and future generations,
and other controlled sources.

Find out more about HarperCollins and the environment at
www.harpercollins.co.uk/green

About the Author

Neil Somerville is one of the leading writers in the West on Chinese horoscopes. He has been interested in Eastern forms of divination for many years and believes that much can be learned from the ancient wisdom of the East. His annual book on Chinese horoscopes has built up an international following and he is also the author of *What's Your Chinese Love Sign?* (Thorsons, 2000; HarperElement, 2013), *Chinese Success Signs* (Thorsons, 2001) and *The Answers* (Element, 2004).

Neil Somerville was born in the year of the Water Snake. His wife was born under the sign of the Monkey, his son is an Ox and daughter a Horse.

TO ROS, RICHARD AND EMILY

As we march through life,
we each have our hopes, our ambitions and our dreams.

Sometimes fate and circumstance will assist us,
sometimes we will struggle and despair,
but march we must.

For it is those who keep going,
and who keep their aspirations alive,
who stand the greatest chance of securing what they want.

March determinedly,
and your determination will, in some way, be rewarded.

Neil Somerville

Contents

Acknowledgements

In writing *Your Chinese Horoscope 2014* I am grateful for the assistance and invaluable support that those around me have given.

I would also like to acknowledge Theodora Lau's *The Handbook of Chinese Horoscopes* (Harper & Row, 1979; Arrow, 1981), which was particularly useful to me in my research.

In addition to Ms Lau's work, I commend the following books to those who wish to find out more about Chinese horoscopes: Kristyna Arcarti, *Chinese Horoscopes for Beginners* (Headway, 1995); Catherine Aubier, *Chinese Zodiac Signs* (Arrow, 1984), series of 12 books; E. A. Crawford and Teresa Kennedy, *Chinese Elemental Astrology* (Piatkus Books, 1992); Paula Delsol, *Chinese Horoscopes* (Pan, 1973); Barry Fantoni, *Barry Fantoni's Chinese Horoscopes* (Warner, 1994); Bridget Giles and the Diagram Group, *Chinese Astrology* (HarperCollins*Publishers*, 1996); Kwok Man-Ho, *Complete Chinese Horoscopes* (Sunburst Books, 1995); Lori Reid, *The Complete Book of Chinese Horoscopes* (Element Books, 1997); Paul Rigby and Harvey Bean, *Chinese Astrologics* (Publications Division, South China Morning Post Ltd, 1981); Ruth Q. Sun, *The Asian Animal Zodiac* (Charles E. Tuttle Company, Inc., 1996); Derek Walters, *Ming Shu* (Pagoda Books, 1987) and *The Chinese Astrology Workbook* (The Aquarian Press, 1988); Suzanne White, *The New Astrology* (Pan, 1987), *The New Chinese Astrology* (Pan, 1994) and *Chinese Astrology Plain and Simple* (Eden Grove Editions, 1998).

Introduction

The origins of Chinese horoscopes have been lost in the mists of time. It is known, however, that oriental astrologers practised their art many thousands of years ago and even today Chinese astrology continues to fascinate and intrigue.

In Chinese astrology there are 12 signs named after 12 different animals. No one quite knows how the signs acquired their names, but there is one legend that offers an explanation. According to this legend, one Chinese New Year the Buddha invited all the animals in his kingdom to come before him. Unfortunately, for reasons best known to the animals, only 12 turned up. The first to arrive was the Rat, followed by the Ox, Tiger, Rabbit, Dragon, Snake, Horse, Goat, Monkey, Rooster, Dog and finally Pig. In gratitude, the Buddha decided to name a year after each of the animals and that those born during that year would inherit some of the personality of that animal. Therefore those born in the year of the Ox would be hardworking, resolute and stubborn, just like the Ox, while those born in the year of the Dog would be loyal and faithful, just like the Dog. While it is not possible that everyone born in a particular year can have all the characteristics of the sign, it is incredible what similarities do occur, and this is partly where the fascination of Chinese horoscopes lies.

In addition to the 12 signs of the Chinese zodiac there are five elements and these have a strengthening or moderating influence upon the signs. Details about the effects of the elements are given in each of the chapters on the signs.

To find out which sign you were born under, refer to the tables on the following pages. As the Chinese year is based on the lunar year and does not start until late January or early February, it is particularly important for anyone born in those two months to check carefully the dates of the Chinese year in which they were born.

Also included, in the appendix, are two charts showing the compatibility between the signs for personal and business relationships and details about the signs ruling the different hours of the day. From this it is possible to locate your ascendant and, as in Western astrology, this has a significant influence on your personality.

In writing this book I have taken the unusual step of combining the intriguing nature of Chinese horoscopes with the Western desire to know what the future holds, and have based my interpretations upon various factors relating to each of the signs. Over the years in which *Your Chinese Horoscope* has been published I have been pleased that so many have found the sections on the forthcoming year of interest and hope that the horoscope has been constructive and useful. Remember, though, that at all times you are master of your own destiny.

I sincerely hope that *Your Chinese Horoscope 2014* will prove interesting and helpful for the year ahead.

The Chinese Years

Ox	6 February	1913	to	25 January	1914
Tiger	26 January	1914	to	13 February	1915
Rabbit	14 February	1915	to	2 February	1916
Dragon	3 February	1916	to	22 January	1917
Snake	23 January	1917	to	10 February	1918
Horse	11 February	1918	to	31 January	1919
Goat	1 February	1919	to	19 February	1920
Monkey	20 February	1920	to	7 February	1921
Rooster	8 February	1921	to	27 January	1922
Dog	28 January	1922	to	15 February	1923
Pig	16 February	1923	to	4 February	1924
Rat	5 February	1924	to	23 January	1925
Ox	24 January	1925	to	12 February	1926
Tiger	13 February	1926	to	1 February	1927
Rabbit	2 February	1927	to	22 January	1928
Dragon	23 January	1928	to	9 February	1929
Snake	10 February	1929	to	29 January	1930
Horse	30 January	1930	to	16 February	1931
Goat	17 February	1931	to	5 February	1932
Monkey	6 February	1932	to	25 January	1933
Rooster	26 January	1933	to	13 February	1934
Dog	14 February	1934	to	3 February	1935
Pig	4 February	1935	to	23 January	1936
Rat	24 January	1936	to	10 February	1937
Ox	11 February	1937	to	30 January	1938
Tiger	31 January	1938	to	18 February	1939
Rabbit	19 February	1939	to	7 February	1940
Dragon	8 February	1940	to	26 January	1941

Snake	27 January	1941	to	14 February	1942
Horse	15 February	1942	to	4 February	1943
Goat	5 February	1943	to	24 January	1944
Monkey	25 January	1944	to	12 February	1945
Rooster	13 February	1945	to	1 February	1946
Dog	2 February	1946	to	21 January	1947
Pig	22 January	1947	to	9 February	1948
Rat	10 February	1948	to	28 January	1949
Ox	29 January	1949	to	16 February	1950
Tiger	17 February	1950	to	5 February	1951
Rabbit	6 February	1951	to	26 January	1952
Dragon	27 January	1952	to	13 February	1953
Snake	14 February	1953	to	2 February	1954
Horse	3 February	1954	to	23 January	1955
Goat	24 January	1955	to	11 February	1956
Monkey	12 February	1956	to	30 January	1957
Rooster	31 January	1957	to	17 February	1958
Dog	18 February	1958	to	7 February	1959
Pig	8 February	1959	to	27 January	1960
Rat	28 January	1960	to	14 February	1961
Ox	15 February	1961	to	4 February	1962
Tiger	5 February	1962	to	24 January	1963
Rabbit	25 January	1963	to	12 February	1964
Dragon	13 February	1964	to	1 February	1965
Snake	2 February	1965	to	20 January	1966
Horse	21 January	1966	to	8 February	1967
Goat	9 February	1967	to	29 January	1968
Monkey	30 January	1968	to	16 February	1969
Rooster	17 February	1969	to	5 February	1970
Dog	6 February	1970	to	26 January	1971
Pig	27 January	1971	to	14 February	1972
Rat	15 February	1972	to	2 February	1973
Ox	3 February	1973	to	22 January	1974
Tiger	23 January	1974	to	10 February	1975
Rabbit	11 February	1975	to	30 January	1976

Dragon	31 January	1976	to	17 February	1977
Snake	18 February	1977	to	6 February	1978
Horse	7 February	1978	to	27 January	1979
Goat	28 January	1979	to	15 February	1980
Monkey	16 February	1980	to	4 February	1981
Rooster	5 February	1981	to	24 January	1982
Dog	25 January	1982	to	12 February	1983
Pig	13 February	1983	to	1 February	1984
Rat	2 February	1984	to	19 February	1985
Ox	20 February	1985	to	8 February	1986
Tiger	9 February	1986	to	28 January	1987
Rabbit	29 January	1987	to	16 February	1988
Dragon	17 February	1988	to	5 February	1989
Snake	6 February	1989	to	26 January	1990
Horse	27 January	1990	to	14 February	1991
Goat	15 February	1991	to	3 February	1992
Monkey	4 February	1992	to	22 January	1993
Rooster	23 January	1993	to	9 February	1994
Dog	10 February	1994	to	30 January	1995
Pig	31 January	1995	to	18 February	1996
Rat	19 February	1996	to	6 February	1997
Ox	7 February	1997	to	27 January	1998
Tiger	28 January	1998	to	15 February	1999
Rabbit	16 February	1999	to	4 February	2000
Dragon	5 February	2000	to	23 January	2001
Snake	24 January	2001	to	11 February	2002
Horse	12 February	2002	to	31 January	2003
Goat	1 February	2003	to	21 January	2004
Monkey	22 January	2004	to	8 February	2005
Rooster	9 February	2005	to	28 January	2006
Dog	29 January	2006	to	17 February	2007
Pig	18 February	2007	to	6 February	2008
Rat	7 February	2008	to	25 January	2009
Ox	26 January	2009	to	13 February	2010
Tiger	14 February	2010	to	2 February	2011

Rabbit	3 February	2011	to	22 January	2012
Dragon	23 January	2012	to	9 February	2013
Snake	10 February	2013	to	30 January	2014
Horse	31 January	2014	to	18 February	2015

Note

The names of the signs in the Chinese zodiac occasionally differ, although the characteristics of the signs remain the same. In some books the Ox is referred to as the Buffalo or Bull, the Rabbit as the Hare or Cat, the Goat as the Sheep and the Pig as the Boar.

For the sake of convenience, the male gender is used throughout this book. Unless otherwise stated, the characteristics of the signs apply to both sexes.

Welcome to the
Year of the Horse

Whether pulling a cart, working on a farm, being ridden for pleasure or sport or displaying the graceful skills of dressage, the horse is a good worker. And has style. Many of these qualities will be evident during the Year of the Horse.

The Horse enjoys activity and a prominent feature of the Horse year is that it favours action. Whether on the world stage or in the arts, media, technology, medicine or other spheres, there will be significant developments this year and the emphasis will be on innovation and pushing the boundaries.

Internationally, too, the focus will be on moving situations forward and some landmark agreements will be forged which will bring hope to troubled regions. Previous Horse years have seen the formal reunification of East and West Germany following the collapse of the Berlin Wall, the release of Nelson Mandela, which led to dramatic change in South Africa, and, in 1918, the ending of the First World War. In 2014 again, important conflict resolutions can lift the shadow of oppression from certain regions. Middle Eastern and African countries will, in particular, continue to experience great change during the year.

Although the accent will be on progress, there will, though, inevitably be flashpoints and sudden acts of aggression, as in the Horse year of 1990, when Iraqi troops invaded Kuwait, but generally the troubles will be of short duration and the reaction from international communities swift.

Another area which will continue to exercise the minds of those in authority will be the world economy. After the austerity and fiscal measures imposed by some governments, 2014 will bring improvement. The green shoots of recovery already seen in some economies will grow stronger during the year, with many governments taking greater measures to stimulate growth and reduce unemployment. With the Horse year favouring initiative, several dynamic approaches will be put forward. Quite a few sectors will see steady growth, but industries which are likely to fare especially well are transport, technology, fashion and those connected with the use and manufacture of renewable energy. Also, while economic considerations will be paramount, attention will again focus on environmental concerns, particularly on reducing pollution in heavily industrialized areas.

This Horse year will also see lively debate in quite a few countries as governmental and constitutional issues are discussed and new ideas put forward. In the UK in particular, great interest will be focused on the Scottish referendum and the constitutional implications. Other countries, too, will see significant issues debated which could affect national identity and ways of governance.

Horse years have energy and passion and focus the mind. They have their lighter sides too, including great successes on stage and screen and in the music industry. This year again some influential new figures could emerge on the music scene and new television series and film releases attract great followings. *Star Trek* and the American reality series *The Osbournes* both started in Horse years, and *Spider-Man* and *The Lord of the Rings: The Two Towers* were especially successful in 2002. Interestingly, it was a Horse year, 1894, when Louis Lumière invented the cinematograph, and another Horse year when Sony made the first Walkman, a device which was to transform the listening habits of so many. The entertainment industry is set to have another pioneering year in 2014.

The fashion industry too will enjoy a revival, with new trends and styles quickly coming to prominence. A more elegant look could well be a feature.

The energy of horses will also be seen in sport. The 2014 Winter Olympics and then the World Cup in Brazil will be colourful and exciting spectacles and there will be historic moments as new sporting milestones are achieved. It was 60 years ago, in a previous Horse year, that Roger Bannister broke the four-minute mile, a record that made sporting history.

As with all years, there will be bleaker moments too. Natural forces and the vagaries of world weather patterns will bring tragedy. There will also be concern about world resources, including the difficulties of meeting ever-growing demands and compensating for crop failures. But while there will inevitably be some problems, the emphasis will be on moving forward and the year will favour growth.

For the individual, too, this is a year for being willing to take that one step further and work towards goals. With willingness and purpose much can become possible this year. While some Chinese signs will fare better than others, the Horse year is essentially a time for action and I sincerely hope that your actions will bring you the results you desire and that you will fare well.

Good luck. Be purposeful and I hope this will be a good year for you.

Your
Chinese
Horoscope
2014

5 February 1924 to 23 January 1925 — *Wood Rat*

24 January 1936 to 10 February 1937 — *Fire Rat*

10 February 1948 to 28 January 1949 — *Earth Rat*

28 January 1960 to 14 February 1961 — *Metal Rat*

15 February 1972 to 2 February 1973 — *Water Rat*

2 February 1984 to 19 February 1985 — *Wood Rat*

19 February 1996 to 6 February 1997 — *Fire Rat*

7 February 2008 to 25 January 2009 — *Earth Rat*

The Rat

The Personality of the Rat

To see,
and to see what others do not see.
That is true vision.

The Rat is born under the sign of charm. He is intelligent, popular and loves attending parties and large social gatherings. He is able to establish friendships with remarkable ease and people generally feel relaxed in his company. He is a very social creature and is genuinely interested in the welfare and activities of others. He has a good understanding of human nature and his advice and opinions are often sought.

The Rat is a hard and diligent worker. He is also very imaginative and is never short of ideas. However, he does sometimes lack the confidence to promote his ideas and this can often prevent him from securing the recognition he deserves.

The Rat is very observant and many Rats have made excellent writers and journalists. The Rat also excels at personnel and PR work and any job that brings him into contact with people and the media. His skills are particularly appreciated in times of crisis, for the Rat has an incredibly strong sense of self-preservation. When it comes to finding a way out of an awkward situation, he is certain to be the one who comes up with a solution.

The Rat loves to be where there is a lot of action, but should he ever find himself in a very bureaucratic or restrictive environment he can become a stickler for discipline and routine. He is also something of an opportunist and is constantly on the lookout for ways in which he can improve his wealth and lifestyle. He rarely lets an opportunity go by and can become involved in so many plans and schemes that he sometimes squanders his energies and achieves very little as a result. He is also rather gullible and can be taken in by those less scrupulous than himself.

Another characteristic of the Rat is his attitude towards money. He is very thrifty and to some he may appear a little mean. The reason for this is purely that he likes to keep his money within his family. He can be most generous to his partner, his children and close friends and relatives. He can also be generous to himself, for he often finds it impossible to deprive himself of any luxury or object he fancies. He is very acquisitive and can be a notorious hoarder. He also hates waste and is rarely prepared to throw anything away. He can be rather greedy and will rarely refuse an invitation to a free meal or a complimentary ticket to a lavish function.

The Rat is a good conversationalist, although he can occasionally be a little indiscreet. He can be highly critical of others – for an honest and unbiased opinion, the Rat is a superb critic – and will sometimes use confidential information to his own advantage. However, as he has such a bright and irresistible nature, most people are prepared to forgive him his slight indiscretions.

Throughout his long and eventful life the Rat will make many friends and will find that he is especially well suited to those born under his own sign and those of the Ox, Dragon and Monkey. He can also get on well with those born under the signs of the Tiger, Snake, Rooster, Dog and Pig, but the rather sensitive Rabbit and Goat will find him a little too critical and blunt for their liking. The Horse and Rat will also find it difficult to get on with each other – the Rat craves security and will find the Horse's changeable moods and rather independent nature a little unsettling.

The Rat is very family orientated and will do anything to please his nearest and dearest. He is exceptionally loyal to his parents and can himself be a very caring and loving parent. He will take an interest in all his children's activities and see that they want for nothing. He usually has a large family.

The female Rat has a kindly, outgoing nature and involves herself in a multitude of different activities. She has a wide circle of friends, enjoys entertaining and is an attentive hostess. She is also conscientious about the upkeep of her home and has good taste in home furnishings. She is most supportive to the other members of her family and, due to her resourceful, friendly and persevering nature, can do well in practically any career she chooses.

Although the Rat is essentially outgoing, he is also a very private individual. He tends to keep his feelings to himself and while he is not averse to learning what other people are doing, he resents anyone prying too closely into his own affairs. He also does not like solitude and if he is alone for any length of time he can easily get depressed.

The Rat is undoubtedly very talented, but he does sometimes fail to capitalize on his many abilities. He has a tendency to become involved in too many schemes and chase after too many opportunities at once. If he can slow down and concentrate on one thing at a time, he can become very successful. If not, success and wealth can elude him. But, with his tremendous ability to charm, he will rarely, if ever, be without friends.

The Five Different Types of Rat

In addition to the 12 signs of the Chinese zodiac there are five elements and these have a strengthening or moderating influence on the signs. The effects of the five elements on the Rat are described below, together with the years in which they were exercising their influence. Therefore Rats born in 1960 are Metal Rats, Rats born in 1972 are Water Rats, and so on.

Metal Rat: 1960

This Rat has excellent taste and certainly knows how to appreciate the finer things in life. His home is comfortable and nicely decorated and he likes to entertain and mix in fashionable circles. He has considerable financial acumen and invests his money well. On the surface he appears cheerful and confident, but deep down he can be troubled by worries that are quite often of his own making. He is exceptionally loyal to his family and friends.

Water Rat: 1972

The Water Rat is intelligent and very astute. He is a deep thinker and can express his thoughts clearly and persuasively. He is always eager to learn and is talented in many different areas. He is usually very popular, but his fear of loneliness can sometimes lead him into mixing with the wrong sort of company. He is a particularly skilful writer, but can get sidetracked very easily and should try to concentrate on just one thing at a time.

Wood Rat: 1924, 1984

The Wood Rat has a friendly, outgoing personality and is popular with his colleagues and friends. He has a quick, agile brain and likes to turn his hand to anything he thinks may be useful. His one fear is insecurity, but given his intelligence and capabilities, this fear is usually unfounded. He has a good sense of humour, enjoys travel and, due to his highly imaginative nature, can be a gifted writer or artist.

Fire Rat: 1936, 1996

The Fire Rat is rarely still and seems to have a never-ending supply of energy and enthusiasm. He loves being involved in some form of action, be it travel, following up new ideas or campaigning for a cause in which he fervently believes. He is an original thinker and hates being bound by petty restrictions or the dictates of others. He can be forthright in his views but can sometimes get carried away in the excitement of the moment and commit himself to various undertakings without thinking through all the implications. Yet he has a resilient nature and with the right support can go far in life.

Earth Rat: 1948, 2008

This Rat is astute and very level-headed. He rarely takes unnecessary chances and while he is constantly trying to improve his financial status, he is prepared to proceed slowly and leave nothing to chance. He is probably not as adventurous as the other types of Rat and prefers to remain in familiar territory rather than rush headlong into something he knows little about. He is talented, conscientious and caring towards his loved ones, but at the same time can be self-conscious and worry a little too much about the image he is trying to project.

Prospects for the Rat in 2014

The Year of the Snake (10 February 2013–30 January 2014) will have been a variable one for the Rat. Problems may have hindered his progress and, as Snake years require a certain amount of patience, more action-loving Rats may have found parts of the year frustrating.

As the Snake year draws to a close, however, the Rat will find some of his efforts paying off and will enjoy a gradual improvement in his situation. In particular he could find himself in increasing demand socially. Many Rats will impress others at this time and make some useful friends and contacts. August and December could be particularly full and enjoyable months.

The Rat will also be active in domestic matters and will not only do much to assist family members but also enjoy arranging some special events and get-togethers. The closing months of the year will be expensive, though, and the Rat should be careful about spending too much on a whim.

Work-wise, he will need to be alert and watch developments closely, although the year's end can provide the opportunity for many Rats to extend their skills and vary their role in what could be a potentially useful manner.

Overall, the Snake year may not have been an easy or smooth one for the Rat, but he will have learned much from it and will emerge with some achievements of which he can be proud.

The Year of the Horse begins on 31 January and will be a mixed one for the Rat. Although it will give him the chance to use his skills to advantage (and for resourcefulness the Rat is among the best), it does require care. Risks can backfire, and while the Rat may like to be at the forefront of activity, he needs to be mindful of prevailing conditions and wary of acting in haste.

However, while the aspects may be cautionary, the Horse year can have its benefits too. Some of the situations the Rat finds himself in will not only bring out his best but also enable him to learn more *and* ultimately make progress. The Horse year can also spring its surprises, and while some plans may not proceed as originally envisaged, better possibilities can arise in their place. In 2014 the Rat would do well to keep his wits about him.

One area which calls for special attention is the Rat's relations with others. Although he has charm and great empathy, this is no time for him to be too independent. To go it alone or be obtuse could leave him isolated and vulnerable. In the Horse year he does need to consult others *and* listen to what they have to say. April, June, September and December could be the most socially active months of the year.

Rats enjoying romance or perhaps looking for romance will need to be especially aware of the feelings of others and not take them for granted. Being inattentive or preoccupied could cause some relationships to founder. By being mindful of such risks, however, the Rat can do a lot to prevent difficulties from arising, and the year will see some Rats both enjoying and strengthening their love for another person.

The need for awareness also applies to domestic situations. Here again, being busy or preoccupied could take its toll. Although the Rat likes to be central to whatever is going on, throughout the year he should consult others and show some flexibility when necessary. When making decisions or dealing with pressures, a joint approach will lead to better solutions. Domestic life can also be greatly helped by spending quality time together. That way, everyone will have the chance to appreciate some of the family news and occasions the Horse year will bring.

At work, the Rat will have plenty of opportunity to use his strengths to advantage and to impress others. At times of pressure or difficulty, his ability both to cope and to find ways round problems will be valued. However, despite his efforts, progress may not always be easy. If promotion opportunities arise or the Rat applies for another position, he could find himself competing against many experienced candidates and it may take considerable effort to make headway.

Rats seeking work will also find the Horse year requires determination. However, the Rat *is* a survivor, and his resourcefulness and commitment will show through and often enable him to secure a position he can build on in the future. Effort will be needed, but opportunities can arise suddenly and the Rat does need to be alert throughout the year. March, June, September and November could see encouraging work developments.

Throughout the year the Rat can help his situation by seizing any opportunities to add to his skills and working knowledge. Whether at work or in his own time, by developing himself in some way he can do much to strengthen his prospects.

Money matters will, however, need close attention. In 2014 the Rat should be wary of risk and examine the implications carefully if he enters into any new agreement. If he has any questions or doubts, he should seek advice before proceeding. With many outgoings and some expensive plans, he also needs to keep a tight rein over spending and, where possible, make advance provision for some of the larger purchases he has in mind. Good budgeting can make an important difference.

Overall, the Rat will need to be on his mettle in the Horse year. Lack of awareness, preoccupation and risk can all give rise to problems, and effort will be needed to make headway. However, it is during more challenging times that strengths can emerge and the Rat can demonstrate some of his finer qualities this year. His achievements will be well deserved, and by sharing them with others, he will not only enjoy them that much more, but also find that many can be built on in the following, more encouraging Goat year.

The Metal Rat

The Metal element can make a sign more resolute and determined, and this is especially the case with the Metal Rat. Always keen to make the most of himself, he is a doer and has considerable ability and presence.

While 2014 will present its obstacles, by taking into account the prevailing conditions and adjusting as required, the Metal Rat can fare reasonably well.

One of the key requirements of the year is awareness. In almost all areas of his life the Metal Rat will need to observe what is going on, listen to others and think carefully about his situation. This is no time to go it alone or take action without adequate thought. Moments of impulsiveness could cost him dear.

In his home life, it is important that the Metal Rat shares any concerns with those close to him. The more liaison and dialogue there is in his household, the better for all. Greater co-operation will also lead to more practical projects in the home being successfully carried through. There may be important events to mark as well, and making arrangements together can help make the occasion more special. This is a year favouring a collective approach. If possible, the Metal Rat should aim to take a holiday with his loved ones too. The latter part of the year could bring additional travel opportunities.

With this likely to be an often busy year, the Metal Rat should also try to keep his lifestyle in balance and allow time for rest and relaxation as well as personal interests. If he feels stressed or that his life is in some way lacking, he should give himself some 'me time'. Personal interests and relaxing pursuits can do the Metal Rat a lot of good this year.

He should also keep in regular contact with friends and, if invited to social occasions or intrigued by certain events, try to attend. This can be another way to achieve that all-important lifestyle balance. Metal Rats who are alone will find new interests can also be an excellent way to come into contact with others. Late March, April, June, September and December will see the most social activity. However, with the aspects as they are, any Metal Rat who is tempted to stray or take risks with a relationship could find problems occurring. Horse years tend not to be forgiving of personal lapses. Metal Rats, take note.

At work this can be a year of important developments. Although progress may be difficult, there will be the chance for many Metal Rats to develop their role, including taking on other responsibilities or adapting to new procedures and technology. With a willingness to embrace what occurs, they can find some aspects of their work particularly satisfying. Those who start the year feeling staid or disenchanted will particularly welcome the chance to take on more fulfilling duties. Securing promotion may not be easy this year, but the developments that do occur will often give the Metal Rat the chance to widen his role.

Metal Rats who are seeking work or looking to change employer will need to remain determined and persistent. With the number of vacancies often limited, these Metal Rats will need to emphasize their skills, experience and willingness to learn. Their communication skills can be very much to their advantage, however, and many will eventually secure a new and satisfying position. March, June, late August, September and November could see encouraging developments, but this is a year requiring effort *and* the willingness to adapt.

The Metal Rat will also need to handle his finances with care, including keeping a watch on outgoings and making early and ample allowance for obligations and more expensive plans. Financially, this is a time for discipline and the avoidance of risk. Throughout the year, if the Metal Rat has concerns over a financial matter, he should check the details and, if appropriate, obtain professional advice.

Overall, the Metal Rat will need to be thorough and careful this year and avoid acting too independently. With support, advice and good liaison with others, he will find problems can be considerably eased. He should also allow time to consider his approach rather than act in haste. But while the year will bring its pressures, the Metal Rat can still accomplish a great deal. Developing his skills and interests can be satisfying and often lead to other opportunities, especially in the following and more auspicious Goat year. The Horse year may be challenging for the Metal Rat, but its lessons can be considerable.

Tip for the Year

Be thorough and disciplined. With effort, awareness and support, you will have more chance of benefiting from the developments that will take place. Care and commitment are required this year.

The Water Rat

The Water Rat has a highly intuitive nature and is particularly adept at gauging situations and the feelings of others. This skill will stand him in good stead this year. It will be a demanding one for him, but by adapting as required, he can help both his present *and* future prospects.

Throughout the year it is important that the Water Rat consults others and listens to their advice. If he is considering any ideas or has any concerns, he will find that by talking these over with those around him, he can benefit from their assistance.

At work this will be a challenging year. New targets or objectives could be set and some Water Rats may have to adjust to new working procedures or new management. The demands and expectations can be high, but while this can be an exacting time and there may be some uncomfortable moments to endure along the way, the Water Rat can gain valuable skills and display his strengths. The importance of what is accomplished now should *not* be underestimated.

For Water Rats who are seeking work or who decide to move on from their present employer, the Horse year can be challenging. Obtaining a position will require considerable effort and it is important that the Water Rat makes the most of the support and information available, including from employment agencies, advisers and contacts. This way he may not only be alerted to more possibilities but also be advised of schemes (including training) that may help. While the competition will be considerable, by being prepared to adapt and learn, quite a few Water Rats will secure an interesting new position that they can subsequently build on. March, June, September and November could be important months for employment matters.

Financially, this is a year for discipline and control. The Water Rat should not only keep a close watch on his spending but also budget in advance for plans he has in mind. He also needs to be thorough when dealing with financial correspondence and seek advice should he have any problems or concerns. To make assumptions or take risks could be to his disadvantage. Money-wise, this is a year for care.

In view of the pressures the Water Rat is likely to face this year, it is also important that he gives some consideration to his lifestyle. This includes taking regular exercise and giving some thought to the quality of his diet as well as spending time on pursuits he enjoys. If a new activity or subject appeals to him, he should follow it up. Not only will this be of benefit now, but it can also open up possibilities for later.

The Water Rat will also value his social contacts during the year. Whether he is meeting friends or going to events that appeal to him, his social life can do him good as well as extend his circle of acquaintances. However, while a lot is set to go well, the Horse year does contain its awkward aspects and the Water Rat should be careful of saying things he may later regret or placing himself in a situation which could rebound on him. These words only apply to a minority of Water Rats, but the Horse year can bring problems for the unwary and lax. April, June, late August, September and December could see the most social activity.

The Water Rat's domestic life will be especially busy this year and in view of the various commitments of family members, there will need to be good organization and some flexibility. Here the Water Rat's attentiveness and ability to gauge the feelings of others will be especially appreciated. However, it is also important that household tasks and decisions are shared and that there is good co-operation between all. In addition, while family members will often be occupied with their own activities, the Water Rat should ensure that time is allowed for joint activities as well as to appreciate individual and family successes. Home life can be rewarding this year, but it does require input and mindfulness.

The Horse year is also capable of springing surprises, with travel being one. It could be that the Water Rat sees a late holiday offer that appeals to him or is invited to visit family and friends at short notice. By embracing such chances, he will find the spontaneity can make them all the more special.

Generally, the Year of the Horse will demand a lot of the Water Rat, but by rising to its challenges and being prepared to adapt and learn, he can benefit from what occurs. Throughout the year, he should liaise closely with those around him. With support and a carefully considered approach, he will get far more from the year and be able to sow seeds for later growth. In many ways this is a year of preparation for the better times that await, especially in 2015.

Tip for the Year
Seize any chances to add to your skills. By building on your experience, you will help new possibilities to open up. Your efforts can make this both a constructive and instructive time.

The Wood Rat

This year is significant for the Wood Rat. Not only does it mark the start of a new decade in his life, but a lot that he does during it can have important implications for his future. The year may not always be easy, but its lessons can prepare the Wood Rat for subsequent success.

One area of concern to many Wood Rats will be their work situation. Some may already be established in a particular career but feel they are not making the progress they would like. However, these Wood Rats should not underestimate their position and the experience they have built up. Their reputation, commitment and judgement are all valued, and as the year progresses many will find they are offered wider responsibilities and the chance of greater involvement. Although this can bring added pressure, it not only shows the faith more senior colleagues have in the Wood Rat's abilities but will also allow him to add to his skills and learn more about his industry. Whenever the Wood Rat has the chance to further his role in some way, he should make the most of it, for what he does now can pave the way to more substantial advances in the future, particularly as opportunities are likely to arise next year.

There will, however, be some Wood Rats who are feeling unfulfilled in their present position and looking for a career change. For these Wood Rats, as well as those currently seeking work, the Horse year will be challenging, but despite some difficult and often disappointing moments, many Wood Rats will be able to secure entry into a new type of work. These Wood Rats will need to be adaptable and show they are willing to learn, but the positions they take on now can often give them the chance to establish themselves in a new career. March, June, September and November could see encouraging work developments.

A further benefit of the year will be the training many Wood Rats receive and the insights they are able to gain into the industry in which they work. Not only can these be helpful in their present position but they can also reveal aptitudes these Wood Rats can build on and can alert them to other possibilities in the future.

Similarly, Wood Rats who are seeking work will find that if they take advantage of any retraining or refresher courses they are eligible for, new ways forward can open up for them. These may not always be easy times, but important seeds for the future can now be sown.

As far as the Wood Rat's personal interests are concerned, however, this can be an encouraging year. Some Wood Rats will already have acquired considerable expertise in a certain hobby or pursuit and will now have the chance to take this further, either by following up new ideas, setting themselves a more ambitious project or sharing their knowledge with others. Some may also find a personal interest of financial benefit. Whatever they do, in the Horse year all Wood Rats should set time aside for pursuits they enjoy. In addition, some may become intrigued by a new interest or form of recreation, including one with a keep-fit element, and what is started this year can have benefits both now and in the near future.

Financially, this is a time for discipline. With the Wood Rat's existing commitments, as well as the plans and hopes he has for the year, he will need to keep a tight rein on spending and set money aside for specific requirements. With good control, he will be able to proceed with many of his ideas, possibly including exciting travel plans, but money does have to be managed well and risks avoided. Also, should the Wood Rat enter into any financial commitment, he should check the terms and obligations. Where financial matters are concerned, this is a year to be thorough and careful.

For personal relations, the Wood Rat will find it an eventful time. With his genial nature, he has a wide range of friends and contacts and over the year some of them can be especially helpful to him. Whenever he has concerns or anxieties, he should not hesitate to talk these over with those around him, who may not only be willing to help but also have experience of their own to draw on. In this sometimes demanding year the Wood Rat could particularly value the assistance he is given.

There will also be excellent opportunity for the Wood Rat to meet new people during the year and he will enjoy an almost immediate rapport with some of them. Late March, April, June, September and December could see the most social activity. However, while the Wood Rat's relations with those around him will generally be positive, the aspects warn against acting thoughtlessly or taking risks. Wood Rats who are newly in love or perhaps looking for romance need to proceed particularly carefully. Time should be allowed to build a relationship, especially if it is to endure.

While the Horse year calls for care, it will also have its high points, including the marking of the Wood Rat's thirtieth birthday. Not only will family and friends be keen to celebrate, but also to underline the affection they have for the Wood Rat. There could also be another personal event which is something of a milestone, possibly a personal decision, a family event or an addition to the family. The Wood Rat may find the Horse year bringing several significant moments. Many will also have important decisions to make concerning their accommodation. By discussing their ideas with their loved ones, these Wood Rats will be pleased with how their plans turn out. Domestically, this can be a full and eventful year.

Overall, the Wood Rat will need to proceed carefully in the Year of the Horse. However, by nature he is practical and alert, and provided he remains mindful of the feelings of others and takes advantage of the opportunities that come his way, he can lay down a firm foundation on which to build in the future. In particular, skills acquired in his work can prepare the way for the opportunities that await in the near future. His thirtieth year will require effort, but what he takes from it can go a long way towards helping him realize some of the aspirations that he has for this new and exciting decade in his life.

Tip for the Year
Be attentive and give time to others. Also, think long term and look to further your skills and talents. Use this year well, for it can prove significant.

The Fire Rat

This will be a full and often demanding year for the Fire Rat, but it will also be one of considerable possibility. He will have the chance to develop both new and existing skills and often gain important qualifications. What he undertakes now can have considerable bearing on the next few years.

For Fire Rats in education, there will be exams to prepare for as well as decisions to make about the direction they would like their life to take. At times the pressure may be considerable and the Fire Rat may feel overwhelmed, but if he gives his best and works in a consistent and organized way, he may be pleased with what he achieves.

During the year he should make the most of the resources available to him. Not only can this help with his studying but, looking ahead, by contacting organizations and advice centres he could find out more about the possibilities available. He should also talk to those at home as well as his tutors. Knowing him as well as they do, they too will have ideas and suggestions he could benefit from as well as practical ways to help. In the Horse year the Fire Rat needs to be receptive to the advice of others.

However, while this can be a constructive time, it is important that the Fire Rat accepts that not all his plans will be easily achieved. The Horse year will require great effort and if he is lax or careless, disappointments could loom.

Many Fire Rats will devote a lot of their time to studying this year, but this can also be an important time for general development. In particular, the Fire Rat will often have the chance to take certain interests further. Whether he is developing his skills, exploring his ideas or just having fun, his personal interests can bring both pleasure and other benefits. Fire Rats who enjoy playing a musical instrument, like sport or are artistically inclined will find that joining others and learning more can lead to them developing their talents and being inspired to take them further. Also, if something new intrigues the Fire Rat during the year, he should follow it up. As with so much this year, it can lead on to other possibilities.

With his lively nature and wide interests, the Fire Rat has a good way with others and gets on well with most. Over the year he will enjoy going out with friends and attending parties and other occasions, and will value certain friendships in particular. However, the year does have its more cautionary aspects. If the Fire Rat finds himself in a situation about which he has misgivings or is tempted to over-indulge, problems could occur. This is no time for risks or personal lapses. Fire Rats, take note. Enjoy the year, but be careful. Late March to early May, June, September and December could see the most social activity.

Another area which requires care is finance. With the Fire Rat likely to want to do a great deal on often limited means, he would do well to take his time when considering purchases and avoid impulse buys. Also, if entering into any financial agreement, he should check the terms and be aware of the obligations. This is no year for risk.

For Fire Rats currently in work, the Horse year can bring the chance to build on their present position and move on to new duties. Although sometimes their work may be repetitive and they may be keen to make more of their abilities, by showing commitment and willingness to learn, they will have the chance to benefit when other openings arise.

For Fire Rats seeking work this can be a difficult time. With many people chasing few vacancies, it will require a special effort to secure an opening. However, by preparing applications with care, including finding out more about the company and duties involved, the Fire Rat will find his initiative *will* show through and may lead to him securing that all-important foothold on the employment ladder. March, June, September and November could see some interesting possibilities.

The element of Fire adds tenacity and drive to a sign and this is especially the case with the Fire Rat. He is purposeful and alert and has style and presence. Provided he is disciplined and prepared to put in the effort, what he achieves this year can be an important foundation for the future. The Horse year will be demanding and not always easy, but it represents a real chance for the Fire Rat to show his qualities and prepare himself for the success that awaits.

Tip for the Year
Make the most of chances to learn. What you do now can often have long-term value. Also, enjoy your personal interests, for these too can benefit you, sometimes in an unexpected way.

The Earth Rat

There is a Chinese proverb which states, 'He who comprehends the times is great.' As 2014 starts, the Earth Rat would do well to reflect on his position and what he would like to see happen. Having ideas in mind will not only give him something to work towards but also allow him to use his time and energy more profitably. The Year of the Horse, while not always easy, does have considerable possibility.

As with all Rats, the Earth Rat is blessed with an enquiring mind. If something intrigues him, he will always endeavour to find out more. His curious nature will serve him well this year. Remarks he hears, subjects he reads about or invitations that come his way may all give him the chance to try new activities, go to new places or take up new interests. This is very much a year to be open-minded and game.

Earth Rats who are newly retired or who retire this year will find that with more free time available they will have more chance to develop their interests. Their actions can make this an often stimulating time. Another encouraging feature of the year will be the support the Earth Rat receives from those around him. Not only will family and friends be encouraging, but other enthusiasts or a local interest group can add to the pleasure his interests bring.

Also, quite a few Earth Rats will have dormant talents just waiting to blossom. It could be they enjoy music, art, writing or another creative activity but have not had the chance to either explore or develop their skills. Now is the time. The Horse year is one of interesting possibility.

The Earth Rat would also do well to give some consideration to his general well-being and take regular and appropriate exercise. He may be tempted to join a keep-fit class, but whatever he does, by remaining active (and sometimes sharing activities with others), he can benefit. However, before starting any new exercise regime or if he has any concerns, it is important he seeks medical guidance.

During the year the Earth Rat will often have social occasions to look forward to and the chance to meet his friends, and April, June, September and December could be particularly full and pleasing months socially.

As always, the Earth Rat will give much attention to his home life, including tackling domestic projects, sorting out maintenance problems and smartening living areas. The Horse year is one for action, and the plans the Earth Rat carries out during it, including some he may have thought about for some while, will bring him considerable pleasure.

Over the year he will also find others, particularly younger relations, seeking his views and grateful for assistance he is able to give. However, while his domestic life can bring him much contentment, there may also be issues that concern him. Minor matters have a tendency to escalate in Horse years and if the Earth Rat detects difficult undercurrents or potential problems, he would do well to address these early on. With dialogue and compromise, awkward situations can often be dealt with, but in the Horse year early action is advised.

This also applies to a possible friendship issue. Here again the Earth Rat should be mindful of the views of others and wary in potentially awkward situations. Fortunately his ability to read people and situations can serve him well and he is a skilled diplomat, but disagreements could arise and risk casting a shadow over some of the year's activities. Earth Rats, be warned and tread carefully.

Another area which requires care is finance. Over the year the Earth Rat needs to watch his spending as well as plan for more major out-goings. Also, when completing paperwork, especially if tax, pension or benefit related, he needs to be thorough and query anything which is not clear. This is a year to be thorough and disciplined.

Despite this, the Earth Rat would do well to try and make provision for travel, if possible. A change of scene could do him a lot of good and he could enjoy new experiences and be inspired by the sights he sees. This is a year which can open the Earth Rat's mind to new possibilities.

Overall, the Earth Rat can derive much personal benefit from the Horse year, although to get the most from it he does need to act upon his ideas and develop his interests. This could include nurturing talents which may have lain dormant for some time. The Horse year does hold considerable scope for the Earth Rat, but money matters need to be handled with care and while the Earth Rat can look forward to many agreeable times with others, the year can give rise to problems, which ideally should be addressed early on. The Earth Rat will need to remain aware of these potentially awkward aspects and proceed with caution. This can be a satisfying year with scope for personal development, but it is also one which requires care.

Tip for the Year

Be open – you can gain a great deal from the support and encouragement you are given as well as enjoy the way many of your ideas develop. Also, make the most of your own special skills. These too can bring pleasure – and a possible surprise.

Famous Rats

Ben Affleck, Ursula Andress, Louis Armstrong, Lauren Bacall, Dame Shirley Bassey, Kathy Bates, Irving Berlin, Kenneth Branagh, Marlon Brando, Charlotte Brontë, Jackson Browne, George H. W. Bush, Glen Campbell, Jimmy Carter, Jeremy Clarkson, Aaron Copland, Cameron Diaz, David Duchovny, Duffy, T. S. Eliot, Eminem, Colin Firth, Clark Gable, Liam Gallagher, Al Gore, Hugh Grant, Lewis Hamilton, Thomas Hardy, Prince Harry, Haydn, Charlton Heston, Buddy Holly, Mick Hucknall, Henrik Ibsen, Jeremy Irons, Samuel L. Jackson, LeBron James, Jean-Michel Jarre, Scarlett Johansson, Gene Kelly, Avril Lavigne, Jude Law, Gary Lineker, Lord Andrew Lloyd Webber, Ian McEwan, Katie Melua, Claude Monet, Richard Nixon, Ozzy Osbourne, Sean Penn,

Katy Perry, Sir Terry Pratchett, Ian Rankin, Lou Rawls, Burt Reynolds, Rossini, William Shakespeare, James Taylor, Leo Tolstoy, Henri Toulouse-Lautrec, Spencer Tracy, the Prince of Wales, George Washington, the Duke of York, Emile Zola.

6 February 1913 to 25 January 1914 — *Water Ox*

24 January 1925 to 12 February 1926 — *Wood Ox*

11 February 1937 to 30 January 1938 — *Fire Ox*

29 January 1949 to 16 February 1950 — *Earth Ox*

15 February 1961 to 4 February 1962 — *Metal Ox*

3 February 1973 to 22 January 1974 — *Water Ox*

20 February 1985 to 8 February 1986 — *Wood Ox*

7 February 1997 to 27 January 1998 — *Fire Ox*

26 January 2009 to 13 February 2010 — *Earth Ox*

The Ox

The Personality of the Ox

The more considered the way,
the more considerable the journey.

The Ox is born under the signs of equilibrium and tenacity. He is a hard and conscientious worker and sets about everything he does in a resolute, methodical and determined manner. He has considerable leadership qualities and is often admired for his tough and uncompromising nature. He knows what he wants to achieve in life and, as far as possible, will not be deflected from his ultimate objective.

The Ox takes his responsibilities and duties very seriously. He is decisive and quick to take advantage of any opportunity that comes his way. He is also sincere and places a great deal of trust in his friends and colleagues. He is, nevertheless, something of a loner. He is a quiet and private individual and often keeps his thoughts to himself. He also cherishes his independence and prefers to set about things in his own way rather than be bound by the dictates of others or influenced by outside pressures.

The Ox tends to have a calm and tranquil nature, but if something angers him or he feels that someone has let him down, he can have a fearsome temper. He can also be stubborn and obstinate and this can lead him into conflict with others. Usually he will succeed in getting his own way, but should things go against him he is a poor loser and will take any defeat or setback extremely badly.

The Ox is often a deep thinker and rather studious. He is not particularly renowned for his sense of humour and does not take kindly to new gimmicks or anything too innovative. He is too solid and traditional for that and prefers to stick to the more conventional norm.

His home is very important to him and in some respects he treats it as a private sanctuary. His family tends to be closely knit and the Ox will make sure that each member does their fair share around the house. He tends to be a hoarder, but he is always well organized and neat. He also places great importance on punctuality and there is nothing that infuriates him more than to be kept waiting, particularly if it is due to someone's inefficiency. The Ox can be a hard taskmaster!

Once settled in a job or house the Ox will quite happily remain there for many years. He does not like change and he is also not particularly keen on travel. He does, however, enjoy gardening and other outdoor pursuits and he will often spend much of his spare time out of doors. He is usually an excellent gardener and whenever possible will make sure he has a large area of ground to maintain. He usually prefers to live in the country rather than the town.

Due to his dedicated and dependable nature the Ox will usually do well in his chosen career, providing he is given enough freedom to act on his own initiative. He invariably does well in politics, agriculture and careers that need specialized training. He is also very gifted artistically and many Oxen have enjoyed considerable success as musicians or composers.

The Ox is not as outgoing as some and it often takes him a long time to establish friendships and feel relaxed in another person's company. His courtships are likely to be long, but once he is settled he will remain devoted and loyal to his partner. He is particularly well suited to those born under the signs of the Rat, Rabbit, Snake and Rooster. He can also establish a good relationship with the Monkey, Dog, Pig and another Ox, but he will find that he has little in common with the whimsical and sensitive Goat. He will also find it difficult to get on with the Horse, Dragon and Tiger – the Ox prefers a quiet and peaceful existence and those born under these three signs tend to be a little too lively and impulsive for his liking.

The female Ox has a kind and caring nature and her home and family are very much her pride and joy. She always tries to do her best for her partner and can be a most conscientious and loving parent. She is an excellent organizer and a very determined person who will often succeed in getting what she wants in life. She usually has a deep interest in the arts and is often a talented artist or musician.

The Ox is a very down-to-earth character. He is sincere, loyal and unpretentious. He can, however, be rather reserved and to some he may appear distant and aloof. He has a quiet nature, but underneath he is very strong-willed and ambitious. He has the courage of his convictions and is often prepared to stand up for what he believes to be right, regardless of the consequences. He inspires confidence and trust and throughout his life he will rarely be short of people who are ready to support him.

The Five Different Types of Ox

In addition to the 12 signs of the Chinese zodiac there are five elements and these have a strengthening or moderating influence on the signs. The effects of the five elements on the Ox are described below, together with the years in which they were exercising their influence. Therefore Oxen born in 1961 are Metal Oxen, Oxen born in 1913 and 1973 are Water Oxen, and so on.

Metal Ox: 1961

This Ox is confident and very strong-willed. He can be blunt and forthright in his views and is not afraid of speaking his mind. He sets about his objectives with a dogged determination, but he can become so involved in his various activities that he can be oblivious to the thoughts and feelings of those around him, and this can sometimes be to his detriment. He is honest and dependable and will never promise more than he can deliver. He has a good appreciation of the arts and usually has a small circle of very good and loyal friends.

Water Ox: 1913, 1973

This Ox has a sharp and penetrating mind. He is a good organizer and sets about his work in a methodical manner. He is not as narrow-minded as some of the other types of Ox and is more willing to involve others in his plans and aspirations. He usually has very high moral standards and is often attracted to careers in public service. He is a good judge of character and has such a friendly and persuasive manner that he usually experiences little difficulty in securing his objectives. He is popular and has an excellent way with children.

Wood Ox: 1925, 1985

The Wood Ox conducts himself with an air of dignity and authority and will often take a leading role in any enterprise in which he becomes involved. He is very self-confident and is direct in his dealings with others. He does, however, have a quick temper and has no hesitation in speaking his mind. He has tremendous drive and willpower and an extremely good memory. He is particularly loyal and devoted to the members of his family and has a most caring nature.

Fire Ox: 1937, 1997

The Fire Ox has a powerful and assertive personality and is a hard and conscientious worker. He holds strong views and has very little patience when things do not go his way. He can also get carried away in the excitement of the moment and does not always take into account the views of those around him. He nevertheless has many leadership quali-ties and will often reach positions of power, eminence and wealth. He usually has a small group of loyal and close friends and is very devoted to his family.

Earth Ox: 1949, 2009

This Ox sets about everything he does in a sensible and level-headed manner. He is ambitious but also realistic in his aims and is often prepared to work long hours to secure his objectives. He is shrewd in financial and business matters and is a very good judge of character. He has a quiet nature and is greatly admired for his sincerity and integrity. He is also very loyal to his family and friends and his views are often sought.

Prospects for the Ox in 2014

The Year of the Snake (10 February 2013–30 January 2014) will have been an interesting one for the Ox and allowed him to make progress as well as enjoy himself. The Snake year generally proceeds at a more measured pace and this will have suited the Ox and given him the chance to set about his activities in his own way. The closing months can be particularly satisfying.

The Ox's relations with others are especially well aspected, and although the Ox often takes his time in getting to know others, in the last quarter of the year he will see an increase in social activity and have good opportunities to extend his circle of friends and acquaintances. Romantic prospects are also excellent and for unattached Oxen there can be exciting times ahead. October and December can be busy months and even Oxen who tend to keep themselves to themselves should make the most of their social opportunities.

The Ox's home life will see much activity at this time and also some pressure, as quite a few arrangements will need making. Good liaison with others and some flexibility will be helpful. While some weeks may be hectic, the Ox will especially enjoy family occasions and may be pleasantly surprised by the way certain plans take shape.

At work many Oxen will find themselves with a heavier workload and the chance to take on additional responsibilities. Some who are seeking work will be successful in securing a position late in the year. Snake years generally encourage Oxen to develop their strengths and can bring some interesting opportunities.

The Year of the Horse begins on 31 January and will be an eventful one for the Ox. Situations may change quickly and to benefit the Ox will need to move swiftly and be prepared to adjust. Failure to do so could leave him languishing or missing out on some fine opportunities. Action, initiative and hard work are very much the keywords for the year.

At work many Oxen will feel the winds of change. There could be new management, new procedures and new technology to adjust to as well as new responsibilities. Being on the conservative side, quite a few Oxen will view the developments with misgiving. However, this is no time to be left behind and the Ox will need to adapt as required. By being involved in the changes and willing to contribute rather than hold back, he could find himself in a good position to make progress. He may not always be comfortable with the situation, but with input and hard work, he can influence matters and, importantly, benefit.

There will be scope for many Oxen to build on their existing position this year and for those keen to move elsewhere as well as those seeking work, the Horse year can open up exciting possibilities. However, considerable effort will be required and these Oxen need to keep alert and act quickly when they see an opening that interests them. To give themselves the best chance, they should also register with employment agencies and, if eligible, consider training initiatives that could assist them. With drive, resolve and tenaciousness, they will find important doors opening, however, and once in a new position (even if initially on a temporary basis), they will soon have the opportunity to prove themselves. The Ox is a redoubtable worker and the Horse year will give him the chance to impress. March, April, July and September could see important work developments.

Progress at work can also lead to a rise in income. While this will be welcome, the Ox does need to manage his financial situation well this year and be particularly careful when entering into long-term commitments. This is a time to be thorough and aware of the implications and obligations involved in any transaction, otherwise misjudgements could be made. Oxen, take note, remain vigilant and avoid unnecessary risk.

Another important consideration this year is the Ox's well-being. Although he likes to keep himself active, he does drive himself hard, and without care, tiredness or tension could take its toll and leave him lacking his usual energy and susceptible to minor ailments. To help counter this, the Ox should make sure his diet is healthy and nutritious and his lifestyle well balanced. This includes setting time aside for relaxation – something not all Oxen are good at doing! Oxen who are sedentary for much of the day should also consider taking some exercise. A little personal attention can make an important difference.

The Ox takes his responsibilities seriously and likes to make his own decisions. However, in this fast-paced year it is important that he shares his thoughts and any concerns with others rather than dwells upon them alone. Similarly, at busy times he should draw on the help of those around him and, in his household, ensure that everyone does their fair share.

In addition he will need to show some patience this year. It could be that certain plans, particularly in his home life, have to be deferred to less busy times or that plans have to be modified as schedules change. Although the Ox likes to proceed in an orderly fashion, this is a year when he will need to show some flexibility. Taking on board the viewpoints of others will be both important and helpful.

While domestic activities will keep the Ox busy, the Horse year can bring many special moments. These could include celebrating some of his own successes and marking the achievements of a loved one as well as welcome family news or a decision that delights everyone concerned. Shared activities are also likely to be appreciated and the Ox and his family could particularly benefit from a holiday or break taken during the year. Some rest and relaxation needs to be factored into busy lifestyles! June and July could see interesting developments in many an Ox household.

Although frequently busy, the Ox will also benefit from his social life. He should keep in regular contact with his friends and be prepared to confide in them if anything is concerning him. March, May, September and November will see the most social activity and if the Ox receives invitations or sees events advertised that appeal to him, he should aim to go. In this busy year his social life can be another way to help achieve that all-important lifestyle balance.

Where matters of the heart are concerned, this is a year for care. With time and attention, many a romance can flourish, but without commitment, relationships may falter.

Overall, the Year of the Horse will be a demanding one for the Ox. It is no time for idling or being resistant to change, and the progress the Ox makes will be the result of effort and commitment. However, one of the Ox's many strengths is that he is hard-working, and by being prepared to adapt as situations require and to add to his skills, he can do well. Throughout the year it is important he keeps his lifestyle in balance and preserves time for his domestic and social life as well as gives some consideration to his own well-being. With care, effort and balance, however, he can make this a constructive and satisfying year.

The Metal Ox

This will be an interesting year for the Metal Ox, but it is also one for care. Events will move swiftly and although the Metal Ox likes to plan ahead, in 2014 he will need to show flexibility and be accommodating. As the Chinese proverb reminds us, 'If you chase after two rabbits, you will catch neither.' In the Horse year the Metal Ox will need to concentrate on priorities rather than spread his energies too widely.

In his work, the Horse year will bring change. New methods of working may be introduced or, by virtue of his experience, he may be given a more specialist role. Some new developments may happen quickly and catch the Metal Ox by surprise, but this is very much a year to adapt and 'go with the flow'. If not, some Metal Oxen run the risk of being passed over and missing out on opportunities. Also, when changes take place, if the Metal Ox is a part of what is happening rather than appearing too removed, he will have more chance to bring his strengths to bear and, in the process, raise his profile and position. This is no year to stand still or let chances slip by.

Most Metal Oxen will remain with their present employer over the year and experience a change in duties. However, for Metal Oxen who would welcome new challenges elsewhere as well as those seeking work, the Horse year can bring important opportunities. To benefit, these Metal Oxen will need to be quick and flexible. Although they may be keen to pursue a certain type of work or remain in a particular industry, by widening their options many could secure a position that offers them the chance to use their strengths in other ways. March to early May, July and September could see encouraging developments.

Another benefit of the Horse year will be the opportunities it will bring for the Metal Ox to extend his knowledge and skills. Often these will come through the new duties he takes on, but if there is an area of his knowledge he would like to improve on or a skill he would like to become more proficient in, he would do well to set time aside to learn more. Whether through research he can do by himself or enrolling on a course, by doing something positive he will not only feel he is moving himself forward but also that he is helping his future prospects. A few Metal Oxen may also decide to take up a new recreational activity, but whatever the area involved, with a willingness to learn, the Metal Ox will find considerable benefits can follow on.

He can also be helped by giving some consideration to his well-being over the year. With the energy he puts into his activities and the long hours he sometimes keeps, it is important he allows time to rest and makes sure he has regular and appropriate exercise. He should also pay attention to the quality of his diet. To be neglectful could leave him lacking his usual energy or prone to minor ailments. If he has any concerns or decides on a keep-fit regime, it would be worth him seeking medical advice.

The Horse year can hold travel opportunities for many Metal Oxen, often arising at short notice, and again they are likely to enjoy the pleasures that travel can bring.

By nature the Metal Ox is thorough and careful, and in the Horse year he does need to be vigilant in money matters. If he takes on new commitments or has doubts over a particular transaction or financial matter, he should seek clarification. This is no time for making assumptions or taking risks.

The Metal Ox is usually selective in his socializing and prefers to keep his social circle relatively small. However, the Horse year can open up interesting possibilities and he should not deny himself the chance to go out, whether to meet friends or to go to events that appeal to him. Also, by keeping informed about what is happening in his area, he could learn of activities that he could enjoy or that could benefit him in some other way. Here again, the year can bring some interesting opportunities, but the Metal Ox does need to act upon them.

For Metal Oxen who are unattached and would welcome company, new activities can also be an excellent way to meet others. For some, the year can have intriguing love prospects, but the Metal Ox will need to be attentive and cannot take the feelings of another for granted or appear unaccommodating, otherwise disagreements could ensue. Awareness is very important this year. March, May, September and November could see the most social activity.

The Metal Ox's home life will be particularly busy this year and there will need to be good co-operation and a willingness to compromise over certain arrangements. Also, where some practical undertakings are concerned, the Metal Ox will need to prioritize rather than attempt too much at once. He may be keen, but as the Chinese proverb warns, spreading his energies too widely could lead to less satisfactory results. In the Horse year he needs to be realistic about what is doable at any one time.

In addition to all he does around his home, the Metal Ox will often help and advise family members as well as give assistance to someone much older than himself. Others especially value his solid and dependable nature and in the Horse year he will earn the gratitude of many. He can also look forward to some notable family events, especially during the summer.

Overall, the Year of the Horse will be an active one for the Metal Ox and although he may be uncomfortable with the pace of events, by being prepared to adapt and widen his perspective, he can greatly benefit from the opportunities the year offers. He will also be able to add to his skills or acquire new ones over the year and this can help open up possibilities in the future. This is a time for moving forward and while the Metal Ox may by nature be cautious, if he is willing to venture forth he can gain a great deal from the Horse year.

Tip for the Year

Concentrate on priorities and be prepared to adapt as required. With your talents and a certain flexibility, you have it within you to accomplish a great deal this year.

The Water Ox

The Water Ox is blessed with a keen and practical nature and as 2014 starts he will be likely to have ideas about what he would like to see happen over the year as well as certain issues he would like to address. As a result, many Water Oxen will start the year in determined spirit.

One particular area of focus may well be their work situation. While many Water Oxen will have made headway in recent times, this period of change is far from over. Horse years are innovative and fast-moving and in many workplaces new procedures will be introduced, policies and objectives reviewed and expectations increased. As situations change, it is important that the Water Ox keeps himself informed and involved. This way he will not only have more chance to contribute but also to benefit from the openings that are created. What many Water Oxen accomplish this year, in sometimes volatile situations, will be very much to their credit and something they can build on in the future.

It is also important that throughout the year the Water Ox works closely with others and seizes any opportunities to build up his contacts and raise his profile, including, if appropriate, joining a professional organization. Again, the more involved he is, the more he stands to gain.

The Horse year can also bring important developments for Water Oxen seeking work or looking to change employer. Events can take an unexpected course and this is a year to be open to possibility. By doing so, many Water Oxen will be able to successfully embark on a new stage in their career. Horse years offer opportunity, but the Water Ox cannot be too narrow-minded or independent in his approach. Late February to early May, July and September could bring some decisive moments, but such is the nature of the year that opportunities could arise at almost any time and will need to be acted on quickly.

A great many Water Oxen can look forward to a modest rise in income during the year, but finances still need to be carefully managed. This includes making allowance for both new and existing commitments as well as keeping a close watch on everyday spending. This is a year to be careful and thorough and avoid risk. If the Water Ox has problems or enters into a long-term agreement it could be helpful to seek professional advice.

With the busy nature of the year it is also important the Water Ox keeps his lifestyle in balance and allows himself time for recreation, personal interests, exercise and just relaxing. To keep pushing himself could lead to stress and leave him susceptible to minor ailments. Water Oxen, do take note and give some consideration to your lifestyle.

The Water Ox can derive much pleasure from his home life this year, and joint pursuits and quality time with his loved ones will not only help mutual understanding but also lead to many enjoyable occasions. It is important that the Water Ox shares what is on his mind with others and with a spirit of openness helpful to all. The summer months could be especially full and interesting. However, in view of the busy nature of the year, practical projects should not be rushed but carried out as and when time allows.

The Water Ox should also make the most of his social opportunities. Contact with others can do him good and be another way to keep his lifestyle in balance. March, May, September and November could see the most social activity.

The Water Ox is certainly set to have a full and eventful year, but throughout he does need to be aware of changing situations and prepared to adapt accordingly. This is not a time to be intransigent or too independent in approach. However, while the year will bring its challenges, it will also bring opportunities for the Water Ox to add to his capabilities and improve on his position. During it, he would do well to give some consideration to his lifestyle and preserve time for those who are important to him. This can be a rewarding year, but it does call for watchfulness and keeping his lifestyle in balance.

Tip for the Year
Value your relations with others. With their support, advice and encouragement your year will be that much easier. Also, allow yourself some 'me time' to relax and enjoy your achievements.

The Wood Ox

This will be an eventful year for the Wood Ox and while the pressures may sometimes be great, there will be much for him to enjoy.

With Wood as his element, this Ox is practical and realistic. He is also patient and prepared to work hard for the things he wants. In the Horse year some of his longer-term hopes will be realized, sometimes in unexpected but fortuitous ways. Indeed, what happens this year can be the culmination of considerable effort combined with an element of luck.

A particularly eventful area may be his private life. Wood Oxen with a partner may well find that plans they have been working towards for some time can now be realized and between them there could be several personal successes to enjoy, including for some an addition to their family. Others may move to somewhere more convenient or, through their own efforts, be able to transform their existing home. An important element of the Horse year is that it favours following up ideas.

Although, like all Oxen, the Wood Ox values his independence, it is also important that he is prepared to discuss his thoughts and any concerns with his partner, friends and more senior relations. If he does so, they will not only be better able to advise but can sometimes assist in unexpected ways. A lot that the Wood Ox sets out to do this year will be helped along by the support of others.

The Horse year can also be significant for the unattached Wood Ox. Again, events can take a surprising course and he may meet someone by chance who will soon become very special to him. Although the Wood Ox likes to take his time in getting to know another person, love could take hold suddenly this year and transform his situation. March, May, September and November could be important months.

In view of accommodation costs, however, plus his other activities and sometimes expensive personal plans, the Wood Ox will need to be disciplined in money matters. When entering into an agreement he does need to check the terms and, if considering expensive purchases, take the time to compare prices. Hurrying, taking risks or ignoring fine print could lead to problems. Money matters require careful handling this year.

At work, the Wood Ox will see important developments. There may well be changes to his responsibilities, objectives and workload. These can often bring increased pressure but at the same time give him the chance to demonstrate his potential and extend his skills. With commitment and hard work, many Wood Oxen can do their reputation a lot of good this year and mark themselves out for future progress. However, as with all Oxen, the Wood Ox does have a stubborn streak, and should he show himself resistant to change, his progress may not be so great. In the Horse year he does need to be willing to learn and to embrace change.

For Wood Oxen who are seeking work or intent on changing their employer, the Horse year can open up some interesting opportunities. Effort will be required and when making applications and at interview these Wood Oxen will need to stress their experience and also demonstrate initiative by finding out more about what is involved. With persistence and determination, however, the Wood Ox can make this a significant and rewarding year. Late February to early May, July and September will be important months for employment matters.

The Wood Ox can derive much satisfaction from his personal interests over the year and if he has ideas he is keen to develop or skills he can put to good use, he should allow himself the time to do so. With a willing attitude, he can look forward to some encouraging achievements. For Wood Oxen who are interested in adding a new element to their lifestyle, it could be well worth considering joining a local activity or social group.

With his busy lifestyle the Wood Ox would also do well to give some thought to his well-being. With so many ambitions to fulfil, in this busy year he does need to keep himself in good form.

Overall, the Horse year will see a lot of activity in the Wood Ox's life and is very much a time for building on his position. He will be assisted by those around him and sometimes the workings of chance as well. As a Wood Ox he is keen and practical, and his efforts will bring some well-deserved results as well as help his continuing progress. A satisfying year.

Tip for the Year

Act on your ideas. Your resolve and determination can lead to a lot opening up for you. Also, do consult others. These can be special times which can see the fulfilment of some important personal hopes.

The Fire Ox

This can be a promising year for the Fire Ox, although just how well he fares is very much in his own hands. With willingness to make the most of his situation and the opportunities that will open up for him, he can make good progress and enjoy some positive developments. However, if he idles or makes little effort, the year can have salutary warnings. This can be a time of great potential, but the Fire Ox does need to seize the moment and apply himself.

For the many Fire Oxen in education this can be an interesting year. Although busy with coursework and preparing for exams, these Fire Oxen will often have the chance to extend their studies as well as tackle certain areas in greater depth. This can not only make their studying more interesting but also bring out certain strengths. Admittedly, the pressures will sometimes be great and there will be times when some may question their abilities, but by concentrating on what needs to be done and organizing their workload well, many will find themselves making great strides.

The Fire Ox can also benefit from making good use of the facilities and support available to him. By being willing and proactive, he can gain a lot from what he does now as well as prepare himself for future possibilities.

He will also have the chance to develop certain interests. Some can have a good social element, with much fun likely to be had. For the sporting and outdoor enthusiast in particular, this can be quite a lively year.

The Fire Ox will value his friendships too and welcome the support and understanding of those around him. In addition new activities or studies can often introduce him to new people over the year. For a few Fire Oxen, affairs of the heart can add moments of excitement, although there may, for some, be painful times as well. The path of true love rarely runs smooth.

In fact the Horse year does have its more awkward aspects and the Fire Ox will need to remain aware of the feelings of others and be particularly careful in any difficult or fraught situation. Although he can be outspoken, words said in haste could rebound on him and he would do well to think before he speaks out.

Another area which will require care will be his finances. With sometimes limited resources, the Fire Ox will need to think carefully about what he spends his money on. With good control, he will manage to do a surprising amount, but if he lacks discipline, some of his activities may have to be curtailed. Also, if he enters into any agreement or makes a large purchase, he needs to be sure of the details and keep the paperwork, including receipts and guarantees, safe. Risks, carelessness and not checking facts fully could all work to his disadvantage.

For Fire Oxen in work or seeking work, even if on a temporary basis, the Horse year can be demanding. Those already in a position will often have the opportunity to do more, and even though this may not always be fulfilling, by showing reliability and commitment, these Fire Oxen will find that more rewarding possibilities can follow on. Also, any Fire Ox who is able to take advantage of an apprenticeship or work placement will find this can give them valuable experience, including insights into the type of work they may want to do in the future as well as where their aptitudes lie. The Horse year will, for many, be instructive and alert them to future possibilities. This also applies to Fire Oxen currently seeking work. Effort will be required, but once given a start, they will have a platform on which to build later. What is accomplished this year can have long-term significance.

Although the Fire Ox generally keeps himself active, he should also give some thought to his well-being. To be at his best he would find it helpful to have a balanced diet and, after busy times or late nights, give himself the chance to catch up on sleep. He should also follow the recommended procedures if involved in any strenuous or hazardous activity. Attention to health and well-being is important this year.

While the Fire Ox will often be occupied with his studies and other activities, he should also make sure he contributes to home life and is open and forthcoming with those around him. His participation will not only be appreciated but will also help build rapport and understanding.

Overall, the Year of the Horse is one of important possibility for the Fire Ox. However, he does need to use his time wisely and make the most of his opportunities. As an ambitious Fire Ox, he is very much laying the foundation for future success.

Tip for the Year
You may have set ideas, but do be open to opportunity. Important developments can often follow on from what you do now. Also, value your relations with others and enjoy the support and good times you can share.

The Earth Ox

This can be an active and generally pleasurable year for the Earth Ox, although he will need to be flexible in approach. To be too rigid over particular plans or unyielding over certain issues could lead to problems as well as undermine some of what he is hoping to do. The Earth Ox does have a firm will, but in 2014 he would do well to adapt to the situations in which he finds himself and to be open and communicative.

One area he will give much attention to this year will be his home. He may be keen to improve certain areas and replace inefficient equipment as well as add new comforts. As he considers various options, if he is prepared to be flexible and open to suggestion, he will be pleased with how his plans develop.

With accommodation being a key feature this year, some Earth Oxen may consider moving to somewhere that better suits their needs. Here again, original plans may alter and this is very much a year to be open to possibility.

In addition to the practical activity that will be seen in many an Earth Ox home, the Earth Ox will take a fond interest in the activities of his family members. Younger relations will often be keen to seek his advice and will benefit from his valuable support. The Earth Ox can also look forward to some pleasing family occasions. Whether celebrating his own or another's retirement, his growing family or a close relation's success, he can enjoy quite a few memorable moments this year.

However, while a lot can go well, no year is ever free of problems. Should the Earth Ox find himself in disagreement with someone or have doubts over certain developments, he would do well to address the issue early on rather than risk it escalating. Often open and honest discussion will help, as will a willingness to compromise.

A further area which needs close attention this year is finance. With home-improvement costs, perhaps including a move, together with his other plans and commitments, the Earth Ox will need to keep a close watch on his financial situation and carefully check the terms of any new commitment he may take on. Also, he needs to take his time when considering more expensive purchases. This is no year for haste or risk.

Although the Earth Ox's various plans will keep him busy, he should also devote time to his own interests. Projects he sets himself over the year can be especially absorbing. Many Earth Oxen will also be attracted by outdoor pursuits. The Horse year can contain an interesting mix of things to do and the Earth Ox may find it worth joining a local interest group or becoming more involved in community activities. Interesting possibilities can open up for the willing and keen.

The Earth Ox will value his close circle of friends during the year, and should he find himself under pressure or have any concerns, he should talk matters over with them. Admittedly, Earth Oxen do like to keep their thoughts close to their chest, but this is a year favouring openness. March, May, September, November and the end of the Horse year could see some fine social occasions, and for some unattached Earth Oxen the year can bring an interesting romantic encounter.

For Earth Oxen in work this can be a time of change. Many will retire, while others will look at reducing their hours or investigate types of work or particular projects they could do on their own. In considering their options, these Earth Oxen should draw on expert advice.

Sometimes opportunities can arise suddenly and it will help if the Earth Ox has already thought through what he wants to do.

Although the Earth Ox usually keeps himself active, it is also important that he gives some consideration to his own well-being over the year. Should he feel out of condition or have any concerns it would be worth him obtaining medical advice.

Overall, the Year of the Horse will be an active one for the Earth Ox as well as being a time of change. It is no time to be too independent-minded or inflexible, and the Earth Ox does need to consult others and listen carefully to their views if he is to make the most of his opportunities. This is a year of considerable possibility, but is also one for increased mindfulness.

Tip for the Year
Be flexible in your undertakings so that you can benefit from the support of others and make the most of the chances that will open up for you. With awareness and an accommodating approach, you can achieve a lot this year.

Famous Oxen

Lily Allen, Hans Christian Andersen, Peter Andre, Gemma Arterton, Johann Sebastian Bach, David Blaine, Napoleon Bonaparte, Albert Camus, Jim Carrey, Charlie Chaplin, George Clooney, Natalie Cole, Bill Cosby, Diana, Princess of Wales, Marlene Dietrich, Walt Disney, Patrick Duffy, Jane Fonda, Edward Fox, Michael J. Fox, Peter Gabriel, Elizabeth George, Richard Gere, Ricky Gervais, Julia Gillard, William Hague, Handel, King Harald V of Norway, Adolf Hitler, Dustin Hoffman, Hal Holbrook, Anthony Hopkins, Billy Joel, King Juan Carlos of Spain, John Key, B. B. King, Keira Knightley, Mark Knopfler, Burt Lancaster, Chloë Moretz, Kate Moss, Eddie Murphy, Jack Nicholson, Leslie Nielsen, Bill Nighy, Barack Obama, Gwyneth Paltrow, Oscar Peterson, Lionel Richie, Wayne Rooney, Tim Roth, Rubens, Meg Ryan, Amanda Seyfried, Jean Sibelius, Bruce Springsteen,

Meryl Streep, Lady Thatcher, Alan Titchmarsh, Scott F. Turow, Vincent van Gogh, Sigourney Weaver, the Duke of Wellington, Arsène Wenger, W. B. Yeats.

26 January 1914 to 13 February 1915 — *Wood Tiger*

13 February 1926 to 1 February 1927 — *Fire Tiger*

31 January 1938 to 18 February 1939 — *Earth Tiger*

17 February 1950 to 5 February 1951 — *Metal Tiger*

5 February 1962 to 24 January 1963 — *Water Tiger*

23 January 1974 to 10 February 1975 — *Wood Tiger*

9 February 1986 to 28 January 1987 — *Fire Tiger*

28 January 1998 to 15 February 1999 — *Earth Tiger*

14 February 2010 to 2 February 2011 — *Metal Tiger*

The Tiger

The Personality of the Tiger

It's
the zest,
the enthusiasm,
the giving the little bit more,
that makes the difference.
And opens up so much.

The Tiger is born under the sign of courage. He is a charismatic figure and usually holds very firm views. He is strong-willed and determined and sets about most of his activities with tremendous energy and enthusiasm. He is very alert and quick-witted and his mind is forever active. He is a highly original thinker and is nearly always brimming with new ideas or full of enthusiasm for some new project or scheme.

The Tiger adores challenges and loves to get involved in anything that he thinks has an exciting future or that catches his imagination. He is prepared to take risks and does not like to be bound either by convention or the dictates of others. He likes to be free to act as he chooses and at least once during his life he will throw caution to the wind and go off and do the things he wants to do.

The Tiger does, however, have a somewhat restless nature. Even though he is often prepared to throw himself wholeheartedly into a project, his initial enthusiasm can soon wane if he sees something more appealing. He can also be rather impulsive and there will be occasions in his life when he acts in a manner he later regrets. If he were to think things through or be prepared to persevere in his various activities, he would almost certainly enjoy a greater degree of success.

Fortunately the Tiger is lucky in most of his enterprises, but should things not work out as he hoped, he is liable to suffer from severe bouts of depression and it will often take him a long time to recover. His life often consists of a series of ups and downs.

He is, however, very adaptable. He has an adventurous spirit and rarely stays in the same place for long. In the early stages of his life he is likely to try his hand at several different jobs and he will also change his residence fairly frequently.

The Tiger is very honest and open in his dealings with others. He hates any sort of hypocrisy or falsehood. He is also well known for being blunt and forthright and has no hesitation in speaking his mind. He can be rebellious at times, particularly against any form of petty authority, and while this can lead him into conflict with others, he is never one to shrink from an argument or avoid standing up for what he believes is right.

The Tiger is a natural leader and can rise to the top of his chosen profession. He does not, however, care for anything too bureaucratic or detailed, and he does not like to obey orders. He can be stubborn and obstinate and throughout his life he likes to retain a certain amount of independence in his actions and be responsible to no one but himself. He likes to consider that all his achievements are due to his own efforts and he will not ask for support from others if he can avoid it.

Ironically, despite his self-confidence and leadership qualities, he can be indecisive and will often delay making a major decision until the very last moment. He can also be sensitive to criticism.

Although the Tiger is capable of earning large sums of money, he is rather a spendthrift and does not always put his money to best use. He can also be most generous and will often shower lavish gifts on friends and relations.

The Tiger cares very much for his reputation and the image that he tries to project. He carries himself with an air of dignity and authority and enjoys being the centre of attention. He is very adept at attracting publicity, both for himself and the causes he supports.

The Tiger often marries young and he will find himself best suited to those born under the signs of the Pig, Dog, Horse and Goat. He can also get on well with the Rat, Rabbit and Rooster, but will find the Ox and Snake a bit too quiet and serious for his liking and will be highly irritated by the Monkey's rather mischievous and inquisitive ways. He will also find it difficult to get on with another Tiger or a Dragon – both partners will want to dominate the relationship and could find it difficult to compromise on even the smallest of matters.

The Tigress is lively, witty and a marvellous hostess at parties. She takes great care over her appearance and is usually most attractive. She can be a very doting mother and while she believes in letting her children have their freedom, she makes an excellent teacher and will ensure that her children are well brought up and want for nothing. Like her male counterpart, she has numerous interests and likes to have sufficient independence and freedom to go off and do the things she wants to do. She has a most caring and generous nature.

The Tiger has many commendable qualities. He is honest, courageous and often a source of inspiration to others. Providing he can curb the wilder excesses of his restless nature, he is almost certain to lead a fulfilling and satisfying life.

The Five Different Types of Tiger

In addition to the 12 signs of the Chinese zodiac there are five elements and these have a strengthening or moderating influence on the signs. The effects of the five elements on the Tiger are described below, together with the years in which they were exercising their influence. Therefore Tigers born in 1950 and 2010 are Metal Tigers, Tigers born in 1962 are Water Tigers, and so on.

Metal Tiger: 1950, 2010

The Metal Tiger has an assertive and outgoing personality. He is very ambitious, and while his aims may change from time to time, he will work relentlessly until he has obtained what he wants. He can, however, be impatient for results and become highly strung if things do not work out as he would like. He is distinctive in his appearance and is admired and respected by many.

Water Tiger: 1962

This Tiger has a wide variety of interests and is always eager to experiment with new ideas or satisfy his adventurous nature by going off to explore distant lands. He is versatile, shrewd and has a kindly nature. He tends to remain calm in a crisis, although he can be annoyingly indecisive at times. He communicates well with others and through his many capabilities and persuasive nature usually achieves what he wants in life. He is also highly imaginative and is often a gifted orator or writer.

Wood Tiger: 1914, 1974

The Wood Tiger has a friendly and pleasant personality. He is less independent than some of the other types of Tiger and more prepared to work with others to secure a desired objective. However, he does have a tendency to jump from one thing to another and can easily become distracted. He is usually very popular, has a large circle of friends and invariably leads a busy and enjoyable social life. He also has a good sense of humour.

Fire Tiger: 1926, 1986

The Fire Tiger sets about everything he does with great verve and enthusiasm. He loves action and is always ready to throw himself wholeheartedly into anything that catches his imagination. He has many leadership qualities and is capable of communicating his ideas and enthusiasm to others. He is very much an optimist and can be most generous. He has a likeable nature and can be a witty and persuasive speaker.

Earth Tiger: 1938, 1998

This Tiger is responsible and level-headed. He studies everything objectively and tries to be scrupulously fair in all his dealings. Unlike other Tigers, he is prepared to specialize in certain areas rather than get distracted by other matters, but he can become so involved in what he is doing that he does not always take into account the opinions of those around him. He has good business sense and is usually very successful in later life. He has a large circle of friends and pays great attention to both his appearance and his reputation.

Prospects for the Tiger in 2014

The Year of the Snake (10 February 2013–30 January 2014) will have had a moderating effect on the Tiger and not all his plans will have proceeded as quickly or as smoothly as envisaged. However, as the year draws to a close, the Tiger can look forward to an upturn in activity.

At work there could be interesting developments. Some Tigers will have the opportunity to extend their duties, vary their role or take on something new. September and October could be key months. Snake years are ideal for developing skills and any way that the Tiger is able to add to his capabilities could be to his future advantage.

If he is looking to make major purchases or buy something specific, especially around the year's end, he could benefit from some good fortune, and it would be worth him keeping alert for special offers and when shopping in more unusual outlets.

With his active and outgoing nature, the Tiger will make the most of the family and social occasions the closing months of the year will bring. However, he does need to be aware of the views and sensitivities of other people. Also, he needs to be realistic in his planning. He may like to do a lot, but Snake years are not ones for rush and it is better to appreciate what he can do rather than rue what he cannot. December, however, could be a particularly active month domestically and socially.

Overall, the Snake year will have brought its challenges and some frustrations, but the Tiger will have gained useful experience and will be able to build on this in 2014.

The Year of the Horse begins on 31 January and will be a favourable one for the Tiger. Tigers thrive on activity and, being resourceful and enterprising, are set to make the most of the opportunities this fast-moving year will bring. Those who have been disappointed with recent progress or are unhappy with their present situation will find the Horse year is very much a time for moving forward. With resolve, effort and willingness, many can see their prospects substantially improve.

At work, the Tiger will often have the chance to make more of his expertise and use the skills he has recently built up. As a result, when promotion opportunities become available or staff are required for specific assignments, many Tigers will be excellently placed to benefit. All Tigers can help their situation by being more involved in their place of work, whether working in a team, starting up initiatives or taking chances to network. The effort the Tiger makes now can do much to enhance his reputation and strengthen his prospects.

For Tigers who have felt held back in recent years, are looking for new challenges or are seeking a position, the Horse year can bring interesting possibilities. By keeping alert, making enquiries and being persistent, many will find doors opening for them. February, April, June and September could see positive developments, but whenever the Tiger sees an opening, has an idea that may help his situation or would like to find out more about a particular type of work or industry, he should investigate. It will be his initiative and drive that will lead him to make headway over the year.

Personal interests are favourably aspected and if the Tiger has a project he wants to start or an idea he is keen to explore, he should give himself the time and opportunity to do so. The Tiger's inventiveness and creative spark will often be whetted during the course of the Horse year, and for Tigers who enjoy following or partaking in sport, there can be exciting times in store.

The Tiger's progress at work can lead to an increase in income and some could also receive a gift or bonus over the course of the year. However, to benefit from any upturn, the Tiger will need to manage his money well and ideally set sums aside for specific requirements and, if he is able, reduce any borrowings. With good management and control, he can improve his financial situation over the year.

The Tiger enjoys company and whether meeting up with friends, going to parties and other social occasions, taking part in interest groups or enjoying events in his area, he will have plenty of opportunity to go out and enjoy himself during the year.

For the unattached, affairs of the heart are splendidly aspected, with existing romances becoming more meaningful or new acquaintances quickly becoming special. These can be busy, exciting and often passionate times. Almost all months of the year will offer social occasions for the Tiger to enjoy, but May, July, September and December could see the most activity.

The Tiger's home life is also pleasingly aspected and during the year there could be several good reasons to celebrate. In keeping with his inventive nature, the Tiger will never be short of ideas and yet again his input will lead to a lot happening. However, while the Tiger is enthusiastic, he does need to avoid spreading his energies too widely, and where practical (and potentially disruptive) undertakings are concerned, he should concentrate on one task at a time. The year will be busy enough without adding further pressure.

In general, the Year of the Horse is filled with great possibility, and the Tiger's drive, ideas and dynamic personality will help to make this an active and fulfilling time. He can also look forward to a certain amount of good fortune. In addition, his relations with others will bring him much happiness and he will greatly benefit from the encouragement and support he receives from those around him. This is a year of considerable opportunity.

The Metal Tiger

The Metal Tiger has a keen and alert nature and as the Horse year starts he will have plans to get underway and hopes to realize. To get the best from the year, he will need to remain focused and resist the temptation of trying to do too much at once. With organization, discipline and concentrated effort, however, he will be able to achieve a great deal.

Foremost in the thoughts of many Metal Tigers will be their work situation. In particular, some will be feeling that they have not been making the most of their potential and will be keen to take on a new role. The Horse year will give many of these Metal Tigers the chance they want.

Those who are well-established in a company may find opportunities arising – sometimes quite suddenly – for them to take on more specialist tasks and use their experience to better advantage. As a result, many will find their work becoming more satisfying. Some will also have the chance to mentor more junior colleagues.

Metal Tigers wanting a complete change – perhaps a position nearer to their home – as well as those seeking work could also benefit from encouraging developments. By keeping in regular contact with employment agencies, talking to contacts and making enquiries, they can find their persistence paying off and bringing them an interesting new opening. Admittedly, there could be adjustments to make and new procedures to learn, but the Metal Tiger often does well when given a challenge. February, April, June and September could see important developments.

The Metal Tiger's financial prospects are also encouraging. Many Metal Tigers will increase their income over the year or benefit from the receipt of something extra. Some may also find a way to supplement their income through an interest or skill. However, to make the most of any upturn, the Metal Tiger does need to manage his situation well rather than proceed on an ad hoc basis. By considering his position and saving for more major purchases, as well as, if possible, making provision for the longer term, he will benefit both now and in the future. In addition, he may decide on an efficiency drive this year, getting his paperwork in better order and sorting through unwanted belongings. Horse years encourage activity and the Metal Tiger may be keen to make quite a few positive changes.

He can also derive considerable pleasure from his interests during the year, particularly from the way he is able to develop certain ideas. He could find it helpful to contact other enthusiasts or at least get feedback on some activity he may be considering. This way he could benefit from a certain synergy and some interests and projects could gain new momentum. A new recreational pursuit could also catch his attention, as the Horse year will bring some interesting possibilities.

The Metal Tiger's social life is also well aspected and he will have plenty of chances to meet up with his friends as well as attend an often interesting mix of occasions. For the unattached, the Horse year has distinct romantic possibilities. Any Metal Tiger who is feeling jaded or unfulfilled and would welcome more company would find it well worth joining an activity group in his area. Late April, May, July, September and December could be active and interesting months socially.

The Metal Tiger's home life is also likely to see a lot of activity during the year. If he is a grandparent, he could find himself helping younger family members more as well as offering pertinent advice. His extensive knowledge can be much appreciated this year. In addition, by talking, listening and spending time with his loved ones, he will not only value the special rapport they share but will find that all sorts of ideas and activities can come about. In addition, he will take pleasure in tackling more practical projects, and provided he does not rush or embark on too many at once, he will be pleased with the improvements made.

With this being a year of positive developments, there could also be a family celebration in many a Metal Tiger household and a holiday or local trip could provide some memorable highlights.

Overall, the Metal Tiger can do well in the Horse year. He will have the chance to put his ideas and strengths to good use, but exactly how he fares is, to some extent, in his own hands. This is a year for effort and taking the initiative, and any Metal Tigers who are tempted to coast or not particularly exert themselves could find chances are missed. With willingness, commitment and his usual enthusiastic nature, however, the Metal Tiger can benefit from the variety of opportunities the year will bring.

Tip for the Year

Act with determination. That way, you can achieve a great deal. Also, whenever possible, join with others. Shared activities are favourably aspected and your relations with others can be meaningful and special.

The Water Tiger

As the Year of the Horse gets underway, many Water Tigers will feel this is a time of change and that by acting purposefully, they will gain results. And this *will* be the case for many. The Horse year requires effort and application and the enterprising Water Tiger will be able to make positive strides. For those who have been feeling unfulfilled or have been hindered by recent circumstances, this can be a particularly welcome change.

In the Water Tiger's work situation there can be significant developments. In view of the expertise and experience he has built up, he will often have the chance to move his career forward, either by taking advantage of promotion opportunities or new openings that arise during the year. Many Water Tigers will find themselves in the right place at the right time in this year of rapidly moving developments. The Water Tiger's strengths can serve him especially well and, being an effective communicator and good at generating ideas, he will often find himself with an increased role to play in many a team. This is a year when he can make his talents count and show others his true potential.

This also applies to Water Tigers who feel there are limited prospects where they are as well as those looking for work. Although the employment situation may be difficult, by considering different ways in which they could use their skills and making an extra effort with their applications and at interview, they will find new doors opening for them. The Water Tiger's drive, talents and personal strengths will impress many this year. February, late March, April, June and September could see interesting developments, but with the aspects as they are, at almost any time of the year the Water Tiger may see an avenue of enquiry which could be worth pursuing.

Another positive aspect concerns his own personal development. Whether through work or his personal interests, he should make the most of any opportunities to learn something new or improve on his skills and knowledge. Much can follow on from this in the future.

In addition, Water Tigers who enjoy creative activities could receive an encouraging response to any ideas or work they may promote this year. As the saying goes, 'Nothing ventured, nothing gained,' and it will reward the Water Tiger to venture.

The progress he makes can also help financially, and with the aspects as they are, he may also benefit from some financial windfalls this year. However, with existing commitments, an often active lifestyle and the likelihood of travel too, his outgoings will be considerable and will need to be watched. Before making any major purchase, the Water Tiger should take the time to consider his choices. With care, he can fare well, but he does need to remain vigilant.

He can look forward to a busy social life in the Horse year and will often have an interesting mix of things to do. Once again, his interest in others and ability to empathize will make him popular company. For Water Tigers who have experienced recent personal difficulty or feel their life is lacking a certain sparkle, the Horse year can be a time of exciting possibility. However, to bring improvement these Water Tigers need to be active and go to events in their area and/or join interest or community groups. Positive action can lead to meeting others and, for some who are currently unattached, exciting romantic possibilities. May, July, September and December could be busy months socially.

The Water Tiger's home life will also be especially active this year, with the possibility of an important family occasion to mark. In view of all the activity, there will need to be good organization, co-operation and flexibility. To help, the Water Tiger should spread out any practical undertakings rather than have a lot concentrated in a short space of time. He should also make sure that quality time does not suffer due to general busyness. With travel well aspected, he should aim to take a holiday with his loved ones over the year as well as take advantage of any travel opportunities that arise at short notice. Horse years do have an element of surprise and spontaneity about them.

Overall, the Year of the Horse can be a favourable one for the Water Tiger. To benefit fully, he will need to keep alert as well as use his ideas and strengths to advantage. However, the Water Tiger has a lot to offer and with a positive 'can do' attitude, he can fare well and enjoy some well-deserved success.

Tip for the Year

Seize your opportunities. Be determined, believe in yourself and enjoy what you do. That way, you can achieve some pleasing results. This year has considerable potential for you – make the most of it.

The Wood Tiger

This will be a full and interesting year for the Wood Tiger. Not only does it mark the start of a new decade in his life, but with his active and enthusiastic nature, he will revel in the excellent opportunities it will bring. For any Wood Tiger who has felt held back or frustrated in recent times, this year can see a welcome improvement in both his situation and prospects.

With Tiger resolve combined with his quick wits, the Wood Tiger can achieve a lot in 2014 as well as set a positive pattern for the next few years. However, to get the best results from the year, he will need to remain focused and concentrate on priorities.

For Wood Tigers who are well established in a career, the Horse year can offer some good opportunities to move ahead. Whether obtaining promotion with their existing employer or moving elsewhere, these Wood Tigers will find this an encouraging time. Also, what many Wood Tigers take on this year will give them the chance to explore and extend their capabilities and, in the process, prepare them for further advances in the future. What is achieved this year can have considerable long-term value.

For Wood Tigers who feel unfulfilled or are seeking work, the Horse year can also bring new opportunities. However in order to benefit, these Wood Tigers will need to be active in making enquiries and quick to follow up any possibilities – Horse years are not ones for delay. However, when committed to an objective, the Wood Tiger will usually achieve what he wants – and changing or finding a job will be a priority for many this year. February, April, June to early July and September could see encouraging developments.

Another factor that will help many Wood Tigers this year will be their ability to relate well to others. Not only can the Wood Tiger be a key member of any workforce or team, but during the course of the year he can particularly impress influential people and establish what can become important contacts. If relevant, he may find it helpful to join a professional organization. By networking and raising his profile he can do a lot to strengthen his position and prospects.

Progress at work will often lead to an increase in income and as a consequence some Wood Tigers will decide to go ahead with accommodation plans or major purchases that they have been considering for some time. By thinking through their requirements, they will often be very pleased with the outcome. An element of good fortune can sometimes help as well.

The Horse year can bring some good travel opportunities and some Wood Tigers will decide to celebrate their fortieth year with a special holiday or treat. If this can be planned and budgeted for in advance, it can be enjoyed all the more and be a memorable highlight of the year.

The Wood Tiger will also make the most of his social opportunities this year. Not only will he value meeting his friends (some of whom will be especially supportive this year), but will also thoroughly enjoy the social events he attends. His personal interests can also bring him into contact with new people. Late April, May, July, September and December are likely to see the greatest level of social activity.

For the unattached Wood Tiger this can be an especially exciting year, with a chance encounter possibly becoming significant. Wood Tigers who have been feeling lonely and would welcome company, a more rewarding social life or possible romance should make it a resolution to go out more and perhaps join a local activity group. This is a year which rewards positive and purposeful action.

The Wood Tiger can also benefit from his personal interests this year. If he has ideas he would like to take further, this would be an ideal time to act. The Wood Tiger is blessed with an imaginative and enquiring nature and some of his undertakings this year will be especially rewarding.

In addition he should give some thought to his well-being and if he feels his level of exercise or the quality of his diet is in any way lacking, he should seek advice on the best action to take.

His home life will be busy and eventful and his loved ones may well be keen to celebrate his fortieth year in style. Over the year the Wood Tiger may also give extra assistance to more senior relations. However, in view of the general activity of the year, flexibility would be advised where more practical activities are concerned and the Wood Tiger should watch his sometimes over-zealous nature. He may be keen and willing, but there are limits to how much can be undertaken at any one time. Overall, however, this can be a full and rewarding year domestically.

The Wood Tiger has many talents, and his determination, quick wits and experience may lead to some good results in the Horse year. To make the most of his opportunities, he does need to concentrate on specific aims and focus on priorities, but he will be helped by the support and goodwill of those around him and his loved ones will be especially important. There are some memorable personal times in store for him in this rewarding year.

Tip for the Year
Celebrate your fortieth year by regarding it as a time for action. Focus on your priorities and use your strengths to advantage. Your efforts – sometimes helped by a certain amount of good fortune – can make this a personally special year. Enjoy it and give it your best.

The Fire Tiger

There is a Chinese proverb that is especially apt for the Fire Tiger this year: 'Hoist your sail when the wind is fair. Seize the opportunity.' This is a highly promising year and by acting in determined and enterprising fashion, the Fire Tiger can accomplish a great deal.

His personal life is particularly well aspected. For Fire Tigers with a partner this can be an often special year, with some marrying, starting a family or reaching a shared goal. Whatever their aspirations, the Horse year will see many Fire Tigers having good cause to celebrate. The Fire Tiger can also benefit from a certain amount of luck this year and once plans are underway, an element of fortune can often help them along.

For Fire Tigers who are alone and may have had some recent personal misfortune to bear, the Horse year can see a transformation in their situation – often through Cupid's arrow being aimed directly at them! Romance could be found through a chance meeting or in some other way, but however it comes about, for many Fire Tigers this will be a year of passion. May, July, September and December to mid-January could see some particularly meaningful developments.

The Fire Tiger will also make the most of the social opportunities of the year. Meeting his friends will often offer him the chance to seek advice and test out ideas as well as enjoy mutual interests. In addition, his work situation and various activities can lead to new friends and important connections being made. This is a year for networking and the congenial Fire Tiger will often be on sparkling form.

The Fire Tiger is also blessed with an inventive streak and if he has interests that are in any way creative or expressive, he should allow himself the time to develop them and, if appropriate, promote what he does. With the encouraging aspects of the year, interesting developments can often follow on. Similarly, Fire Tigers who enjoy sport or more outdoor activities will find the Horse year bringing them much pleasure. All Fire Tigers can also benefit from the sometimes unexpected travel opportunities that will arise during the year.

Although the Fire Tiger keeps himself active, he should give some consideration to his well-being this year. To be at his best and keep his energy levels high, he should ensure his diet is balanced and nutritious.

The Horse year can also see important developments in the Fire Tiger's work situation. For Fire Tigers pursuing a specific career, there can be some unexpected opportunities. Although these Fire Tigers may have their sights set on a particular position or type of work, they may be offered the chance to broaden their experience by taking on different responsibilities or, if in a large organization, transferring to another section. The Horse year very much encourages progress, but this may not always come about in the precise way the Fire Tiger envisaged. However, by making the most of his opportunities, he can not only make important headway but also improve his prospects for the future.

For Fire Tigers who are unfulfilled in their present position, as well as those seeking work, again the Horse year can offer considerable possibility. Although the job-seeking process can be wearying, the Fire Tiger's determination and personality can make a great difference and by using his initiative to make enquiries, he may ultimately be successful in his quest. He could also be helped by some of his contacts. With his often impressive manner, he may well find others keen to assist, including sometimes putting in recommendations on his behalf. In the Horse year the Fire Tiger could have quite a few people rooting for him. February, April, June, September and early October could see some good opportunities, but whenever the Fire Tiger identifies a possible opening he should act upon it quickly. Horse years are not ones for delay.

This can be an important year for financial matters, with the Fire Tiger having to make some major spending decisions as well as sometimes take on a new long-term commitment. He will need to be thorough and seek professional advice as well as be aware of the terms and obligations involved in any new agreement. He would also do well to make early allowance for any expensive personal projects and/or travel plans. However, while care is needed, the Fire Tiger can also enjoy some financial luck. He may be fortunate in locating items he wants at an advantageous price or in receiving extra funds, either through an increase in income or a gift.

The Fire Tiger has a strong will and engaging manner, and both will serve him well this year. By looking to move forward and seizing his opportunities, he can make important headway. His personal life is splendidly aspected and romantic prospects and personal relationships can bring him much happiness. Overall, he has a lot in his favour this year, but it does call on him to put in the effort and use his talents well. This is not a year to waste, especially in view of some of the hopes and aspirations he is so keen to realize.

Tip for the Year

Your relations with others can be of special value this year. Consult those around you and seize any chances to build up contacts. Their support can often be significant. Also, act with purpose. With self-belief and initiative, you can achieve a lot and enjoy many happy times.

The Earth Tiger

For the Earth Tiger born in 1998 this can be a dynamic year. There will be opportunities aplenty and by putting in the effort, the Earth Tiger can make important progress.

In his education the young Earth Tiger will often be grappling with many different subjects as well as preparing for exams. On occasions there could be a bewildering amount to do and it would benefit the Earth Tiger to stay well organized. With focus and discipline, he can accomplish a great deal and may achieve impressive results. Also, while he may sometimes feel daunted by the pressures of studying, it is by being challenged that he will have the chance to develop his knowledge and highlight certain aptitudes. The Horse year can be both instructive and illuminating.

Throughout the year the Earth Tiger should be open to opportunity and if he has the chance of extra tuition or training he should make the most of it. If he takes his chances and is receptive to what is offered him, he can not only benefit now but also invest in his future. The Horse year will require effort, but it can help provide the skills and qualifications that can be of so much value later.

During the year the Earth Tiger should also make the most of any opportunity he has to talk over future study choices and possible career options with tutors and advisers. By forming some idea of what he wants to do later, he can not only be alerted to areas he needs to concentrate on but also particular qualifications he should aim for.

In addition to the academic progress he makes, the Earth Tiger will have the chance to develop his skills and interests in other areas, whether sporting, creative, musical or some other sphere. The Horse year has considerable potential, but to benefit, the Earth Tiger needs to make the most of his opportunities. They may not come his way again. Earth Tigers, take note.

With his genial nature the Earth Tiger enjoys good relations with many people and over the year can look forward to some great times with his friends. Not only will he appreciate the support they can give one another but also the fun they can have. Some activities the Earth Tiger pursues can lead to him meeting new people and, especially for any Earth Tiger who may be shy or not as much a part of the social scene as he would like, an important new friendship can be forged. The year is favourably aspected for relations with others.

There will also be opportunities for the Earth Tiger to travel. Whether he is on holiday or an educational visit, he will often delight in the places he sees and the activities he has the chance to try out. With more active pursuits, however, he does need to pay heed to the advice and instructions given. This may be a good year, but it is not one for foolhardiness.

The Earth Tiger will also need to be receptive to the views and advice of family members. Although he may have his own ideas, those around him do have his best interests at heart and extensive experience behind them, and the young Earth Tiger would do well to listen to what they suggest or recommend. Rapport and understanding will also be helped by the Earth Tiger assisting more in the home and contributing to family life. While he will often be involved in studying and other activities, anything he can do to help will be appreciated.

Overall, this will be a valuable year for the young Earth Tiger and can prove to be an important stage in his development. If he seizes his opportunities and gives his best he can grow considerably in confidence this year and in the process highlight his future potential.

For Earth Tigers born in 1938, this will also be an interesting year. However, to get the best from it these Earth Tigers should decide on their priorities and concentrate on these. With focus, effort and the support of others, they will find many of their activities going well and bringing them considerable satisfaction.

The more senior Earth Tiger's thinking may concern modifications to his home and visits to places of interest he would like to make as well as ways in which he can use his skills and enjoy his interests. Whatever he chooses to focus on, he will rarely be at a loss for things to do, and the more he can share his thoughts and activities with those around him, the better.

The Earth Tiger will also follow family activities with fond interest and, despite a considerable gap of years, the rapport he has with a much younger relation can be especially gratifying.

He will also welcome the social opportunities of the year. Some of his friends will prove especially supportive, particularly with certain activities the Earth Tiger may be involved with or decisions he may have to take. Local activities can be another source of interest and the Earth Tiger would do well to keep informed about what is happening in his area.

Financial matters will need care and the Earth Tiger does need to be thorough when dealing with important correspondence. This should not be rushed, and advice should be obtained if needed. However, despite this need for vigilance, many Earth Tigers could enjoy some luck this year, including a possible competition win.

Whether born in 1938 or 1998, the Earth Tiger will find the Horse year an encouraging one and can accomplish and enjoy a great deal. If he draws on the support of those around him and seizes his opportunities, he can make this a year of fine personal achievement.

Tip for the Year

Decide on your objectives and concentrate on them. With focus, effort and support, a lot of your aims can be achieved. Earth Tigers born in 1998, be open-minded and make good use of your resources and opportunities. This has the potential for being a significant and rewarding year. Use it well.

Famous Tigers

Paula Abdul, Amy Adams, Kofi Annan, Sir David Attenborough, Christian Bale, Queen Beatrix of the Netherlands, Victoria Beckham, Beethoven, Jamie Bell, Tony Bennett, Tom Berenger, Chuck Berry, Usain Bolt, Jon Bon Jovi, Sir Richard Branson, Matthew Broderick, Emily Brontë, Garth Brooks, Mel Brooks, Isambard Kingdom Brunel, Agatha Christie, Charlotte Church, Robbie Coltrane, Bradley Cooper, Sheryl Crow, Tom Cruise, Penelope Cruz, Charles de Gaulle, Leonardo DiCaprio, Emily Dickinson, David Dimbleby, Drake, Dwight Eisenhower, Queen Elizabeth II, Enya, Roberta Flack, Frederick Forsyth, Jodie Foster, Megan Fox, Lady Gaga, Crystal Gayle, Buddy Greco, Germaine Greer, Ed Harris, Hugh Hefner, William Hurt, Ray Kroc, Shia LaBeouf, Stan Laurel, Jay Leno, Matt Lucas, Groucho Marx, Karl Marx, Marilyn Monroe, Demi Moore, Alanis Morissette, Rafael Nadal, Robert Pattinson, Jeremy Paxman, Marco Polo, Beatrix Potter, Renoir, Nora Roberts, Kenny Rogers, the Princess Royal, Dylan Thomas, Liv Ullman, Jon Voight, Julie Walters, H. G. Wells, Oscar Wilde, Robbie Williams, Tennessee Williams, Sir Terry Wogan, Stevie Wonder, William Wordsworth.

14 February 1915 to 2 February 1916 — *Wood Rabbit*

2 February 1927 to 22 January 1928 — *Fire Rabbit*

19 February 1939 to 7 February 1940 — *Earth Rabbit*

6 February 1951 to 26 January 1952 — *Metal Rabbit*

25 January 1963 to 12 February 1964 — *Water Rabbit*

11 February 1975 to 30 January 1976 — *Wood Rabbit*

29 January 1987 to 16 February 1988 — *Fire Rabbit*

16 February 1999 to 4 February 2000 — *Earth Rabbit*

3 February 2011 to 22 January 2012 — *Metal Rabbit*

The Rabbit

The Personality of the Rabbit

Whenever
Wherever
With whoever.
Always I try to understand.
Without this, one flounders.
But with understanding,
at least you have a chance.
A good chance.

The Rabbit is born under the signs of virtue and prudence. He is intelligent, well mannered and prefers a quiet and peaceful existence. He dislikes any sort of unpleasantness and will try to steer clear of arguments and disputes. He is very much a pacifist and tends to have a calming influence on those around him. He has wide interests and usually a good appreciation of the arts and the finer things in life. He also knows how to enjoy himself and will often gravitate to the best restaurants and nightspots in town.

The Rabbit is a witty and intelligent speaker and loves being involved in a good discussion. His views and advice are often sought by others and he can be relied upon to be discreet and diplomatic. He will rarely raise his voice in anger and will even turn a blind eye to matters that displease him just to preserve the peace. He likes to remain on good terms with everyone, but he can be rather sensitive and takes any form of criticism very badly. He will also be the first to get out of the way if he sees any form of trouble brewing.

The Rabbit is a quiet and efficient worker and has an extremely good memory. He is very astute in business and financial matters, but his degree of success often depends on the conditions that prevail. He hates being in a situation which is fraught with tension or where he has to make sudden decisions. Wherever possible he will plan his various activities with the utmost care and a good deal of caution. He does not like to take risks and does not take kindly to change. Basically, he seeks a secure, calm and stable environment, and when conditions are right he is more than happy to leave things as they are.

The Rabbit is conscientious and because of his methodical and ever-watchful nature he can often do well in his chosen profession. He makes a good diplomat, lawyer, shopkeeper, administrator or priest, and he excels in any job where he can use his superb skills as a communicator. He tends to be loyal to his employers and is respected for his integrity and honesty, but if he ever finds himself in a position of great power he can become rather intransigent and authoritarian.

The Rabbit attaches great importance to his home and will often spend a lot of time and money maintaining and furnishing it and fitting it with all the latest comforts – the Rabbit is very much a creature of comfort! He is also something of a collector and there are many Rabbits who derive much pleasure from collecting antiques, stamps, coins, *objets d'art* or anything else which catches their eye or particularly interests them.

The female Rabbit has a friendly, caring and considerate nature, and will do all in her power to give her home a happy and loving atmosphere. She is also very sociable and enjoys holding parties and entertaining. She has a great ability to make the maximum use of her time and although she involves herself in numerous activities, she always manages to find time to sit back and enjoy a good read or a chat. She has a great sense of humour, is very artistic and is often a talented gardener.

The Rabbit takes considerable care over his appearance and is usually smart and well turned out. He also attaches great importance to his relations with others and matters of the heart are particularly important to him. He will rarely be short of admirers and will often have several serious romances before he settles down. He is not the most faithful of signs, but he will find that he is especially well suited to those born under the signs of the Goat, Snake, Pig and Ox. Due to his sociable and easy-going manner he can also get on well with the Tiger, Dragon, Horse, Monkey, Dog and another Rabbit, but he will feel ill at ease with the Rat and Rooster, as both these signs tend to speak their mind and be critical in their comments and the Rabbit just loathes any form of criticism or unpleasantness.

The Rabbit is usually lucky in life and often has the happy knack of being in the right place at the right time. He is talented and quick-witted, but he does sometimes put pleasure before work and wherever possible will opt for the easy life. He can at times be a little reserved and suspicious of the motives of others, but generally will lead a long and contented life and one which – as far as possible – will be free of strife and discord.

The Five Different Types of Rabbit

In addition to the 12 signs of the Chinese zodiac there are five elements and these have a strengthening or moderating influence on the signs. The effects of the five elements on the Rabbit are described below, together with the years in which they were exercising their influence. Therefore Rabbits born in 1951 and 2011 are Metal Rabbits, Rabbits born in 1963 are Water Rabbits, and so on.

Metal Rabbit: 1951, 2011

This Rabbit is capable, ambitious and has very definite views on what he wants to achieve in life. He can occasionally appear reserved and aloof, but this is mainly because he likes to keep his thoughts to himself. He has a quick and alert mind and is particularly shrewd in business matters. He can also be very cunning in his actions. He has a good appreciation of the arts and likes to mix in the best circles. He usually has a small but very loyal group of friends.

Water Rabbit: 1963

The Water Rabbit is popular, intuitive and keenly aware of the feelings of those around him. He can, however, be rather sensitive and take things too much to heart. He is very precise and thorough in everything he does and has an exceedingly good memory. He tends to be quiet and at times rather withdrawn, but he expresses his ideas well and is highly regarded by his family, friends and colleagues.

Wood Rabbit: 1915, 1975

The Wood Rabbit is likeable, easy-going and very adaptable. He prefers to work in a group rather than on his own and likes to have the support and encouragement of others. He can, however, be rather reticent in expressing his views and it would be in his own interests to become a little more open and let others know how he feels on certain matters. He usually has many friends, enjoys an active social life and is noted for his generosity.

Fire Rabbit: 1927, 1987

The Fire Rabbit has a friendly, outgoing personality. He likes socializing and being on good terms with everyone. He is discreet and diplomatic and has a very good understanding of human nature. He is also strong-willed and provided he has the necessary backing he can go far in life. He does, not, however, suffer adversity well and can become moody and depressed when things are not working out as he would like. He has a particularly good manner with children, is very intuitive and there are some Fire Rabbits who are even noted for their psychic ability.

Earth Rabbit: 1939, 1999

The Earth Rabbit is a quiet individual, but nevertheless very astute. He is realistic in his aims and prepared to work long and hard in order to achieve his objectives. He has good business sense and is invariably lucky in financial matters. He also has a most persuasive manner and usually experiences little difficulty in getting others to fall in with his plans. He is held in high esteem by his friends and colleagues and his views are often sought and highly valued.

Prospects for the Rabbit in 2014

The Year of the Snake (10 February 2013–30 January 2014) will have been a reasonable one for the Rabbit, although as it draws to a close he could find a lot being asked of him. To help, he should keep well organized as well as draw on the assistance of others. With good planning and support, he can accomplish a great deal.

At work he could find he has a heavy workload and needs to prioritize what has to be done. November could be an important month and perhaps bring new objectives or a new opportunity.

The Rabbit's domestic and social life will also become busier in the closing months of the year, with events, parties and other get-togethers to enjoy. However, while usually so skilful in handling his relations with others, the Rabbit does need to remain aware of the views of those around him and be alert to any gossip or mischief-making that is taking place. A rumour or personal difficulty could concern him. Rabbits, do take note, and if you are worried, check the facts and keep matters in perspective.

The Rabbit could be fortunate in some purchases he makes at this time, however, and his alert nature and fine taste can reward him well.

Overall, the Snake year will have been a generally satisfying one for the Rabbit, with a lot of activity concentrated in the closing months.

The Year of the Horse begins on 31 January and the high level of activity will continue. Although this may sometimes be more than the Rabbit is comfortable with, the year will also contain some excellent opportunities and many fine personal times.

The Rabbit's relations with others are especially well aspected and he will have the chance to meet many new people this year. Some will quickly become part of his social circle, while others, often met in work situations, will be particularly taken with his qualities and be keen to assist him in some way. As has often been found, the more people you know and who know of you, the more likely it is that you will benefit from opportunities, and this will be very much the case for the Rabbit this year. His social skills will not only reward him well but also allow him to enjoy the year that much more. February, March, August and October could see the most social activity, although at most times of the year the Rabbit will have opportunities go out and meet others.

For Rabbits who are alone, perhaps having moved to a new area, and would welcome more company, the Horse year can bring an improvement in their situation. By immersing themselves in local activities, possibly by joining societies, helping in their community or going to events, they will get to meet others and brighten their situation. For the unattached, the Horse year also has exciting romantic prospects, even though the path of true love may not always run smoothly. Love can bring great happiness for many Rabbits this year, though, with some of the more challenging moments being overcome.

The Rabbit's domestic life can also see much activity. This is a year that favours togetherness and joint effort and the Rabbit's attentive nature can be an important factor in his home life. However, for all to go smoothly, it is important that plans are agreed in advance and decisions talked through. Also, while the Rabbit and other family members will often have work and other commitments, time should be preserved for joint activities and perhaps the occasional treat or holiday.

It is also important that the Rabbit does not neglect his personal interests. These can be a tonic for him and give him the chance to relax too. Outdoor and activity pursuits are particularly well aspected this year.

The Rabbit can also look forward to making progress in his work, even though the pressures will sometimes be great. Horse years are times of often intense activity and the Rabbit could be set challenging objectives or find his workload considerably heavier. Also, while he may like to proceed at a more considered pace, he could be caught up in fast-moving situations and need to act quickly in order to benefit. If, for instance, a promotion opportunity suddenly arises or staff are required for new undertakings, the Rabbit should waste no time in putting himself forward. Speed is of the essence this year.

For Rabbits who feel there are limited opportunities where they are and would welcome new challenges, as well as those seeking work, the

Horse year can have important developments in store. By making enquiries, considering different ways in which they can use their skills and being quick in putting forward applications, these Rabbits can find their efforts leading to a new position, and often one with the potential for future development. The Horse year favours initiative and many Rabbits will be able to make some well-deserved headway.

With personal relations favourably aspected this year, the Rabbit should also take any chances to get himself better known. Some of his contacts could give him useful advice or be instrumental in some of his achievements. March, June, August and November could see key work developments.

Progress at work can help the Rabbit's earnings, but with his domestic commitments, travel plans and social opportunities, he will have considerable demands on his resources. Accordingly, he does need to watch his spending and be wary of too many unplanned outgoings. Financially, this is a year requiring good control.

In general, the Horse year will be a full and active one and to do well the Rabbit will need to work hard and act quickly. He may not always welcome the speed with which events happen or the pressure this causes, but this is still a year of considerable potential, and the Rabbit can improve both his current situation and future prospects. His relations with others are well aspected, and whether making new friends, forging connections in his work and personal interests or enjoying a rewarding domestic life, he will find himself in demand and appreciating a lot of what he does. For the unattached, romance, too, can help make the year special. Overall, a busy and rewarding year.

The Metal Rabbit

One of the strengths of the Metal Rabbit is his perceptive nature. He not only reads people and situations well but is often able to gauge the right course of action to take. This ability will serve him well in this fine and encouraging year.

The Metal Rabbit's relations with others are set to go particularly well and during the year he can look forward to some special times. In his home life there could be pleasing developments in store, with the Metal Rabbit playing an important part in what takes place. His loved ones will frequently seek his opinion and younger relations will be grateful for his guidance.

In addition to helping others and keeping tabs on a generally busy domestic life, the Metal Rabbit could have some ambitious plans for his home. These could include replacing equipment, making modifications to particular items and refurbishing certain rooms. With his eye for detail, the Metal Rabbit will be keen to get everything right, but he should avoid rush and be receptive to the views of those around him and the advice given by experts. In some cases, modifications to existing ideas could lead to better outcomes. Also, by waiting for favourable buying opportunities rather than proceeding too hastily, the Metal Rabbit could save himself unnecessary outlay as well as make more suitable purchases.

In addition to all the practical activity, the Metal Rabbit should encourage joint interests and, if possible, take a holiday or break with his loved ones. Domestic life can have a special quality this year.

The aspects are also promising for the Metal Rabbit's social life. He will once more value meeting his friends and could particularly benefit from the assistance or expertise a certain friend may offer. The Metal Rabbit will do a lot for others this year, but will receive much in return.

With his wide interests, he could be attracted by events happening in his area or become involved in a local group or community project or give help to a cause he supports. Whatever he does, the indications are that he will get to know quite a few new people this year and will get on especially well with those who share similar outlooks. New friends can add new meaning to the year and for some Metal Rabbits who are currently unattached, romance is a distinct possibility. February, March, August and October could see the most social activity.

During the year the Metal Rabbit could also find it helpful to give some consideration to his general well-being. If he feels he does not get sufficient exercise, he should seek advice on what activities may be most suitable. In some cases a new form of exercise could become a new hobby, with a possible social element an added bonus.

For Metal Rabbits in work this will be a busy year. With events often happening quickly and a heavy workload to deal with, the Metal Rabbit's ability to focus and remain organized will be of considerable help. However, while this can be a demanding time, the Metal Rabbit can look forward to some notable successes. In addition, he will be helped by the excellent working relations he has with many of his colleagues and his guidance will often be sought on certain matters.

The Horse year can offer change as well as the opportunity for the Metal Rabbit to make good use of his skills and act on his ideas. Some Metal Rabbits may choose to retire this year, while those looking for work could find a part-time situation or have the opportunity to try something different.

The Metal Rabbit can fare reasonably well in financial matters, but with domestic plans and tempting travel opportunities, as well as socializing and other activities, he could find it an expensive year. Spending will need to be watched and the Metal Rabbit should be wary about making large purchases too hurriedly. More time and consideration will lead to better decisions.

Overall, though, the Year of the Horse can be a rewarding one for the Metal Rabbit. It will give him the chance to take his ideas forward, develop his interests and enjoy good times with those around him. To get the best from the year he will need to put in the effort, but with Metal as his element, he is by nature resourceful and his many abilities will help him to do well in this encouraging and active year.

Tip for the Year

Seize your opportunities and follow up your ideas. Also, value your relations with others. The support you receive, backed by your own initiative, will allow you to accomplish and enjoy a lot this year.

The Water Rabbit

The element of Water can strengthen a sign's abilities as a communicator and this is especially true for the Water Rabbit. Not only is he an effective speaker, but he listens well and picks up on a great deal. In addition he has a genuine interest in others which is appreciated by those who come into contact with him. His personal talents can not only help in a lot of what he sets out to do this year but can also give rise to some memorable occasions.

The Water Rabbit's domestic life may see a lot happen over the year and those close to him will often be grateful for his care and assistance. This applies to both younger and more senior relations, who will often look to him for advice. Indeed, the Water Rabbit may not always realize how much impact his words and actions can have.

With the year favouring joint undertakings, this can be a good time for family activities. There will, however, also be pressures, especially if working routines change or plans run into problems. Here some flexibility will be needed, but discussion and compromise can help to ease the more difficult or trying moments of the year.

Travel is favourably aspected and the Water Rabbit should, if possible, aim to take a holiday with loved ones at some time during the year. Even if he does not travel too far, a change of scene can benefit all concerned.

In addition, there could be a special occasion to mark that could give the Water Rabbit the chance to meet some family members he has not seen for some while.

He will also take considerable pleasure in his social life and will value the support some close friends are able to give, especially if he finds himself with important decisions to make. Often he will know someone with the right knowledge or skills to help, and he should not hesitate to ask. Friendships and other contacts can prove especially helpful this year.

There will also be some good social opportunities, with the Water Rabbit's interests and other activities often bringing him into contact with new people. Water Rabbits who would welcome a more active social life or are perhaps looking for romance will find the Horse year can bring quite a transformation in their situation. It is a time which can highlight the Water Rabbit's personal qualities and he may well find himself in increasing demand. February, March, August and October could see the most social activity as well as be good for meeting others.

Although the Water Rabbit will often have a lot to do, he should try not to let his own interests get sidelined during the year. These can help him relax, give him the chance to do something different and perhaps be an outlet for his creative talents. In this active year the Water Rabbit does need to preserve some time just for himself.

Work-wise, this can be an interesting year. Although many Water Rabbits will be well established in a certain type of work, the Horse year can offer the opportunity to switch to new duties or use their talents in different ways. For some this may include taking on a more managerial role and/or progressing to a new stage in their career. There may be times when the Water Rabbit may feel daunted by what is asked of him or the sheer volume of information he has to familiarize himself with, but while some parts of the year can be exacting, the Water Rabbit will have the chance to acquire and demonstrate skills which can be to his present and future benefit.

Water Rabbits seeking work should not only keep alert for possible vacancies and stay informed of developments in major industries in their area, but also keep in regular contact with employment agencies and former colleagues and contacts. By being active and quick to follow up opportunities, they can be successful in their quest. Although some of the work offered these Water Rabbits may be different from what they have done before, they will often revel in the chance to prove themselves in a new capacity. Here again skills and knowledge gained this year can have long-term value. March, mid-May to the end of June, August and November could see particularly encouraging developments.

The Water Rabbit's progress at work can help financially, but he should keep track of his spending and make early provision for more major expenses. He also needs to be thorough when dealing with financial paperwork. A mistake or delayed response could be to his disadvantage. His lifestyle may keep him busy, but he cannot be dilatory when dealing with money matters. Water Rabbits, take note.

Overall, the Year of the Horse is one of great possibility for the Water Rabbit. He will enjoy good support as well as rewarding times in both his domestic and social life. He may also have the chance to move ahead in his work and although pressures may sometimes be great, he too will have the opportunity to demonstrate and extend his skills. A busy but potentially significant year.

Tip for the Year

Use your personal skills to good effect. The more people you know and who know of you, the more your position and prospects can be helped. Also, extend your capabilities. Skills acquired now can help your subsequent progress. This is a good year of often far-reaching significance for you.

The Wood Rabbit

This will be a busy year for the Wood Rabbit, with some encouraging developments.

One of the Wood Rabbit's strengths is his ability to converse and empathize with others. People value his company and think highly of his judgement, and throughout the year his ability to forge connections can be an important factor in his success.

This is particularly the case in his work. Wood Rabbits who have been in the same position or organization for some time will have built up a solid reputation and when the opportunity arises for promotion, their experience can make them a strong candidate. This is very much a year for building on their current position. For those whose work involves communication and liaison with others, this can be an especially successful time.

There can also be encouraging developments for Wood Rabbits seeking change or looking for work. Although the job-seeking process will not be easy, by remaining persistent, making enquiries and talking to contacts and advisers, these Wood Rabbits may be successful in their quest. Admittedly, adjustments will be needed when taking on a new position and there may be much to learn, but by showing commitment and rising to the challenge, these Wood Rabbits will soon become established in their role and an important member of any team. For all Wood Rabbits, the Horse year can be a demanding one, but it will give them the chance to demonstrate their strengths and many will make deserved headway. March, June, August, late October and November could be important months for work matters.

Progress at work can also help financially, but with an often busy lifestyle, together with other commitments, the Wood Rabbit will need to keep his outgoings under strict control. He can proceed with many of his plans this year, but it will require careful budgeting. Also, when considering major purchases, particularly for the home, he should take the time to investigate different options. With patience and thoroughness, he could save himself unnecessary outlay as well as acquire items which can be a source of pleasure both to himself and others.

An encouraging aspect of the year will be the opportunities it will bring for the Wood Rabbit to develop his skills and expertise. These will partly come as a result of the new duties he takes on, but as far as personal interests are concerned, if there is something the Wood Rabbit wants to learn or improve on, this would be an excellent year to do so. Creative pursuits can be particularly rewarding and, with travel well aspected, some Wood Rabbits may also decide to visit places connected to their interests or attend special events.

Quite a few will also find their interests have a good social element to them and this can make them all the more enjoyable. Wood Rabbits who are feeling lonely would find it well worth considering joining a local group. For the unattached, the Horse year has excellent romantic possibilities. February to early April, August and October could see the most social activity, although at most times of the year there will be things of interest for the Wood Rabbit to look forward to.

The Wood Rabbit's home life will also see considerable activity this year. Here his ability to organize, find consensus and keep tabs on many different activities at once can be of particular value. With practical undertakings, however, flexibility will be needed. In view of changing work schedules and other commitments, sometimes projects may take longer than envisaged or have to be postponed to quieter times.

While this will be an active year domestically, there will, though, be much to enjoy. Wood Rabbits who are parents could be particularly proud of the achievements of their children. Shared activities, including, if possible, a holiday or break away, are favourably aspected, and the Wood Rabbit's care and attentiveness can add meaning and pleasure to his home life. Wood Rabbits with more senior relations will again do much to help them over the course of the year – although such help could turn out to be reciprocal, as senior relations may in turn be able to offer time or support. Domestically, the Horse year will be a full one, but will contain some special moments.

In such an active year, however, the Wood Rabbit will often find himself leading long and tiring days, and to remain at his best he would find it helpful to give some consideration to his well-being, including his diet and level of exercise. The attention he can give to this area can make an appreciable difference, especially to his energy levels.

Overall, the Year of the Horse is filled with great possibility for the Wood Rabbit and by seizing his opportunities he can make important headway. Many Wood Rabbits will be able to make progress at work, and developing interests and learning new skills can be personally satisfying. However it is the Wood Rabbit's relations with others that can make this year so special and provide some very gratifying times.

Tip for the Year

As a Wood Rabbit, you know you have it within you to achieve a great deal in life. Now is the time to use your strengths to advantage. Be purposeful – your efforts can reward you well this year. Also, value those who are close to you. They are special – and special for a reason.

The Fire Rabbit

The element of Fire increases a sign's resolve and the Fire Rabbit is certainly keen to make the most of himself. In 2014 he can look forward to some pleasing results. Any Fire Rabbits who start the Horse year disappointed with recent developments will find this is very much a time to draw a line under what has gone before and concentrate on the present and near future.

One important factor in the Fire Rabbit's favour will be the support he will enjoy during the year. Family, friends, colleagues, contacts and new acquaintances may all be keen to encourage and assist when they can. The Fire Rabbit possesses a very personable nature and over the year he should make the most of the good relations he enjoys with so many people as well as take any opportunities to meet others. His efforts will reward him well. Joining a professional organization or a group in connection with one of his personal interests might well be of benefit. This will not only give him the chance to meet like-minded people but also to benefit from their assistance.

The Fire Rabbit's work situation can see some particularly encouraging developments. With many organizations likely to be involved in change this year, new positions could be created, and the Fire Rabbit may find himself ideally placed to apply. Alternatively, he could be offered promotion and/or the chance to extend his current duties. This is certainly a year when the commitment and skills of many Fire Rabbits will be recognized and encouraged.

For Fire Rabbits who are unfulfilled in their present line of work and would welcome a new challenge, as well as those seeking work, the Horse year can have far-reaching significance. By widening the scope of positions they are prepared to consider, talking to employment officials, professional organizations and, if possible, taking advantage of refresher courses, many of these Fire Rabbits could be successful in obtaining a new type of work with the potential for future development. Late February, March, June, August and November could see important developments, but such is the fast-moving nature of the Horse year that opportunities need to be seized the moment they occur. This is no time for delay.

In view of some of the ambitions the Fire Rabbit will have, he should also use any chances he has to study and extend his knowledge, possibly by enrolling on a course or securing another qualification. What he does now can strengthen his prospects and open up possibilities for the future.

Some of the Fire Rabbit's personal interests can also have unexpected benefits. Creative and expressive interests could add to his personal and presentational skills as well as give him greater confidence, while more outward bound pursuits may help fitness levels. Although the year will often be busy, it is important that the Fire Rabbit sets time aside to enjoy his own interests and, in many cases, shares them with others.

Progress at work can lead to many Fire Rabbits increasing their income over the year, and some will also benefit from the receipt of additional funds. However, with often costly plans and many commitments, the Fire Rabbit will need to keep careful control over his spending. He should also check the terms of any new agreement he enters into.

While money will require careful management, if possible the Fire Rabbit should, however, try to take a holiday at some time during the year. Travel is well aspected and a change of scene can do him good as well as enable him to visit some often interesting destinations.

Socially, there is likely to be an increase in activity this year and any Fire Rabbit who has had a recent personal problem to contend with and would welcome a more fulfilling social life will find the Horse year full of exciting potential. By being active and taking up any chances to go out, many of these Fire Rabbits will soon get to meet others and find their personal and social life becoming much more satisfying as a result. Romantic prospects are also excellent and potentially significant. February, March, August and October could be particularly pleasing months, but at most times of the year the Fire Rabbit will have a variety of interesting occasions to look forward to.

His domestic life is also favourably aspected. With this being a year favouring joint decisions and combined effort, shared plans and activities can bring particular pleasure. An element of luck can also come into play and it may be that items for the home are secured on favourable terms or assistance with a project appears from an unexpected quarter. Over the year there could also be a cause for celebration and the Fire Rabbit will find his home life active but rewarding.

Overall, the Year of the Horse can be an exciting one for the Fire Rabbit. There will be some personally pleasing times to look forward to and some good possibilities will emerge. To benefit, the Fire Rabbit will need to be active and put in the effort, but he knows he has the skills and wherewithal to accomplish a great deal in life and his prospects this year are especially bright.

Tip for the Year

Make the most of your relations with others. With the support and encouragement of those around you, your success can be that much greater. Also, look to increase your skills. This can often lead on to other possibilities.

The Earth Rabbit

'Diligence leads to riches', as the Chinese proverb reminds us, and this holds true for the Earth Rabbit this year. If he uses his time well and sets about his activities with diligence, he will have a lot to gain from this promising year.

For Earth Rabbits born in 1939 the Horse year can give rise to some interesting developments. To take advantage of these, however, the Earth Rabbit will need to show flexibility and be prepared to make the most of his situation. In his home life, he could have ideas which could increase comfort and efficiency, and it is important that he talks over his options with those around him and obtains appropriate advice. Often initial thoughts can just be the starting-point of something better.

Also, if engaged in any practical undertaking, the Earth Rabbit does need to follow the recommended procedures. If in doubt, he should seek assistance. Similarly, he should be careful if lifting heavy weights or moving cumbersome objects. He may be willing, but a sprain could cause him considerable discomfort. Earth Rabbits, take careful note.

In addition to possible alterations to his home, the Earth Rabbit could also be tempted to acquire new equipment or gadgetry, possibly a new computer, television, smartphone or something related to a personal interest. Whatever he chooses, he can derive considerable pleasure from exploring its capabilities. Family members, too, will often be keen to help and to be involved.

There will be good travel opportunities this year, with some arising quite suddenly. The Earth Rabbit could be invited to visit family or close friends, be intrigued by a special event some distance away or just decide to go away on a whim. The surprise nature of some of these trips can add to the fun, and travel can be among the highlights of the Earth Rabbit's year.

He will also follow family activities with much interest and his loved ones will value his kindness and assistance as well as the wisdom of his words. An eloquent speaker, the Earth Rabbit has a wonderful way of imparting advice. There will also be occasions during the year which bring family members together, and the Earth Rabbit will welcome the chance to meet up with those who live some distance away. In addition some family members could have special surprises in store as the Earth Rabbit celebrates his seventy-fifth birthday.

Another source of pleasure will be his personal interests. Not only will he enjoy the projects he tackles but also the way in which he is able to put his knowledge and skills to satisfying use. Creative activities are particularly well aspected and if the Earth Rabbit is able to share his interests with other enthusiasts this can often add to their meaning. For those who enjoy writing, this could be a rewarding way to record their thoughts and experiences.

The Earth Rabbit is usually careful when dealing with paperwork and financial matters, and while this may be a good year, he must not be lax when attending to potentially important correspondence. Although some forms may be irksome, to delay or miss details could be to his disadvantage. He should also keep guarantees and receipts carefully. This is a year that rewards vigilance.

The Earth Rabbit's social life is well aspected and he will again appreciate the contact he has with his good and long-standing friends. Any Earth Rabbits who have been feeling lonely recently would do well to consider joining in with more local activities. As with so much this year, positive action can bring rewards.

Earth Rabbits born in 1999 would also do well to remember that diligence leads to riches. Over the year some important chances will come their way and to get the most benefit from them they will need to be willing and put in the effort. This applies to both education and personal interests.

In their studying, the young Earth Rabbits will not only be laying an important foundation for more advanced studies to come but will also have the chance to make greater use of resources and equipment. Embracing current opportunities will also help them to be a part of school life and, in some instances, make new friends. The young Earth Rabbit may appear reserved, but he can have high ambitions beneath his quiet exterior, and this year can help bring out some of his personal qualities and increase his level of confidence.

Personal interests can go well and for Earth Rabbits who enjoy activities which involve participation, including music, drama and sport, this can be an active and inspired time.

In fact the Earth Rabbit will often have a lot to do and may sometimes be in a quandary about how best to organize his time or worried that he has insufficient means to do all he wants. At such times he does need to speak to others and seek advice. This way they will be better able to assist him. The young Earth Rabbit does have good support and those around him are keen for him to make the most of himself.

Overall, this is a year of considerable potential for the Earth Rabbit, and whether born in 1939 or 1999, he will find that if he sets about his activities with diligence, riches of all kinds can follow. This is a year favouring effort and practical activity. The Earth Rabbit will also be encouraged by the support and assistance he is given, and his relations with others and personal interests will be a source of much pleasure.

Tip for the Year
Be open-minded and willing to try out new activities. Also, look to develop your interests and put your skills to good use. What you do now can often develop in satisfying ways.

Famous Rabbits

Margaret Atwood, Drew Barrymore, David Beckham, Harry Belafonte, Pope Benedict XVI, Ingrid Bergman, St Bernadette, Jeff Bezos, Kathryn Bigelow, Michael Bublé, Nicolas Cage, Lewis Carroll, John Cleese, Confucius, Marie Curie, Johnny Depp, Novak Djokovic, Albert Einstein, George Eliot, W. C. Fields, James Fox, Sir David Frost, Cary Grant,

Ashley Greene, Edvard Grieg, Oliver Hardy, Seamus Heaney, Tommy Hilfiger, Bob Hope, Whitney Houston, Helen Hunt, John Hurt, Anjelica Huston, Chrissie Hynde, Enrique Iglesias, Henry James, Sir David Jason, Angelina Jolie, Michael Jordan, Michael Keaton, John Keats, Enda Kenny, Lisa Kudrow, Gina Lollobrigida, George Michael, Sir Roger Moore, Andrew Murray, Mike Myers, Brigitte Nielsen, Graham Norton, Michelle Obama, Jamie Oliver, George Orwell, Sarah Palin, Edith Piaf, Brad Pitt, Sidney Poitier, Romano Prodi, Emeli Sandé, Elisabeth Schwarzkopf, Neil Sedaka, Jane Seymour, Maria Sharapova, Neil Simon, Frank Sinatra, Sting, Quentin Tarantino, J. R. R. Tolkien, KT Tunstall, Tina Turner, Luther Vandross, Sebastian Vettel, Queen Victoria, Muddy Waters, Orson Welles, Hayley Westenra, Walt Whitman, Will-i-Am, Robin Williams, Kate Winslet, Tiger Woods.

3 February 1916 to 22 January 1917 — *Fire Dragon*

23 January 1928 to 9 February 1929 — *Earth Dragon*

8 February 1940 to 26 January 1941 — *Metal Dragon*

27 January 1952 to 13 February 1953 — *Water Dragon*

13 February 1964 to 1 February 1965 — *Wood Dragon*

31 January 1976 to 17 February 1977 — *Fire Dragon*

17 February 1988 to 5 February 1989 — *Earth Dragon*

5 February 2000 to 23 January 2001 — *Metal Dragon*

23 January 2012 to 9 February 2013 — *Water Dragon*

The Dragon

The Personality of the Dragon

I like giving things a go.
Sometimes I succeed,
sometimes I fail.
Sometimes the unexpected happens.
But it is the giving things a go
and the stepping forward
that make life so interesting.

The Dragon is born under the sign of luck. He is a proud and lively character and has a tremendous amount of self-confidence. He is also highly intelligent and very quick to take advantage of any opportunity. He is ambitious and determined and will do well in practically anything he attempts. He is also something of a perfectionist and will always try to maintain the high standards he sets himself.

The Dragon does not suffer fools gladly and will be quick to criticize anyone or anything that displeases him. He can be blunt and forthright in his views and is certainly not renowned for being either tactful or diplomatic. He does, however, often take people at their word and can occasionally be rather gullible. If he ever feels that his trust has been abused or his dignity wounded, he can sometimes become very bitter and it will take him a long time to forgive and forget.

The Dragon is usually very outgoing and is particularly adept at attracting attention and publicity. He enjoys being in the limelight and is often at his best when he is confronted by a difficult problem or tense situation. In some respects he is a showman and he rarely lacks an audience. His views are highly valued and he invariably has something interesting – and sometimes controversial – to say.

He also has considerable energy and is often prepared to work long and unsocial hours in order to achieve what he wants. He can, however, be rather impulsive and does not always consider the consequences of his actions. He also has a tendency to live for the moment and there is nothing that riles him more than to be kept waiting. The Dragon hates delay and can get extremely impatient and irritable over even the smallest of hold-ups.

The Dragon has an enormous faith in his abilities, but he does run the risk of becoming over-confident and unless he is careful he can sometimes make grave errors of judgement. While this may prove disastrous at the time, he does have the tenacity and ability to bounce back and pick up the pieces again.

The Dragon has such an assertive personality, so much willpower and such a desire to succeed that he will often reach the top of his chosen profession. He has considerable leadership qualities and will do well in positions where he can put his own ideas and policies into practice. He is usually successful in politics, show business, as the manager of his own department or business, and in any job that brings him into contact with the media.

The Dragon relies a tremendous amount on his own judgement and can be scornful of other people's advice. He likes to feel self-sufficient and there are many Dragons who cherish their independence to such a degree that they prefer to remain single throughout their lives. However, the Dragon will often have numerous admirers and many will be attracted by his flamboyant personality and striking looks. If he does marry, he will usually marry young, and will find himself particularly well suited to those born under the signs of the Snake, Rat, Monkey and Rooster. He will also find that the Rabbit, Pig, Horse and Goat make ideal companions and will readily join in with many of his escapades. Two Dragons will also get on well together, as they will understand each other, but the Dragon may not find things so easy with the Ox and Dog, as both will be critical of his impulsive and somewhat extrovert manner. He will also find it difficult to form an alliance with the Tiger, for the Tiger, like the Dragon, tends to speak his mind, is very strong-willed and likes to take the lead.

The female Dragon knows what she wants in life and sets about everything she does in a determined and positive manner. No job is too small for her and she is often prepared to work extremely hard to secure her objectives. She is immensely practical and somewhat liberated. She hates being bound by routine and petty restrictions and likes to have sufficient freedom to go off and do what she wants to do. She will keep her house tidy, but is not one for spending hours on housework – there are far too many other things that she prefers to do. Like her male counterpart, she has a tendency to speak her mind.

The Dragon usually has many interests and enjoys sport and other outdoor activities. He also likes to travel and often prefers to visit places that are off the beaten track rather than head for popular tourist destinations. He has a very adventurous streak in him and providing his financial circumstances permit – and the Dragon is usually sensible with his money – he will travel considerable distances during his lifetime.

The Dragon is a very flamboyant character and while he can be demanding of others and in his early years rather precocious, he will have many friends and will nearly always be the centre of attention. He has charisma and so much confidence that he can often become a source of inspiration to others. In China he is the leader of the carnival and he is also blessed with an inordinate share of luck.

The Five Different Types of Dragon

In addition to the 12 signs of the Chinese zodiac there are five elements and these have a strengthening or moderating influence on the signs. The effects of the five elements on the Dragon are described below, together with the years in which they were exercising their influence. Therefore Dragons born in 1940 and 2000 are Metal Dragons, Dragons born in 1952 and 2012 are Water Dragons, and so on.

Metal Dragon: 1940, 2000

This Dragon is very strong-willed and has a particularly forceful personality. He is energetic, ambitious and tries to be scrupulous in his dealings with others. He can also be blunt and to the point and usually has no hesitation in speaking his mind. If people disagree with him or are not prepared to co-operate, he is more than happy to go his own way. He usually has very high moral values and is held in great esteem by his friends and colleagues.

Water Dragon: 1952, 2012

This Dragon is friendly, easy-going and intelligent. He is quick-witted and rarely lets an opportunity slip by. However, he is not as impatient as some of the other types of Dragon and is prepared to wait for results rather than expect everything to happen at once. He has an understanding nature and is willing to share his ideas and co-operate with others. His main failing is a tendency to jump from one thing to another rather than concentrate on the job in hand. He has a good sense of humour and is an effective speaker.

Wood Dragon: 1964

The Wood Dragon is practical, imaginative and inquisitive. He loves delving into all manner of subjects and can quite often come up with some highly original ideas. He is a thinker and a doer and has the drive and commitment to put many of his ideas into practice. He is more diplomatic than some of the other types of Dragon and has a good sense of humour. He is very astute in business matters and can also be most generous.

Fire Dragon: 1916, 1976

This Dragon is ambitious, articulate and has a tremendous desire to succeed. He is a hard and conscientious worker and is often admired for his integrity and forthright nature. He is very strong-willed and has considerable leadership qualities. He can, however, rely a bit too much on his own judgement and fail to take into account the views and feelings of others. He can also be rather aloof and it would certainly be in his own interests to let others join in more with his various activities. He usually enjoys music, literature and the arts.

Earth Dragon: 1928, 1988

The Earth Dragon tends to be quieter and more reflective than some of the other types of Dragon. He has a wide variety of interests and is keenly aware of what is going on around him. He also has clear objectives and usually has no problems in obtaining support and backing for any of his ventures. He is very astute in financial matters and often able to accumulate considerable wealth. He is a good organizer, although he can at times be rather bureaucratic and fussy. He mixes well with others and has a large circle of friends.

Prospects for the Dragon in 2014

As Chinese signs, the Dragon and Snake get on well and in the Snake year (10 February 2013–30 January 2014) the Dragon can benefit from the Snake's supportive influence.

However, in the closing months of the Snake year the Dragon will have a lot to do and will need to remain organized and concentrate on priorities, otherwise he could find his lifestyle getting out of balance and causing problems and sometimes resentment. Dragons, do take note and try to spread out your commitments rather than having everything happening at once.

This is especially the case in the Dragon's domestic life. If certain plans can be decided upon early, this can help relieve pressure later on. This also applies to purchases the Dragon may be keen to make, including gifts for others and items for his home. By looking ahead and taking the time to consider these, he could make far better acquisitions than if he leaves everything to the last moment.

The Dragon's workload can increase in the closing months of the year. However, his skills and efforts can lead to some encouraging results and he can emerge from the Snake year with his reputation considerably enhanced. For work opportunities, November could hold important possibilities.

Both his domestic and social life will be busy and for Dragons enjoying newfound romance, these can be special times. However, they will need to be attentive and aware of the feelings of others. If they are preoccupied or sacrifice quality time with their loved one, problems could arise. Maintaining a good lifestyle balance is especially important for all Dragons at this time.

Overall, the Year of the Snake has considerable scope for the Dragon and its closing months will be active and rewarding.

The Dragon is strong-willed and always keen to make the most of himself. Sometimes circumstances are not in his favour, but through determination and sheer strength of character he is able to accomplish a great deal. His qualities can again serve him well in the Year of the Horse, which begins on 31 January. This can be a generally good year for him, although he does need to be careful of overstepping the mark or taking one risk too many. The Horse year can have salutary warnings for the unwary or careless.

At work there can be good opportunities for the Dragon to build on his present position. Staff movements can lead to new openings arising and many Dragons will have the opportunity to take on greater responsibilities. Also, as new projects and schemes are introduced, there could be the chance for the Dragon to become involved and broaden his experience. This is a year offering steady progress, *but* should any Dragon take shortcuts or risks or ignore guidelines, problems could arise. The Horse year calls for care and thoroughness.

Most Dragons will remain with their present employer over the year, but for those who feel their prospects could be improved by looking elsewhere, as well as those seeking work, the Horse year can bring surprising developments. Although the job-seeking process will be difficult, the Dragon's resourcefulness could open up a potentially good opportunity. This could come about by chance and require some adjustment on the Dragon's part, but it may offer a welcome and interesting new challenge. With the Horse year encouraging personal development, the training many Dragons receive in their work can also alert them to future possibilities. March, May, July and October could see some encouraging developments, but the determined Dragon can benefit from opportunities at almost any time of the year.

Progress at work can help the Dragon's financial position too, and although his outgoings will be considerable, he could fare well in some important transactions. If he wants to make any major purchases, he will find that by budgeting in advance and seeking advice, he could make some excellent decisions. With travel plans, too, by planning ahead and investigating options, he could benefit from a particularly attractive offer. But while he may enjoy some luck in financial matters this year, he should not tempt fate by taking unnecessary risks or ignoring fine print. At all times, Horse years require vigilance.

Being outgoing, the Dragon will make the most of his social opportunities this year, and for the partygoer and keen socializer, this can be an especially lively time. April, May, September and December could see the most social activity.

For the unattached, there will be excellent romantic possibilities, although circumstances may not always make things easy. With care and time, though, new relationships can often become meaningful.

However, although the Dragon will be kept busy and enjoy a lot of what he does, he also needs to be on his guard. At times a rumour or disturbing news could be upsetting and the Dragon would do well to check the facts himself rather than believe all he is told. Also, if he has any problems or dilemmas, rather than keep them to himself, he should confide in people he trusts. Sometimes worries could be dispelled or certain concerns prove groundless. A worry shared is so often a worry halved.

This need for openness also applies to his home life. With the Dragon himself and those in his household often leading busy lifestyles, there will need to be good liaison and co-operation and, at particularly busy times, greater understanding and assistance. Good communication will be paramount. It could also be helpful to spread practical projects out during the year. This way, more time can be allowed for preparation and the results may be more satisfying.

However, while the Dragon's domestic life will be busy, it will contain an interesting mix of things to do and there will be some good family times to share.

The Dragon should also aim to preserve some time for his own interests as well as give some consideration to his general lifestyle. His personal interests can be good ways for him to relax as well as sometimes be an outlet for his talents and ideas. Ensuring his diet is balanced and nutritious can also make a difference, especially to his energy levels. In this busy year the Dragon should not neglect his own well-being.

The Year of the Horse is a generally encouraging one for the Dragon and will bring some good opportunities for him to move forward. His relations with others can also be helpful, although the Dragon does need to watch his independent tendencies and be prepared to consult others rather than rush ahead on his own. He also needs to remain vigilant. Risks and carelessness could cause problems. Fortunately, though, the Dragon is perceptive and his firm resolve will enable him to gain a lot from this full and interesting year.

The Metal Dragon

There is a Chinese proverb that reminds us, 'Roses too have thorns.' While the Horse year is favourably aspected for the Metal Dragon, it too can have its pitfalls, and the Metal Dragon will need to be alert.

For Metal Dragons born in 1940 the Horse year holds interesting prospects. The Metal Dragon is clear-sighted, knows what he wants to do and plans a lot in advance. In 2014 he will certainly have ideas he is keen to carry through. However, as he will quickly find, the Horse year can bring unexpected developments and open up new choices. Over the year the Metal Dragon would do well to be flexible and be prepared to modify his initial plans if something better arises.

This especially applies to decisions concerning the home. If the Metal Dragon discusses his thoughts with his loved ones and those with expert knowledge, a lot of his plans can be realized, even if in slightly altered form. Also, where large purchases are concerned or before authorizing any work, the Metal Dragon does need to check the costs, details and implications of what he is about to carry out. Without care, misunderstandings could arise. Horse years do require vigilance.

This need for thoroughness also applies to financial matters. If the Metal Dragon is required to complete any forms, he needs to check that the correct information is supplied and the relevant sections completed, otherwise he could find himself with some burdensome correspondence. Horse years can be good ones, but the moment errors occur, problems will ensue. Metal Dragons, take note.

However, while there is this need for extra care and attention, the year will also contain many highlights. In the Metal Dragon's home life, there could be a special occasion involving a younger family member to look forward to and this will be a source of much pride to the Metal Dragon. Over the year he will also value the rapport he enjoys with some family members and this can help make certain activities all the more meaningful. Although sometimes the Metal Dragon may feel he is on the edge of wider family activities, he is very much at the family's heart and is appreciated by many.

The Horse year can also bring some good travel opportunities, including some unexpected ones. It could be that the Metal Dragon decides to make the most of a good spell of weather to go away or decides to attend a special event. Throughout the year there can be an element of spontaneity to what takes place.

The Metal Dragon can also derive considerable pleasure from some of his long-held interests and will have the chance to put his knowledge to greater use. Many Metal Dragons will once again have projects lined up or plans they particularly want to carry out, and by taking action, they will delight in what they achieve. Some may be tempted by activities available in their area and may benefit from finding out more.

The Metal Dragon's interests can often have a good social element to them and during the year he will once more value his friends and enjoy the social occasions he attends. Lonely Metal Dragons could find that there are more social opportunities in their area than they realized and may see something of a transformation in their situation as a result. Here again, positive action can make a difference.

Overall, the Year of the Horse certainly holds good prospects for Metal Dragons born in 1940. However, the more senior Metal Dragon will need to remain alert and be wary about making decisions or taking action without all the necessary information. Roses may be beautiful but they do have thorns, and Horse years can be good but they too can have their difficulties.

For Metal Dragons born in 2000, the Horse year can be lively and interesting. With his keen nature, the young Metal Dragon can make good progress as well as enjoy a range of different activities and experiences. For those who are particularly keen to develop interest-related skills, the year can bring some especially good opportunities, but to benefit, the young Metal Dragon will need to be active and ready. Some chances may not be available for long and should not be wasted. Also, if a new interest or activity appeals to him at any time, the Metal Dragon should tell others and see what can be arranged. Horse years encourage initiative and participation.

During the year the Metal Dragon will also have a large amount to study on a wide range of subjects. Some topics could especially appeal, and could reveal aptitudes the Metal Dragon would do well to develop. By listening to advice and being prepared to put in the effort, he can gain knowledge and skills which can be of both present and future value.

With his outgoing nature the Metal Dragon will also enjoy the camaraderie and friendship of those around him. Although he may already have a close circle of friends, he could meet someone who is destined to become very important over the next few years.

Generally, a lot can go well for the young Metal Dragon in 2014, but the year does call for effort and care. He should not waste his opportunities and should pay heed to the advice he is given. Stubbornness or moments of awkwardness could put him at a disadvantage. Metal Dragons, take note, for this is a year offering scope and opportunity.

Whether born in 1940 or 2000, the Metal Dragon will have the chance to enjoy many activities this year. But throughout he would do well to consult others and take their feelings into account. When necessary, he should be flexible and take advantage of situations *as they are* rather than as he may want them to be. Socially and domestically, this can be a rewarding year with some special times to enjoy. Overall, the Metal Dragon's prospects are good, but to prevent problems, he does need to be attentive and aware.

Tip for the Year
Seek the opinions of others. With their input and encouragement, many of your plans can be realized. Also, be thorough. Carelessness and risk could undermine your prospects in this otherwise promising year.

The Water Dragon

One of the strengths of the Water Dragon is his ability to put his talents and time to good use and this will be very much the case this year. The Horse year can open up quite a few interesting possibilities as well as spring some surprises and to benefit fully the Water Dragon will need to show flexibility.

His home life is likely to see considerable activity and Water Dragons who are grandparents or become grandparents this year will often delight in following the progress of younger family members. With the Water Dragon's experience and ability to empathize, he will also be able to offer quite a few relations both practical assistance and moral support. He will enjoy sharing many activities with those close to him and the year favours joint undertakings. For family developments, this can be a busy and special time.

However, while this can be a full and interesting year, problems can still arise. Sometimes these could be caused by making assumptions or by tension caused by tiredness and pressure. At such times, the Water Dragon should recognize that greater understanding or more discussion is needed. Fortunately these awkward moments will be relatively few, but they should not be allowed to overshadow this potentially rewarding year.

With his sociable nature, the Water Dragon will appreciate meeting up with his friends over the year and many of his interests and activities will have a good social element too. Many Water Dragons will enjoy playing an increased role in organizations or groups, and those who would welcome new friendships would do well to consider activities in their area and groups they could join. Positive action can lead to some special friendships being formed. Late March to early June, September and December could see the most social activity.

Also, the Horse year can proceed in curious ways and should the Water Dragon become intrigued by a new subject, see a course that appeals to him or welcome a new challenge, this would be an ideal time to follow this up.

The Horse year can also bring important choices as far as the Water Dragon's work situation is concerned. As a result of initiatives and changes in their workplace, many Water Dragons will find their objectives and role changing. As a consequence, some parts of the year can give rise to uncertainty, but what opens up will allow many Water Dragons to draw on their experience and to have a positive impact on their place of work.

The majority will continue with their present employer, but some could decide to take up retirement options or feel ready for change and look elsewhere. For those who do seek another position or are currently looking for work, the Horse year can have surprising developments in store. Although the job-seeking process will be difficult, by talking to contacts and keeping themselves informed about what is available, many Water Dragons could be alerted to an ideal opportunity that is possibly something very different from what they have done before. Admittedly, considerable adjustment will be involved, but these Water Dragons will welcome the challenge before them. Here again the Horse year can proceed in curious ways, with late February, March, May, July and October likely to see some interesting developments.

The progress the Water Dragon makes at work may well lead to an increase in income, but over the year he could also find himself making some substantial purchases. Here his fine judgement and eye for quality will be to his advantage. However, he does need to be vigilant with paperwork and keep records, receipts and financial documents carefully. Lapses can delay matters and be to his disadvantage. Water Dragons, be warned.

If possible, the Water Dragon should make allowance for a holiday over the year, as he may have the chance to visit some interesting destinations.

In view of the busy nature of the year he should also give some thought to his well-being. If he feels either the quality of his diet or his general level of exercise is deficient, he should seek advice on the best way to proceed. Some Water Dragons may find themselves both enjoying and benefiting from the activities suggested.

Overall, the Water Dragon will see a lot happen this year and some of what occurs could involve unexpected change. By being open-minded and flexible, however, the Water Dragon can gain a lot from the events of the year. He can also derive much pleasure from his home and social life, and his relations with others will often be special and encouraging.

Tip for the Year

This can be a satisfying year, but to make the most of it, do be prepared to take on new challenges. This is a year of considerable possibility for you. Enjoy it and make the most of it.

The Wood Dragon

This will be an important year for the Wood Dragon and will contain some fine opportunities as well as a few surprises. As it marks the start of a new decade in his life, he may well find himself reflecting on his current situation and what he would like to see happen. This is very much a year to set his plans in motion.

One area to which the Wood Dragon will give much consideration will be his work situation. Many Wood Dragons who have been in the same position or type of work for some time will now feel ready for a new challenge. If working in a large organization, they could take up the chance to transfer to another department or put in for promotion and greater responsibility. Whatever they do, once they start to make enquiries and submit applications, they can set important developments in motion. This is a year to actively seek change.

Wood Dragons who are established on a certain career path can also do well this year and many will benefit from an unexpected opportunity. Whenever an opening occurs, they should be quick to act. This is a fast-moving year and it is those who seize their chances who will fare the best.

For Wood Dragons seeking work, the Horse year can also bring interesting opportunities. Some may find themselves eligible for training or refresher courses, and by taking advantage of these, they could be successful in securing a new position. Friends and contacts could also be helpful in alerting them to possible vacancies. With support, initiative and determination, the Wood Dragon can find his career and prospects being given a new lease of life. March, May, late June to early August and October could see some important developments.

With the year also encouraging personal growth, the Wood Dragon will enjoy the way he is able to take certain interests further. Whether through study, practice or setting himself a new project, he can find purposeful action bringing him both pleasure and considerable satisfaction. For Wood Dragons who enjoy creative pursuits, this can be a particularly inspiring time. Some may also be tempted to try something new, feeling that their fiftieth year is a good one for a fresh challenge.

Travel is also favourably aspected this year and many Wood Dragons may decide to celebrate their fiftieth year with a special holiday or a visit to an attraction or area that has long appealed to them. In addition, the year can bring unexpected travel opportunities and give rise to several spontaneous and enjoyable occasions.

Family and friends will also be keen to mark the Wood Dragon's fiftieth birthday in style and this can be an active year both domestically and socially. With a general willingness to pool together and be flexible over certain arrangements, family life can go well and the Wood Dragon will have many activities to look forward to. He will offer support to both younger and more senior relatives and benefit from the help he receives in return. Good co-operation between family members can make an important difference in this busy year.

The Wood Dragon's social life will also see an increase in activity and he will often have the chance to add to his social circle. For the unattached, the prospect of romance can add excitement to the year. Late March to early June, September and December could see the most social activity.

The Wood Dragon's progress at work can often bring an increase in income, but with a busy lifestyle, the possibility of travel and his existing commitments, he will need to be disciplined in his spending. If he controls his budget he will be able to carry through many of his plans, but should he proceed on a more ad hoc basis, then there is a risk that some of them may not come to fruition. The Horse year does call for careful financial management.

Generally, however, the year can be a full and often satisfying one for the Wood Dragon, and as it marks a new decade in his life, he will feel more impelled to make things happen. He may make good headway in his work, while time spent on personal interests can also be satisfying and travel prospects are good. The Wood Dragon's relations with others will also be of special value and he can enjoy a rewarding social life. The ambitious and personable Wood Dragon has it within him to accomplish a great deal and set this new decade in his life off to an encouraging start.

Tip for the Year

Be purposeful. Decide on what you want to do and then set about your aims. Also, value your relations with others. There will be good times to enjoy this year, and your loved ones, friends and contacts will all be helpful and supportive.

The Fire Dragon

As the Horse year starts, many a Fire Dragon will feel that change is in the air and be ready to move forward. Very early on, their feelings will be justified, as they see encouraging developments taking place. The Horse year will be busy and sometimes pressured, but can ultimately be a very successful one for the Fire Dragon.

Throughout the year the Fire Dragon will enjoy good support from others and if he is open and discusses his thoughts and concerns, he can receive much useful assistance. In some instances, just the process of talking can help clarify certain ideas in his mind. Although some Fire Dragons can be independent-minded, this is a year favouring openness and joint endeavour.

In the Fire Dragon's home life in particular, sharing his thoughts and ideas with those around him will lead to better outcomes. For some time the Fire Dragon may have been thinking about improvements he would like to make, including, in some cases, a move to somewhere better suited to his requirements. Often he will find that once these ideas have been aired, they can quickly get underway, and by the end of the year the Fire Dragon may look back and be surprised and delighted by how much has been accomplished.

In addition to all the practical activity, the Fire Dragon will do much to assist family members, and his judgement and collected manner may be especially appreciated. Several generations will have excellent reason to be thankful to him this year. He will also be the chief instigator of many activities, including some special family occasions, and his thoughtfulness and input will add richness and variety to family life.

His social life will also see an increase in activity. With his genial manner, he is set to impress those he meets over the year and some could prove helpful with his plans. April to mid-June, September, December and January 2015 could see the most social activity, but in most months of the Horse year the Fire Dragon will have opportunities to go out and interesting things to do.

The aspects are particularly encouraging for Fire Dragons who are alone and may have experienced some recent personal difficulty. In some cases this is a time to draw a line under what has gone before and start a new chapter. The Horse year is also capable of springing a few surprises, and a chance meeting could lead to a glorious romance.

The Fire Dragon can derive considerable pleasure from his personal interests this year and it is important that he preserves time for these. Not only can they keep his lifestyle in balance but sometimes they can also give him the opportunity to get additional exercise and/or enjoy something different. Any Fire Dragons who have let their interests lapse of late do need to allow themselves some 'me time' this year and perhaps consider taking up a new recreational activity. This can make a surprising difference to their lifestyle.

Travel is favourably aspected and some opportunities may arise with little warning. If possible, the Fire Dragon should try to take advantage of them, as he could delight in some of the places he gets to see.

With the considerable activity of the year, the Fire Dragon will have many demands on his resources. However, he may benefit from some shrewd decisions and purchases, and with good budgeting and control, he will be able to go ahead with many of his plans.

The Horse year can also be eventful as far as work prospects are concerned. Fire Dragons who are well established where they are could find staff movements bringing chances to progress, even though this could mean a substantial change in duties. However, the Horse year will allow many Fire Dragons to broaden their experience and, in the process, help their overall prospects. It is a time for swift and sometimes surprising developments and the Fire Dragon will need to remain alert and be quick to act. Throughout the year it is also important that he seizes any chances to raise his profile, as his participation and personality can impress others. Some Fire Dragons who benefit from opportunities early on in the year will find further chances arising late in 2014 or early in 2015.

For Fire Dragons who feel their prospects would be helped by changing employer, as well as those seeking work, the Horse year can also have important developments in store. Although the job-seeking process will be difficult, by talking to advisers, contacts and former colleagues, these Fire Dragons could learn of possibilities they had not yet considered. With effort, persistence and initiative, they can find significant doors opening for them. Late February, March, May, July and October could see encouraging developments.

Overall, this will be a very busy 12 months for the Fire Dragon and the key message is that he must not expect to do everything himself. It is by seeking advice and drawing on the support of others that he will be able to enjoy some well-deserved success. The Horse year will bring some surprising developments and for the active and enterprising Fire Dragon, a great deal is possible.

Tip for the Year

You have a great personal manner. Enjoy your relations with those around you and seize your chances to meet others. The more people you know, the more possibilities can arise, and this fast-moving year will contain some excellent possibilities.

The Earth Dragon

'He who comprehends the times is great', as the Chinese proverb states, and one of the Earth Dragon's strengths is his perception. He is always observant and quick to pick up on opportunities, and this fast-moving year has considerable potential for him.

The Earth Dragon's personal life is especially well aspected, and if he has a partner, this can be a year of exciting developments. There will be many plans and hopes to share and the Earth Dragon will often find that once decisions are made, plans can take shape fairly quickly. There is a strong element of serendipity to the year and, particularly with practical endeavours, good fortune will often help matters along. More senior relations too can be helpful and if the Earth Dragon has decisions to make at any time, he would do well to talk these over with them and benefit from their experience. By spending time with his partner and loved ones, he can also enjoy some memorable times this year. In addition, he could find himself attracted to a new interest or pursuit, and if he shares this with others and learns alongside them, he could make encouraging progress and have fun at the same time. This is a favourable year for personal relationships and will contain many special moments.

For the unattached, the Horse year can bring wonderful romantic possibilities. Chance can play a big part and a meeting in sometimes unlikely circumstances could become significant. Earth Dragons who start the Horse year feeling lonely or dispirited could see a substantial change in their fortunes.

The Earth Dragon is also set to make the most of his social opportunities. His interests can have a good social element, but he will also appreciate the chances just to meet up with his friends and talk. Some he has known for a considerable time could provide reassuring support.

For socializing and meeting others late March to early June, September and December are favourable times, but with the active nature of the year the Earth Dragon will have social occasions to look forward to in most months.

With a busy social life, plus accommodation costs, personal activities, transport and travel, this will be an expensive year for the Earth Dragon. However, while he will need to control his spending, he will be able to proceed with many of his plans and could also make some important purchases during the year. He could even benefit from some luck, including finding some real bargains. However, care will be needed when dealing with important paperwork. Carelessness could be to his disadvantage. Earth Dragons, take note and do seek advice when appropriate.

Horse years move at a fast pace and, with this one likely to see change in many working environments, the Earth Dragon may be presented with some significant new opportunities. By being swift to respond, he can often successfully advance his career or secure a new job. As with so much this year, events may take a curious course and the Earth Dragon may find himself obtaining work in a totally different capacity or industry, but he may turn out to be well suited to it. Throughout the year he should have faith in his capabilities. In addition, if there are skills and qualifications he feels could help his situation, he should take advantage of any training opportunities that come his way or see if there are any courses he could study in his own time. This can pay dividends later. March, May, July and October could see some interesting work developments.

Overall, the Year of the Horse will give the Earth Dragon the chance to make progress at work as well as develop new strengths and enjoy his special relations with others. His perception and determination will help and he can also benefit from some moments of good fortune. With initiative and purpose, he can make this an important and personally significant year.

Tip for the Year

Be open to opportunity. This is a favourable time for you, but do not miss out through delay – seize the moment! Also, value your relations with those who are special to you. They are special for a reason.

Famous Dragons

Adele, Maya Angelou, Jeffrey Archer, Joan Armatrading, Joan Baez, Count Basie, Maeve Binchy, Sandra Bullock, Michael Cera, Courteney Cox, Bing Crosby, Russell Crowe, Roald Dahl, Salvador Dali, Charles Darwin, Neil Diamond, Bo Diddley, Matt Dillon, Christian Dior, Placido Domingo, Fats Domino, Kirk Douglas, Faye Dunaway, Dan Fogler, Sir Bruce Forsyth, Sigmund Freud, Graham Greene, Rupert Grint, Che Guevara, James Herriot, Paul Hogan, Joan of Arc, Boris Johnson, Sir Tom Jones, Immanuel Kant, Martin Luther King, John Lennon, Abraham Lincoln, Elle MacPherson, Michael McIntyre, Hilary Mantel, Queen Margrethe II of Denmark, Liam Neeson, Florence Nightingale, Nick Nolte, Sharon Osbourne, Al Pacino, Gregory Peck, Pelé, Edgar Allan Poe, Vladimir Putin, Nikki Reed, Keanu Reeves, Ryan Reynolds, Sir Cliff Richard, Rihanna, Shakira, George Bernard Shaw, Martin Sheen, Alicia Silverstone, Ringo Starr, Karlheinz Stockhausen, Emma Stone, Shirley Temple, Maria von Trapp, Louis Walsh, Andy Warhol, Mark Webber, Raquel Welch, the Earl of Wessex, Mae West, Sam Worthington.

23 January 1917 to 10 February 1918 — *Fire Snake*

10 February 1929 to 29 January 1930 — *Earth Snake*

27 January 1941 to 14 February 1942 — *Metal Snake*

14 February 1953 to 2 February 1954 — *Water Snake*

2 February 1965 to 20 January 1966 — *Wood Snake*

18 February 1977 to 6 February 1978 — *Fire Snake*

6 February 1989 to 26 January 1990 — *Earth Snake*

24 January 2001 to 11 February 2002 — *Metal Snake*

10 February 2013 to 30 January 2014 — *Water Snake*

The Snake

The Personality of the Snake

I think
And think some more.
About what is,
About what can be,
About what may be.
And when I am ready,
Then I act.

The Snake is born under the sign of wisdom. He is highly intelligent and his mind is forever active. He is always planning and always looking for ways in which he can use his considerable skills. He is a deep thinker and likes to meditate and reflect.

Many times during his life he will shed one of his famous Snake skins and take up new interests or start a completely different job. The Snake enjoys a challenge and he rarely makes mistakes. He is a skilful organizer, has considerable business acumen and is usually lucky in money matters. Most Snakes are financially secure in their later years, provided they do not gamble – the Snake has the distinction of being the worst gambler in the whole of the Chinese zodiac!

The Snake generally has a calm and placid nature and prefers the quieter things in life. He does not like to be in a frenzied atmosphere and hates being hurried into making a quick decision. He also does not like interference in his affairs and tends to rely on his own judgement rather than listen to advice.

At times the Snake can appear solitary. He is quiet, reserved and sometimes has difficulty in communicating with others. He has little time for idle gossip and will certainly not suffer fools gladly. He does, however, have a good sense of humour and this is particularly appreciated in times of crisis.

The Snake is certainly not afraid of hard work and is thorough in all that he does. He is very determined and can occasionally be ruthless in order to achieve his aims. His confidence, willpower and quick thinking usually ensure his success, but should he fail it will often take a long time for him to recover. He cannot bear failure and is a very bad loser.

The Snake can also be evasive and does not willingly let people into his confidence. This secrecy and distrust can sometimes work against him and these are traits that all Snakes should try to overcome.

Another characteristic of the Snake is his tendency to rest after any sudden or prolonged bout of activity. He burns up so much nervous energy that he can, if he is not careful, be susceptible to high blood pressure and nervous disorders.

It has sometimes been said that the Snake is a late starter in life and this is mainly because it often takes him a while to find a job in which he is genuinely happy. However, he will usually do well in any position that involves research and writing and where he is given sufficient freedom to develop his own ideas and plans. He makes a good teacher, politician, personnel manager and social adviser.

The Snake chooses his friends carefully and while he keeps a tight control over his finances, he can be particularly generous to those he likes. He will think nothing of buying expensive gifts or treating his friends or loved ones to the best theatre seats in town. In return he demands loyalty. The Snake is very possessive and can become extremely jealous and hurt if he finds his trust has been abused.

The Snake is also renowned for his good looks and is never short of admirers. The female Snake in particular is most alluring. She has style, grace and excellent (and usually expensive) taste in clothes. A keen socializer, she is likely to have a wide range of friends and the happy knack of impressing those who matter. She has numerous interests and her opinions are often highly valued. She is generally a calm person and while she involves herself in many activities, she likes to retain a certain amount of privacy in her undertakings.

Affairs of the heart are very important to the Snake and he will often have many romances before he finally settles down. He will find that he is particularly well suited to those born under the signs of the Ox, Dragon, Rabbit and Rooster. Provided he is allowed sufficient freedom to pursue his own interests, he can also build up a very satisfactory relationship with the Rat, Horse, Goat, Monkey and Dog, but he should try to steer clear of another Snake as they could very easily become jealous of each other. The Snake will also have difficulty in getting on with the honest and down-to-earth Pig, and will find the Tiger far too much of a disruptive influence on his quiet and peace-loving ways.

The Snake certainly appreciates the finer things in life. He enjoys good food and often takes a keen interest in the arts. He also enjoys reading and is invariably drawn to subjects such as philosophy, political thought, religion or the occult. He is fascinated by the unknown and his enquiring mind is always looking for answers. Some of the world's most original thinkers have been Snakes, and although he may not readily admit it, the Snake is often psychic and relies a lot on intuition.

The Snake is certainly not the most energetic member of the Chinese zodiac. He prefers to proceed at his own pace and to do what he wants. He is very much his own master and throughout his life he will try his hand at many things. He is something of a dabbler, but at some time – usually when he least expects it – his hard work and efforts will be recognized and he will invariably meet with the success and the financial security he so desires.

The Five Different Types of Snake

In addition to the 12 signs of the Chinese zodiac there are five elements and these have a strengthening or moderating influence on the signs. The effects of the five elements on the Snake are described below, together with the years in which they were exercising their influence. Therefore Snakes born in 1941 and 2001 are Metal Snakes, Snakes born in 1953 and 2013 are Water Snakes, and so on.

Metal Snake: 1941, 2001

This Snake is quiet, confident and fiercely independent. He often prefers to work on his own and will only let a privileged few into his confidence. He is quick to spot opportunities and will set about achieving his objectives with an awesome determination. He is astute in financial matters and will often invest his money well. He has a liking for the finer things in life and a good appreciation of the arts, literature, music and food. He usually has a small group of extremely good friends and can be generous to his loved ones.

Water Snake: 1953, 2013

This Snake has a wide variety of interests. He enjoys studying all manner of subjects and is capable of undertaking quite detailed research and becoming a specialist in his chosen area. He is highly intelligent, has a good memory and is particularly astute when dealing with business and financial matters. He tends to be quietly spoken and a little reserved, but he does have sufficient strength of character to make his views known and attain his ambitions. He is very loyal to his family and friends.

Wood Snake: 1965

The Wood Snake has a friendly temperament and a good understanding of human nature. He is able to communicate well and often has many friends and admirers. He is witty, intelligent and ambitious. He has numerous interests and prefers to live in a quiet, stable environment where he can work without too much interference. He enjoys the arts and usually derives much pleasure from collecting antiques and other items that appeal. His advice is often highly valued, particularly on social and domestic matters.

Fire Snake: 1917, 1977

The Fire Snake tends to be more forceful, outgoing and energetic than some of the other types of Snake. He is ambitious, confident and never slow in voicing his opinions, and he can be very abrasive to those he does not like. He does, however, have many leadership qualities and can win the respect and support of many with his firm and resolute manner. He usually has a good sense of humour, a wide circle of friends and a very active social life. He is also a keen traveller.

Earth Snake 1929, 1989

The Earth Snake is charming, amusing and has a very amiable manner. He is conscientious and reliable in his work and approaches everything he does in a level-headed and sensible way. He can, however, tend to err on the cautious side and never likes to be hassled into making a decision. He is adept in dealing with financial matters and is a shrewd investor. He has many friends and is very supportive towards the members of his family.

Prospects for the Snake in 2014

The Year of the Snake (10 February 2013–30 January 2014) is one of considerable potential for the Snake himself and the closing months will present him with some good opportunities and also some moments of good fortune.

Although the Snake can be reserved and tends not to be the most active of socializers, the closing months of the year will give him more opportunity to go out and there will be some interesting occasions to look forward to. For the unattached, romantic prospects are promising.

There will also be an increase in domestic activity and quite a few Snake households will see a keynote celebration taking place. Given the general level of activity, it would be helpful if some arrangements were decided early on and everyone persuaded to do their fair share, as otherwise pressure and tiredness could lead to a few disagreements.

The Snake will also have an increasing number of outgoings to contend with at this time and, where possible, should try to spread out his purchases. He would also benefit from budgeting in advance and giving himself time to make selections rather than doing everything in a rush.

His work situation could see important developments as the year draws to a close and he may have the opportunity to extend his role or take on new duties. His experience can bring some pleasing results, with September being a potentially important month.

Overall, the Snake's own year will have brought him some fine opportunities and by putting himself forward and using his strengths to advantage he will have been able to accomplish – and enjoy – a good deal.

The Horse year starts on 31 January and will be a mixed one for the Snake. Events move swiftly in Horse years and at times the Snake could feel unsettled by developments and find himself under increased pressure. However, while this may not be the best of years for him, he can still emerge from it with some well-deserved achievements to his credit.

In his work the Snake can make reasonable progress, although he will need to keep alert. With change afoot, this is no time to be on the periphery of events or pay insufficient heed to current developments. Horse years favour action and involvement rather than the thinking, planning and theorizing that many Snakes prefer.

However, while the changes may be disturbing, many Snakes will have the chance to build on their current duties and gain greater insight into the industry in which they work. Such knowledge can prove very useful, not least in preparing the Snake for the opportunities that will arise later in the Horse year and in the more favourable Goat year that follows.

Snakes who are hoping to make a change or seeking work will need to act quickly whenever an opportunity arises. They can strengthen their prospects by finding out more about the work being offered and emphasizing their experience. April, May, October and November could see important developments.

The Snake is generally careful in money matters and can fare reasonably well this year. Some Snakes may find ways to supplement their income, perhaps through a hobby or enterprising idea. However, while the financial aspects are generally positive, the Snake does need to be wary of rushing purchases and should avoid entering into any commitments until he is ready and satisfied. If possible, he should try to make provision for travel, including a holiday. In this active year, a break and change of scene can do him considerable good.

It is also important that he preserves some time for himself. Having the chance to chill out and unwind is important and necessary for the Snake psyche. Without this, there is a risk that the Snake could become prone to stress and, if overly tired, susceptible to niggling ailments. In this busy year it is essential that he takes care of himself and gets any concerns checked out.

With his enquiring nature, the Snake can derive considerable satisfaction from developing his ideas over the year, or giving himself some projects to do. It is also important that he does not deny himself the chance to go to any social events that appeal to him. The Snake is not the most active socializer, but going out now and then can do him good as well as bring important balance to his lifestyle. March, June, August and October will see the most social activity.

For Snakes who are enjoying romance or who find romance this year, however, care is advised. Preoccupation or a minor difference of opinion could lead to problems. In some situations, especially social ones, the Snake would do well to watch his words and be discreet. Although generally a good diplomat, he may have to tread carefully in volatile or delicate situations this year.

This need for awareness also applies to his domestic life. A lot will be happening, and preoccupation, pressure and tiredness could lead to a few awkward moments. However, with awareness and the willingness to be open and communicative, the Snake can find problems can often be averted. Shared activities will not only help rapport but can also lead to some enjoyable occasions. Spending time with loved ones is very important this year. If possible, a holiday and, at busier times, an occasional treat can do everyone a lot of good.

Overall, the Year of the Horse will be a demanding one for the Snake and he will need to be mindful of those around him as well as preserve time for rest and recreation. However, the year will have its positive side too and the Snake will benefit from adjusting to situations and acquiring new skills and knowledge. In the Horse year challenges can often be opportunities in disguise and with care the Snake will find it will prepare him well for the improved times that await in the more favourable Goat year that follows.

The Metal Snake

One of the many strengths of the Metal Snake is his determination. Whenever he has ideas or particular objectives, he does his best to see them through. In the Horse year, his purposeful manner can lead to him accomplishing a great deal. However, he can also be independent and this year favours working with others. Metal Snakes, take note.

As the Horse year starts, Metal Snakes born in 1941 are already likely to have some objectives in mind. No matter what area these thoughts may concern, the Metal Snake does need to talk them through with his loved ones and, when appropriate, professionals rather than forge ahead on his own. With the input of others, far more will become possible.

This particularly applies to home projects. Whether choosing new equipment, altering living areas or having a major sort out, the Metal Snake will find that if he shares his thoughts and carries out his undertakings with others, not only will some tasks be accomplished more easily but everyone will be better able to appreciate the results.

Mutual interests can also bring pleasure, as can local events, and by keeping active and informed the Metal Snake and his close family members can find themselves with a good mix of things to do.

During the year the Metal Snake will also do a lot to help family members. With some likely to be under pressure or facing important decisions, he can not only offer a listening ear but also valued judgement. Many Metal Snakes could also assist by spending additional time with grandchildren or great grandchildren. The Metal Snake's family means a lot to him and while, as with any year, there may be a few awkward moments, his care, support and involvement can have special significance.

The Metal Snake will also appreciate the social opportunities that arise over the year and any Metal Snakes who would welcome more chance to go out would find local activities well worth investigating. The Metal Snake may have an independent streak, but this is a year for reaching out and participating.

The Metal Snake is generally careful in money matters and by taking his time when considering purchases, he can look forward to making some pleasing and useful acquisitions over the year. If possible, he should also try to make provision for a holiday. By planning this carefully, he can have some fascinating experiences.

Although the Metal Snake generally keeps himself active, he would also do well to give some consideration to his well-being, including taking suitable exercise and having a balanced diet. If he has any concerns or feels some modifications to his lifestyle might help, he should seek medical advice.

For Metal Snakes born in 2001, the Horse year again offers considerable scope. As they further their education, they will find new chances opening up for them, allowing them to do more and gain in confidence. The Horse year encourages progress, but to fully benefit the young Metal Snake does need to be open to instruction. If he is forthcoming and shares his thoughts, hopes and any concerns, he will find that those around him can do a lot to help. But for this to happen, openness is key.

The Metal Snake chooses his friends with care and over the year will especially value the bond he has with one or two special friends, although in some cases a certain matter may lead to a disagreement or some awkward moments. The minority of Metal Snakes affected would do well to try and heal any rift as quickly as they can. The Horse year does call for mindfulness as well as for the Metal Snake to watch his occasionally stubborn tendencies.

The young Metal Snake will also have some interesting travel opportunities over the year and will enjoy some of the places he sees and the (often outdoor) activities he gets to try out. The Horse year can open up exciting possibilities for the keen and willing.

All Metal Snakes, whether born in 1941 or 2001, can benefit from the opportunities that come their way over the Horse year and from the encouragement they are given by those around them. It is, however, important that the Metal Snake consults others and is mindful of their views. To be headstrong, obtuse or do his own thing could limit what he is able to do and sometimes affect his relations with others. With this proviso, this can be a richly varied year with a lot to offer.

Tip for the Year

Value your relations with others. The Horse year is one for involvement and participation. Also, be receptive to new ideas and possibilities. An open-minded approach can help make this an interesting and personally rewarding year.

The Water Snake

This can be a varied and interesting year for the Water Snake, although to get the most from it he will need to be flexible in outlook. This is no time to ignore what is going on around him or fail to capitalize on opportunities, even if what is happening does not fit in with his plans or way of thinking.

At work many Water Snakes will be firmly established in a particular type of position and have extensive experience behind them. Although quite a few will be content to remain where they are, the Horse year is a time of change. Many workplaces will see new systems being introduced, duties altered and objectives set, and the Water Snake will need to remain alert and adapt as required. While he may have misgivings about some of what is taking place, amid the volatility opportunities can open up and he may be well placed to benefit. Many Water Snakes will be successful in moving their career forward over the year.

There will also be some who will be keen to change the nature of their work, perhaps looking for a position involving less commuting and/or with more convenient hours. These Water Snakes, as well as those looking for work, need to remain alert. Although opportunities may be limited, by considering what is available and adapting their skills accordingly, quite a few could take on a very different type of work. Horse years can proceed in curious ways and provided the Water Snake remains flexible and willing, he can often benefit. Late March to May, October and November could see potentially important developments.

A few Water Snakes may also take advantage of early retirement options. Here again the Horse year can be a time of change that leads to new and interesting opportunities.

The progress the Water Snake makes at work can often help financially, but while this will be welcome, he does need to watch his spending levels and, if applicable, reduce his borrowings. With good management he can improve his overall position as well as make some pleasing acquisitions. Where some home purchases are concerned, his eye for quality, style and practicality will serve him well.

Also, if possible, he should make provision for a holiday at some time during the year. With his busy lifestyle, a break can do him good.

He will also enjoy the chances he will have to use and extend his knowledge and skills. These may be related to his work or to other, sometimes diverse, areas. The Water Snake does possess an enquiring mind, and setting time aside to read, research and explore, or possibly enrolling on a course or study programme, can bring him a great deal of pleasure.

To be on good form, however, he should give some consideration to his well-being and if he does not take regular exercise or have a particularly balanced diet, seek advice on changes he could introduce. Ignoring this could leave him lacking his usual sparkle and susceptible to minor ailments. Water Snakes, take note.

The Water Snake prefers to keep his social circle relatively small and be selective in the events he attends, but in the Horse year it is important he does not close his mind to social opportunities. Going to local events or those related to his interests could be to his benefit and some of his friends and other contacts could help him in a sometimes surprising way.

It is also important that Water Snakes who are alone do not withdraw into themselves but give themselves the chance to meet others and attend events of interest. Their willingness to participate can add a new dimension to their lifestyle. March, June, August and October could see the most social activity.

The year will also bring romantic possibilities for the unattached, although for some Water Snakes their current circumstances will mean the path of true love is not smooth or straightforward. Here some patience and increased understanding are advisable.

The Horse year can also see much domestic activity and there could be a special family event in many a Water Snake household. In addition, the year can bring change. Some members of the household could alter their routines or commitments and adjustments will be needed. With understanding and co-operation, however, new patterns can be established, family successes enjoyed and some pleasing (and sometimes ambitious) home projects accomplished. Dialogue and openness can enable more to be achieved as well as prevent possible misunderstandings.

The Year of the Horse offers much scope for the Water Snake, but to benefit, he does need to seize the moment and be open to the new. However, whether in a new working role or exploring new interests, with willingness and a certain open-mindedness, he can fare well.

Tip for the Year

Watch your independent tendencies. Be involved, be a part, share, communicate and be open! That way a lot more can happen for you this year. Also, do not be resistant to change. These are fast-moving times and you need to act accordingly.

The Wood Snake

The Wood Snake has charm, style and great awareness. He also enjoys the support of many and this, together with his keen nature, can help make this an interesting and potentially important year. However, he will need to accept that events can happen quickly in the Horse year and can be subject to some curious twists and turns.

This can especially be the case at work. For the many Wood Snakes who are well established in a particular career, there could be the opportunity to move ahead – but in a different capacity. This may not be what these Wood Snakes were envisaging, but for quite a few the Horse year can give their career a welcome lift.

For Wood Snakes who feel they have been drifting recently, are unfulfilled in what they do or are seeking work, the Horse year can also bring some good, if sometimes unexpected opportunities. The job-seeking process will be difficult, but by making enquiries and being quick to follow up any vacancies, they may well find their enthusiasm catching the eye of prospective employers and leading to a new position being offered. Effort and persistence will be required, but once the right chance is presented, events can move surprisingly quickly. One day the Wood Snake may be despondent, the next ecstatic, such is the way of the Horse year. Late March to May, October and November could see important developments, but at almost any time if the Wood Snake sees a possibility worth pursuing he should do so promptly.

The progress many Wood Snakes will make at work can also help financially, although with existing commitments and possibly some ambitious plans in mind, the Wood Snake will need to manage his outgoings well. This is a year which rewards good planning and financial discipline.

With it also being a time of development and opportunity, however, the Wood Snake can get much satisfaction from his personal interests. If there are ideas he would like to pursue, personal objectives he is keen to reach or skills he would like to learn, he should allow himself the time to do so. Any Wood Snakes who would welcome new challenges or who have, because of commitments, neglected their interests of late would find this an ideal time to start something new.

Some Wood Snakes will take up physical activities or keep-fit pursuits over the year. As well as benefitting their well-being, these activities could also have a sometimes pleasing social element. Should the Wood Snake have concerns or questions about his well-being at any time during the year, he should get these addressed.

The Horse year can also give rise to some unexpected travel opportunities. It could be that the Wood Snake takes advantage of a last-minute offer or has the chance to go away at relatively short notice. The spontaneity can make some of his trips particularly memorable. In addition, if there is a place the Wood Snake is keen to see or an event he would like to attend, he should make enquiries and see what can be arranged. Positive action can pay off.

Although the Wood Snake is selective in his socializing, he will also have the chance to go out and meet others and there could be local events that appeal to him. By making the most of these opportunities, he can not only enjoy himself but also help keep his lifestyle in balance.

Any Wood Snakes who have experienced recent personal difficulty will find the Horse year is a time for moving forward, and for the unattached, romance can beckon. However, while affairs of the heart can generally go well, the Wood Snake should avoid becoming involved in potentially complicated situations. Without care, difficulties could lie ahead. Those affected, take note.

The Wood Snake's domestic life is set to be busy this year and it is important that there is good dialogue and co-operation between all involved. Pressure and tiredness can sometimes lead to irritability, and this needs to be watched. However, while, as with all years, there may be fraught moments, there will also be special times, and shared interests may be particularly valued this year. Some of the Wood Snake's loved ones will also be involved in some important and far-reaching decisions and his support and quiet, considered manner may be especially appreciated.

Overall, the Wood Snake will see a tremendous amount happen this year and at the year's end may look back and be surprised by how many changes have taken place and the curious way in which some plans have moved forward and some opportunities have arisen. This is a year rich in possibility, but it is one when the Wood Snake will need to act quickly and look to move ahead. However, he will have the opportunity to take his skills, knowledge and interests further, and this can help both his current situation and future prospects. The Year of the Horse can bring some surprising (and often fortuitous) developments and have far-reaching significance.

Tip for the Year
Keep your lifestyle in balance. Set aside time for your own interests and your loved ones. Also, seize any chances to develop your skills and knowledge. What you do now can have future significance.

The Fire Snake

The Fire Snake will have seen a lot happen in recent years and this will be yet another full and eventful one. However, while the Fire Snake may have definite ambitions and hopes, in 2014 he will need to be adaptable and make the most of the situations in which he finds himself. This is no time to risk falling behind or losing out for the sake of fixed plans. Horse years require flexibility and an open mind.

The Fire Snake's work prospects are particularly well aspected, but the many new schemes, initiatives and changes that characterize Horse years can arise in some unexpected ways. As a result, some months could be unsettling, but the changes can give rise to new opportunities. Staff may be required to implement new procedures or take on specific tasks, for example, and, by being willing and putting himself forward, the Fire Snake can often benefit. This is a time to stay alert and keep himself informed. In this fast-moving year opportunities may not be available for long.

Many Fire Snakes will remain with their current employer this year, but will be able to move their career forward and add considerably to their skills and experience. Their work can also bring them into contact with new colleagues and they can build up useful connections as well as impress influential people.

For Fire Snakes who decide to move elsewhere or are looking for work, the Horse year can again bring some interesting developments. However, to benefit these Fire Snakes would do well to widen the scope of positions they are prepared to consider. In addition, talking to employment officials and friends could help. It could be that the Fire Snake is alerted to growth areas or companies looking to recruit. With resolve and initiative, many Fire Snakes will be able to secure a position that offers an interesting new career challenge. In typical Horse year fashion, their quest can sometimes proceed in unexpected ways but deliver potentially significant opportunities. Late March to early June, October and November could be important for work matters.

The progress the Fire Snake makes at work may well enable him to increase his income and some Fire Snakes could also benefit from a gift or the receipt of extra funds. However, while any improvement will be welcome, the Fire Snake will need to remain disciplined in his spending and make ample allowance for existing commitments and any deposits he may be required to put down. With care, he will be able to carry out many of his plans, but the Horse year does require careful financial management.

In view of his various commitments, the Fire Snake also needs to keep his lifestyle in balance. To be continually busy and always driving himself could take its toll. Also, as with many of his sign, he does burn up a lot of nervous energy and needs to give himself the chance to relax and unwind. Here personal interests and recreational pursuits can be of considerable benefit and, busy though the year may be, it is important that the Fire Snake allows time for these. Any Fire Snake who has let his interests lapse should try to rectify this early on in the year. Time spent on pleasurable and relaxing activities can do the Fire Snake a lot of good. For those who are sedentary for much of the day, suitable keep-fit activities could also be worth considering. And if at any time during the year the Fire Snake feels below par or has any concerns, he should get these checked out.

Social opportunities can also be good ways for the Fire Snake to relax and he will value meeting up with his friends this year. March, June, August and October could see the most social activity.

For Fire Snakes who start the year alone and unattached, a sudden and glorious romantic opportunity can present itself and, in the process, throw their emotional world into turmoil. Romantic dealings do, though, need to be kept honourable, otherwise problems could result.

The Fire Snake's home life promises to be busy and there will need to be good co-operation between family members. Changes in routine will require adjustment and time should be allowed to attend to plans and home purchases properly. Also, despite all the activity, quality time should not be sacrificed. Should this happen, tensions could arise. Fire Snakes, take note and be mindful. However, the Horse year will have its domestic highlights, including some personal achievements for the Fire Snake and the possible academic success of someone close. Special occasions and shared activities can be especially appreciated and an important ingredient of family life.

The Fire Snake is ambitious and likes to make the most of his situation. In the Horse year some excellent opportunities will come his way but they will call for effort and adjustment. If the Fire Snake is prepared to give this, then he can not only benefit now but also improve his future prospects. There are important gains to be had this year. The Fire Snake should also keep his lifestyle in balance, preserving time for his own interests and for his loved ones. With care, effort and good time management, he can make this a successful and rewarding year.

Tip for the Year

Value your relationships. Family, friends and colleagues can be particularly helpful this year. Do consult them. Also, make the most of your chances to further your skills and experience. This will be important both for now *and* the near future.

The Earth Snake

This can be a generally happy and eventful year for the Earth Snake and with care he will be able to make progress at work as well as enjoy some pleasing developments in his personal life. However, the Horse year will be a fast-moving one and the Earth Snake will need to act quickly and adapt as situations require. Admittedly, he may prefer more time to think and plan, but hesitation or delay could deny him some good opportunities.

An important feature of the year will be the chance the Earth Snake will have to further his knowledge. Whether in his working situation or his personal interests, he will be able to acquire new skills as well as expand and explore his capabilities. If there are certain skills he feels could help his future progress, he should look at ways of obtaining these, including study courses he could take. Positive action now can often improve his current situation as well as widen his options for later.

Another area worth considering is his general well-being. Although the Earth Snake may keep himself active, he does need to make sure he takes sufficient exercise, eats healthily and gives himself the chance to rest after he has been busy and under pressure. To neglect his own well-being could leave him feeling below par, and should he have problems or concerns at any time during the year, he should get these checked out.

In his personal life, he can look forward to some memorable times. Earth Snakes with a partner will be keen to spend a great deal of their time together and move their hopes and plans forward. Events can sometimes move more quickly than anticipated, with the Earth Snake benefiting from fortunate developments and, in some instances, unexpected offers of assistance. This could especially apply to accommodation matters and purchases the Earth Snake is keen to make.

Joint projects can also be satisfying and lead to a lot being accomplished. However, while a lot will go well, the year does call for openness and good communication. Decisions and concerns do need to be talked through, and extra help and consideration given at busy times. By nature the Earth Snake is attentive and caring, but preoccupation or irritability (caused by pressure) may lead to some awkward moments this year.

Earth Snakes who start the year alone can experience sudden and dramatic developments. A chance meeting could change everything and the Earth Snake's emotional world may be sent into a whirl by the speed with which events happen and the way love takes hold. However, for it to endure, time needs to be allowed for each person to get know the other and so put the relationship on a firm foundation. Also, the Earth Snake does need to remain his honourable self. Lapses can lead to heartache. March, June, August and October could be important and special months for personal matters.

While the Earth Snake tends to keep his own counsel (a typical Snake trait), he would do well to draw on the help and expertise of friends this year. Particularly if in a personal dilemma, considering ideas or facing a problem, he will find the support and input of those he trusts of great value. In this busy year he should remember that he is not alone and others will often be willing to assist.

The Horse year may see important developments in the Earth Snake's work situation and in view of skills recently demonstrated, he may be encouraged to take on wider-ranging duties. The emphasis this year is very much on career development. Opportunities can arise with little warning, maybe through the absence of colleagues or internal reorganization, and by being fully involved in the workplace and indicating interest, the Earth Snake may be well placed to benefit.

The Horse year can also open up important possibilities for Earth Snakes who feel their career prospects can be improved by moving elsewhere or who are seeking work. To benefit fully, these Earth Snakes should not be too restrictive in the type of work they are prepared to consider. By keeping alert and being willing to adapt their skills and acquire new ones, many can be successful in securing a new position, and often one that is in a different capacity from what they have done before. April to early June, October and November could see important developments.

Headway made at work can help financially, but in view of the Earth Snake's personal activities, commitments and ambitions, this will be an expensive year. Throughout he needs to be disciplined and keep a careful watch on spending. With care, he will be able to proceed with many of his plans, however, and his shrewd nature can lead to him making some good acquisitions and decisions.

There could also be some good travel opportunities during the year and the Earth Snake should try to take these up. A break and change of scene can do him good.

Overall, the Year of the Horse will be an eventful one, with some fine opportunities coming the Earth Snake's way. These do need to be seized and the Earth Snake also needs to adapt as situations require. However, he will find there is much to be gained this year and his efforts now can help both his current situation and his future prospects. A positive and significant year.

Tip for the Year

Be open to opportunity. Look to move forward and build on your skills and experience. What you do now can lay the foundation for future success. Also, pay attention to your relations with others. The support of those around you can assist in many undertakings.

Famous Snakes

Muhammad Ali, Ann-Margret, Kim Basinger, Ben Bernanke, Björk, Tony Blair, Michael Bloomberg, Michael Bolton, Brahms, Pierce Brosnan, Casanova, Jessica Chastain, Jackie Collins, Tom Conti, Cecil B. de Mille, Robert Downey Jr, Bob Dylan, Elgar, Michael Fassbender, Sir Alex Ferguson, Sir Alexander Fleming, Mahatma Gandhi, Greta Garbo, Art Garfunkel, J. Paul Getty, W. E. Gladstone, Johann Wolfgang von Goethe, Princess Grace of Monaco, Tom Hardy, Stephen Hawking, Audrey Hepburn, Jack Higgins, Elizabeth Hurley, James Joyce, Stacy Keach, Ronan Keating, J. F. Kennedy, Chaka Khan, Carole King, Courtney Love, Rory McIlroy, Mao Tse-tung, Chris Martin, Henri Matisse, Robert Mitchum, Piers Morgan, Alfred Nobel, Mike Oldfield, Jacqueline Onassis, Sarah Jessica Parker, Pablo Picasso, Mary Pickford, Daniel Radcliffe, Franklin D. Roosevelt, Mickey Rourke, J. K. Rowling, Jean-Paul Sartre, Franz Schubert, Charlie Sheen, Paul Simon, Delia Smith, Ben Stiller, Taylor Swift, Madame Tussaud, Shania Twain, Dionne Warwick, Mia Wasikowska, Charlie Watts, Kanye West, Oprah Winfrey, Virginia Woolf.

11 February 1918 to 31 January 1919 — *Earth Horse*

30 January 1930 to 16 February 1931 — *Metal Horse*

15 February 1942 to 4 February 1943 — *Water Horse*

3 February 1954 to 23 January 1955 — *Wood Horse*

21 January 1966 to 8 February 1967 — *Fire Horse*

7 February 1978 to 27 January 1979 — *Earth Horse*

27 January 1990 to 14 February 1991 — *Metal Horse*

12 February 2002 to 31 January 2003 — *Water Horse*

31 January 2014 to 18 February 2015 — *Wood Horse*

The Horse

The Personality of the Horse

There are many worn paths,
but the most rewarding
is the one you decide on and forge yourself.

The Horse is born under the signs of elegance and ardour. He has a most engaging and charming manner and is usually very popular. He loves meeting people and likes attending parties and other large social gatherings.

The Horse is a lively character and enjoys being the centre of attention. He has many leadership qualities and is much admired for his honest and straightforward manner. He is an eloquent and persuasive speaker and has a great love of discussion and debate. He also has a particularly agile mind and can assimilate facts remarkably quickly.

He does, however, have a fiery temper and although his outbursts are usually short-lived, he can often say things that he will later regret. He is also not particularly good at keeping secrets.

The Horse has many interests and involves himself in a wide variety of activities. He can, however, get involved in so much that he can often waste his energies on projects that he never has time to complete. He also has a tendency to change his interests rather frequently and will often get caught up in the latest craze or 'in thing' until something more exciting turns up.

The Horse also likes to have a certain amount of freedom and independence. He hates being bound by petty rules and regulations and as far as possible likes to feel that he is answerable to no one but himself. But despite this spirit of freedom, he still likes to have the support and encouragement of others in his various enterprises.

Due to his many talents and likeable nature, the Horse will often go far in life. He enjoys challenges and is a methodical and tireless worker. However, should things go against him and he fail in any of his enterprises, it will take a long time for him to recover and pick up the pieces again. Success to the Horse means everything. To fail is a disaster and a humiliation.

The Horse likes to have variety in life and will try his hand at many different things before he settles down to one particular job. Even then, he will probably remain alert to see whether there are any better opportunities for him to take up. He has a restless nature and can easily get bored. He does, however, excel in any position that allows him sufficient freedom to act on his own initiative or brings him into contact with a lot of people.

Although the Horse is not particularly bothered about accumulating great wealth, he handles his finances with care and will rarely experience any serious financial problems.

The Horse also enjoys travel and loves visiting new and faraway places. At some stage during his life he may be tempted to live abroad for a short period of time and due to his adaptable nature will find that he will fit in well wherever he goes.

The Horse pays a great deal of attention to his appearance and usually likes to wear smart, colourful and rather distinctive clothes. He is very attractive to others and will often have many romances before he settles down. He is loyal and protective to his partner, but despite his family commitments he still likes to retain a certain measure of independence and have the freedom to carry on with his own interests and hobbies. He will find that he is especially well suited to those born under the signs of the Tiger, Goat, Rooster and Dog. He can also get on well with the Rabbit, Dragon, Snake, Pig and another Horse, but he will find the Ox too serious and intolerant for his liking. He will also have difficulty in getting on with the Monkey and the Rat – the Monkey is very inquisitive and the Rat seeks security, and both will resent the Horse's rather independent ways.

The female Horse is usually most attractive and has a friendly, outgoing personality. She is highly intelligent, has many interests and is alert to everything that is going on around her. She particularly enjoys outdoor pursuits and often likes to take part in sport and keep-fit activities. She also enjoys travel, literature and the arts, and is a very good conversationalist.

Although the Horse can be stubborn and rather self-centred, he does have a considerate nature and is often willing to help others. He has a good sense of humour and will usually make a favourable impression wherever he goes. Provided he can curb his slightly restless nature and keep tight control over his temper, he will go through life making friends, taking part in a multitude of different activities and generally achieving many of his objectives. His life will rarely be dull.

The Five Different Types of Horse

In addition to the 12 signs of the Chinese zodiac there are five elements and these have a strengthening or moderating influence on the signs. The effects of the five elements on the Horse are described below, together with the years in which they were exercising their influence. Therefore Horses born in 1930 and 1990 are Metal Horses, Horses born in 1942 and 2002 are Water Horses, and so on.

Metal Horse: 1930, 1990

This Horse is bold, confident and forthright. He is ambitious and a great innovator. He loves challenges and takes great delight in sorting out complicated problems. He likes to have a certain amount of independence and resents any outside interference in his affairs. He has charm and a certain charisma, but he can also be very stubborn and rather impulsive. He usually has many friends and enjoys an active social life.

Water Horse: 1942, 2002

The Water Horse has a friendly nature and a good sense of humour and is able to talk intelligently on a wide range of topics. He is astute in business matters and quick to take advantage of any opportunities that arise. He does, however, have a tendency to get easily distracted and can change his interests – and indeed his mind – rather frequently, and this can often work to his detriment. He is nevertheless very talented and can often go far in life. He pays a great deal of attention to his appearance and is usually smart and well turned out. He loves to travel and also enjoys sport and other outdoor activities.

Wood Horse: 1954, 2014

The Wood Horse has a most agreeable and amiable nature. He communicates well with others and is able to talk intelligently on many different subjects. He is a hard and conscientious worker and is held in high esteem by his friends and colleagues. His opinions are often sought and, given his imaginative nature, he can often come up with some very original and practical ideas. He is usually widely read and likes to lead a busy social life. He can also be most generous and often holds high moral views.

Fire Horse: 1966

The element of Fire combined with the temperament of the Horse creates one of the most powerful forces in the Chinese zodiac. The Fire Horse is destined to lead an exciting and eventful life and to make his mark in his chosen profession. He has a forceful personality and his intelligence and resolute manner bring him the support and admiration of many. He loves action and excitement and his life will rarely be quiet. He can, however, be rather blunt and forthright in his views and does not take kindly to interference in his own affairs or to obeying orders. He is a flamboyant character, has a good sense of humour and will lead a very active social life.

Earth Horse: 1918, 1978

This Horse is considerate and caring. He is more cautious than some of the other types of Horse, but is wise, perceptive and extremely capable. Although he can be rather indecisive at times, he has considerable business acumen and is very astute in financial matters. He has a quiet, friendly nature and is well thought of by his family and friends.

Prospects for the Horse in 2014

The Horse is action-oriented and likes to see the results of those actions coming through quickly. However, the Snake year (10 February 2013–30 January 2014) tends to proceed at a more measured pace and during it the Horse will need to show greater patience than usual. Although he can fare reasonably well, he needs to keep his expectations modest.

In the remaining months of the Snake year the Horse will see a general increase in activity and can prepare himself for some of the opportunities that await in his own year.

In his work, changing situations and increased pressures will often allow him to demonstrate his judgement and broaden his skills and, in the process, enhance his reputation. For Horses hoping to move their career forward or seeking work, September and November could hold interesting possibilities.

The closing months of the year will see an increase in expenditure and Horses will need to be careful when making large transactions and watch their spending levels. This is a time for discipline.

Domestically and socially, the Horse will be much in demand. There will be friends to meet, occasions to attend and plans to be agreed, with October and December being particularly busy months. A bonus could be that the Horse gets to spend time with some people he does not often see. He may also enjoy some special family news. However, while he will delight in a lot of what takes place, he does need to be mindful of the views of others. Without care, a possible difference of opinion may arise. The Year of the Snake can be a generally constructive one, but it does require the Horse to be attentive and keep his wits firmly about him.

The Horse sets about life with gusto. He has commitment, drive and an engaging personality, and in his own year he will see a lot happen. The Horse year starts on 31 January and has the potential for being a brilliant year for the Horse himself but also – *and here lies a warning* – a disastrous one too! In their own year Horses need to be careful *not* to overreach themselves or push their luck or the goodwill of others too far. With care and good judgement, the majority can look forward to a highly successful year, but the aspects do warn against complacency and unnecessary risk.

One of the most promising features of the year will be the chance it brings for the Horse to build on his strengths. Whether in his career or more personal interests, he will see some encouraging developments.

At work, the way many Horses have been carrying out their responsibilities – often under pressure – will have impressed others, and many will now be well placed to apply for promotion. Those who work in large organizations will find their in-house knowledge can be a definite advantage and many Horses will be able to make deserved headway in their career.

Horses are usually ambitious and for those who are keen to take on new challenges elsewhere, as well as those looking for work, their own year can open up important possibilities. By actively making enquiries and following through ideas (and here their own initiative can bear considerable fruit), many will be successful in finding a position which offers change, the chance to develop their skills and potential for the future. For many, this year can mark a new stage in their working life. February, April, June and September could see encouraging developments, but the Horse's own efforts could pay off at almost any time.

Work colleagues will often be supportive this year and some senior colleagues or contacts could prove helpful in providing advice or references. However, while the aspects may be good, the Horse does need to watch his independent and sometimes self-willed tendencies. To immerse himself so much in his own activities that he becomes isolated or on the periphery of a team risks undermining his situation. This has the potential for being a successful year, but there are quite a few ingredients to success, with good relations with colleagues being one. The Horse does need to remain aware of this.

The progress the Horse makes at work can lead to an increase in income and financially this can be an improved year. The Horse can be successful in some purchases he makes and can enjoy a certain amount of luck in his own year, *but* should he be tempted to take risks, rush transactions or spend his money too readily, he could come to rue his haste. The Horse year has good financial prospects for the Horse himself, but without care these can be undermined. So much in 2014 rests in the Horse's own hands.

With his alert and adventurous nature, however, he should, if possible, make provision for travel this year. He could particularly enjoy visiting places that are new to him. Even if he is not able to travel too far in distance, there could be attractions and events nearby he could enjoy.

He will also have the chance to develop his own interests this year and could find them leading him in new directions. He will rarely be short of ideas or things to do and this can be an inspiring time. In addition, many Horses who lack regular exercise or rely on fast foods will give more attention to their well-being and make improvements to their lifestyle. By seeking advice and following guidance, they may find their actions not only benefitting them but, in some instances, introducing them to new activities or keep-fit disciplines.

The Horse's home life can be eventful this year. The Horse will have many plans he is keen to carry out, but yet again he should be careful not to proceed without proper consideration and consultation. He may be enthusiastic, but haste can bring problems and sometimes dissension. Horses, take note. Also, in such a busy year, it is important that time is set aside for shared activities. In 2014 the Horse does need to strike a sensible balance in all he sets out to do. In many a Horse household, however, there will be special occasions to enjoy and some proud moments. The summer and last few weeks of the year could be busy and interesting.

The likeable and engaging Horse will also make the most of his social opportunities and can look forward to an interesting mix of things to do. New and existing interests can bring him into contact with others and many a Horse will enjoy a flourishing social life. March, June, late July, August and December could be particularly lively months.

Romantic prospects are also good, although while passion can be incredibly strong, it would be worth Horses who are newly in love to show patience and let any new relationship develop gradually.

Active, enterprising and ambitious, the Horse will be determined to do a lot in his own year and will have some good opportunities to do so. He can benefit from some strokes of good fortune as well as the support of others. Domestically and socially, the year will see much activity. However, it is important that the Horse keeps his lifestyle well balanced and gives time both to himself and to others. He also needs to watch his independent tendencies and be careful of acting in haste. In his own year he will be very much the architect of his own fortune. Commitment, good judgement and willingness can bring success, but risk, rush or a poor attitude can undermine so much. Horses, take note, and do make the most of this year which is so rich in possibility.

The Metal Horse

As the Horse year gets underway, many a Metal Horse will feel this is the start of a full and exciting time. For many, it *can* be a highly significant year, but it does call for effort. To make the most of his chances the Metal Horse will need to be determined and have faith in himself. As a Metal Horse, he has many capabilities and this year will not only give him the chance to prove himself but also to enjoy some well-deserved success.

For Metal Horses in work, this can be a significant time. If following a particular career, the Metal Horse could be given the chance of additional training or the opportunity to take on greater responsibilities. Although this can be daunting, by making the most of his opportunities, the Metal Horse will not only add to his skills but also lay the foundation for future success. He is at the start of his working life and his potential will be noticed and encouraged. Horse years reward industry and commitment.

For Metal Horses who are unfulfilled in what they currently do, as well as those seeking work, again the year can bring interesting opportunities. To benefit, these Metal Horses will need to be active in following up vacancies and approaching organizations for information. By nature, however, the Metal Horse is tenacious, and in 2014 his initiative may well lead to him securing a position. Once installed, he may revel in the opportunity and delight in the potential for future development. February, April, June to mid-July and September could see encouraging developments, but such is the pace of the year that opportunities need to be seized without delay.

There will also be many Metal Horses studying for qualifications. A lot will be asked of these Metal Horses and effort and discipline will be required, but by applying themselves, many of these Metal Horses will not only enjoy successful outcomes but also secure the qualifications needed for certain professions.

The Metal Horse's personal interests can bring him considerable pleasure over the year. The Metal Horse delights in activity and this Horse year will offer him the chance to take some of his ideas and talents further. Many will feel in inspired form.

There will also be opportunities for him to travel and, even though funds may sometimes be limited, he will enjoy the places he gets to see and the diverse activities his travels make possible.

However, in view of his many commitments and activities, the Metal Horse will need to manage his finances with care. With good planning he will be able to do a surprising amount, but should he be indulgent or carefree, certain plans may need to be curtailed. The Horse year does require a disciplined approach.

With his many interests, the Metal Horse has an active social life and during the year he will particularly value the support of long-standing friends and the chance to talk over any concerns. Some Metal Horses will change their location this year and have the opportunity to form a new social circle. For any who start the year alone and possibly nursing personal hurt, the Horse year does offer brighter prospects. March, June, late July to early September and December could see the most social activity.

For quite a few Metal Horses the year could also be marked by a significant personal decision, with some getting engaged, marrying or settling down with another person. For the unattached, romantic prospects are also excellent, but new relationships do need time to become established. Also, should strains appear in an existing relationship, it would be best if these were talked through. Hastily made decisions could be regretted. This can be a special year for personal relationships, but is still one for proceeding carefully.

Throughout the year the Metal Horse also needs to draw on the willingness of his family to support and advise him. He may be independent-minded, but the input of others can make an important difference. His family will also be happy to share in his achievements.

Although the Metal Horse generally keeps himself active, he should also give some consideration to his well-being and allow himself the time to rest after stressful periods as well as watch the quality of his diet. Neglecting this could leave him susceptible to colds and other niggling ailments. Metal Horses, take note and care.

Overall, the Year of the Horse has exciting prospects for the Metal Horse. His personal life can be busy and rewarding, with love, achievements and various activities bringing him considerable pleasure. This is also a time for personal development and whether through work experience, qualifications or building on his capabilities in other ways, the Metal Horse can create some good opportunities to move forward. Used well, this Horse year can leave a powerful legacy and prepare him for the successful times ahead.

Tip for the Year

Value the support, love and friendship of those around you. Their help can be significant. Also, take any chances to develop your skills. What you are able to learn now can help both your current situation and future prospects.

The Water Horse

This will be a full and interesting year for the Water Horse, with many of his plans working out well.

For the Water Horse born in 1942, the Horse year encourages practical activity, and if there are plans he wants to set in motion, now is the time to do so. With resolve, he can accomplish a lot this year.

Throughout the year he will also be encouraged by the support of those around him and will benefit from discussing his ideas and seeking advice.

With the synergy of combined effort, some plans and hopes can proceed much faster and in ways the Water Horse may not have envisaged.

The Water Horse's thinking may concern various aspects of his life, although one prominent area will be his home. Over the year many Water Horses will be keen to make modifications, rectify problems, replace equipment and enhance living areas. A few may even decide to move to accommodation that better suits their requirements. A lot of what is completed this year will be both satisfying and appreciated by the entire household. The year will see a lot of practical activity and the Water Horse will never be short of projects to do or ideas to carry out.

The year can also contain some family highlights and there may be several achievements to celebrate. In addition many Water Horses will assist younger relations and, should they be under pressure or facing difficult decisions, the Water Horse's experience and empathy will be much appreciated. In turn the Water Horse himself will be grateful for the assistance of others at times over the year and will appreciate his family bonds.

If possible, he should take advantage of opportunities to travel, and whether he is on holiday or visiting others, he will often enjoy his times away. He can also derive considerable pleasure from his personal interests this year and will be pleased with how many of his projects and ideas can move forward. Horse years can be inspiring.

The Water Horse's interests can often have a social element to them and if he is a member of a group of enthusiasts or decides to join one during the year, he will benefit from being encouraged to do more as well as from spending time with like-minded people. Some Water Horses may also decide to help in their community in some way. The Horse year favours participation. March, June, late July to early September and December could see the most social activity.

In view of his various activities and expenses, the Water Horse will need to watch his financial situation and, where large transactions are concerned, seek additional advice. This is a year which rewards discipline and planning ahead.

The Water Horse should also take good care of his own well-being. This includes taking suitable exercise, watching his diet and following the correct procedures if lifting heavy weights or tackling anything strenuous. Should he have any concerns, he would do well to seek advice.

Overall, the more senior Water Horse will do a lot this year and will be pleased with how his plans develop. However, he does need to liaise well with those around him. The more support he has, the more he will be able to do.

For the Water Horse born in 2002, this is again a year rich in possibility. Quite a few young Water Horses will change their school during the year and many will also be studying new subjects for the first time. Accordingly, the Horse year can be exciting but daunting. However, the young Water Horse has a tenacious nature and by doing his best can not only make encouraging headway but also grow in confidence.

In both his education and personal interests, he will be encouraged to make more of certain aptitudes and by putting in the effort and being willing to learn, he will enjoy the way his skills improve and his ability to do more.

However, while active and game, the Water Horse does need to listen carefully to instructions and, when involved in sport or any potentially hazardous activity, follow the correct procedures. Young Water Horses, take note. Enjoy the year but do not be foolhardy.

The young Water Horse will also value the support of his family and friends this year. If he is open and talks over his ideas and plans, his family members can give him much useful assistance as well as help at times of change and pressure. The Water Horse will also enjoy the company of his friends and, when starting new activities, have the chance to make new ones.

Overall, the Horse year favours activity and the Water Horse, whether born in 1942 or 2002, will enjoy advancing his plans, furthering his interests and using his skills to good effect. This is a year of possibility, but to benefit fully the Water Horse would do well to draw on the support of those around him. With help, backed by his own 'can do' approach, he can make this a personally rewarding year and enjoy some special occasions as well.

Tip for the Year
Follow up your ideas and seize your opportunities. Once wheels are set in motion, interesting developments can quickly follow on. Also, enjoy and develop your personal interests. This can be a satisfying and inspiring year for you.

The Wood Horse

This is the Wood Horse's own year and it promises to be a special one. Not only can it bring some good opportunities but it will also have its surprises, and the Wood Horse will be encouraged and inspired by its developments.

At work in particular, many Wood Horses will be affected by change. Although they may feel settled in their position, this is a time of innovation and development and over the year many will experience changes in their role. These will often require them to adapt to new procedures and technologies and, in view of their seniority, some may also be required to implement developments as well, but by being willing to embrace change and make the most of what occurs, they can make significant headway.

Some Wood Horses will, though, seek to make a complete change in their working lives, either to work nearer to where they live or to fulfil another aspiration. For these Wood Horses, as well as those seeking work, their own year can offer encouraging developments. The job-seeking process will be difficult, but by talking to contacts and advisers, many Wood Horses will be alerted to possibilities worth pursuing. The Wood Horse's resourcefulness can also be to his advantage, with prospective employers being impressed by his drive, experience and willingness to adapt. With persistence, he may well win through and be offered an important opportunity. February, April, June and September could be important months for work matters.

There will also be some Wood Horses who choose to retire this year and this will mark the start of a new chapter in their life.

Also, with this being their sixtieth year, many Wood Horses will be keen to make it a special one. This could be through travel, treating themselves to something they have been wanting for a long time or starting ideas they may have been nurturing. In addition, just as the new year can be a time for making new resolutions, some Wood Horses will resolve to make their sixtieth year a time for positive change. Their improvement programme could include starting a fitness regime, being more efficient in certain undertakings, taking up a new interest or joining a local community group, but by acting on ideas, not only will they enjoy what they do but also the additional benefits that will so often follow on.

The Wood Horse will also have important financial decisions to make this year and will need to think these thorough carefully and, if applicable, seek professional advice. If he proceeds with care and checks the details and implications, he will be pleased with the decisions he takes. With travel likely to be on the agenda, budgeting ahead would be useful.

The Wood Horse also needs to give some consideration to his own well-being this year. While he keeps himself active, should he have concerns at any time over the year, he should get these checked out. Also, if engaged in any strenuous or hazardous activity, he should follow the recommended procedures. This year may be a good one, but it is not one for neglecting his well-being or taking unnecessary risks.

In the Wood Horse's home life, in addition to the often special marking of his own birthday, the year can see the launch of many plans. These can include home improvements, replacing certain pieces of equipment and carrying out a variety of other projects. However, while the Wood Horse will be keen to get a lot done, it will be best to spread projects out rather than have too much happening at once. In addition, throughout the year there needs to be good dialogue and liaison, otherwise amid all the activity and decision-making, disagreements could occur. Wood Horses, take careful note. Overall, though, this is a year of many positive domestic developments.

During the year the Wood Horse will also be attracted by a variety of cultural, sporting or other occasions and, whenever possible, should try to attend. He will also appreciate the social events that take place over the year and sharing news and views with his friends. Again, though, he does need to be aware of the views of others and, in particular, to pay heed to the advice a close friend may give, for they do speak with his interests at heart. For Wood Horses who are alone, new activities can be particularly good ways to meet others and the year will not be without romantic possibilities. March, June, late July to early September and December could be active and rewarding months.

This is the Year of the Wood Horse, and the Wood Horse himself can help make it a memorable one. By following through his ideas and making the most of his opportunities, he can enjoy some very satisfying results. He will also be encouraged by the support and affection of those around him and the year will bring some special times as well as some surprises to enjoy. The active and alert Wood Horse always has a lot to offer and his own year will offer him a lot in return.

Tip for the Year

Be open to the new. This is a year of considerable possibility and can bring you much personal satisfaction. Also, enjoy your relations with those who are special to you – and do listen to their advice. They are keen to assist – and to help make your own year special.

The Fire Horse

The Fire Horse has great drive and tenacity and can look forward to accomplishing a great deal in the Horse year. It can offer some interesting possibilities, and by making the most of these, the Fire Horse will have the chance to do even more. In many areas of his life the Year of the Horse has *great* potential for him.

Any Fire Horses who start the year dissatisfied with their current situation or feeling they have been languishing of late should take heart. This is a time to take the initiative and work towards the improvements they want to see happen. With purpose, backed by the encouraging aspects of the year, these Fire Horses will find positive results quickly following on from their actions. In the Horse year, effort is well rewarded.

The aspects are particularly encouraging as far as the Fire Horse's work situation is concerned. In some instances, as senior colleagues move on the Fire Horse can secure promotion or, as new ideas or procedures are introduced, he can apply for new responsibilities or specialist projects.

Many Fire Horses will be able to make important headway in the organization they work for this year, while those who feel their situation would be helped by moving to another employer, as well as those seeking work, can benefit from some interesting and sometimes surprising developments. Although the job-seeking process will be difficult, by thinking of different ways in which they could use their skills and keeping alert for opportunity, many of these Fire Horses will secure what can be an ideal new position. This could arise in a surprising way but nevertheless seem as if it was meant to be. February, April, June and September to early October could see encouraging developments.

Progress at work will also help financially and many Fire Horses could also benefit from the receipt of extra funds. However, in view of some of the commitments and expensive plans the Fire Horse is likely to have, he will need to manage his outgoings well. This is a year favouring financial discipline. The Fire Horse should also be thorough when dealing with financial correspondence. Haste or carelessness could be to his disadvantage.

With his often active lifestyle, the Fire Horse would also do well to give some consideration to his own well-being this year. To help keep himself on good form, he should allow time for rest and recreation rather than continually drive himself and should give some attention to his diet and level of exercise. If he feels improvements could be made or has concerns at any time, he should seek advice.

With this a year of possibility, he should also set time aside to develop his personal interests. These can often inspire him and do him considerable good. Any Fire Horse who has let his interests lapse due to a busy lifestyle should aim to redress this in the Year of the Horse.

Travel is favourably aspected and if possible the Fire Horse should aim to take a holiday over the year or at least give himself a break. Local activities and attractions can also be pleasurable and it would be worth the Fire Horse keeping informed about events in his locality. Some could surprise and delight him.

Socially, this year is likely to be busier than more recent ones, with March, June, late July to early September and December seeing the most activity.

For the unattached, this can be a time of exciting romantic possibility, although where new romance is concerned it may be best to allow time for the relationship to develop rather than rush into a commitment.

Domestically, change will be occurring in many Fire Horse households. It could be that a relation leaves home for educational purposes or due to another change in circumstances, and parts of the year could be unsettling, but the Fire Horse's ability to organize, prioritize and assist will prove an important asset. However, while this will be an active year, there will be some notable family successes to enjoy and shared activities will often go well.

Overall, the Year of the Horse can be a generally pleasing one for the Fire Horse and by acting determinedly he can make good headway as well as benefit from emerging opportunities. This is a year favouring initiative and action.

Tip for the Year

Be receptive to the changes that take place and seize your opportunities. What you do now can bring you considerable satisfaction and possible future gain. Also, keep your lifestyle in balance and preserve time for your loved ones.

The Earth Horse

The Earth Horse is perceptive and is able to read and adapt to situations well. In this fast-moving year his abilities will prove especially useful. The Horse year will encourage him to make more of his strengths, and the skills and knowledge he has built up will now come into their own.

For any Earth Horse who is feeling staid or unsatisfied or who would welcome new opportunities, this is a year to focus on making some changes. With purpose and commitment, he may well be able to improve his situation.

One of the features of the Horse year is that it is capable of bringing unexpected opportunities and this can be especially evident in the Earth Horse's work situation. Although many Earth Horses will be established in a particular line of work, some could be tempted by a more remunerative position elsewhere or take advantage of promotion or other opportunities. Over the year many will advance their career and, in the process, considerably widen their skills and experience.

A factor in the Earth Horse's favour is the good working relations he enjoys with his colleagues and over the year he can benefit from their support as well as sometimes from the advice of someone more senior. He should also make the most of any networking opportunities.

Earth Horses who are considering changing the nature of their work, as well as those seeking a position, will find that by keeping alert for opportunities, they may well be successful in gaining entry into a new type of work. Although the early days may be demanding and adjustment will be required, by rising to the challenge and showing commitment, many Earth Horses will not only quickly establish themselves but also be encouraged by the prospects that open up for them. The jobseeking process can be wearying, but events this year can take the Earth Horse by surprise and many a breakthrough will come on the back of disappointment. February, April, June to early July and September could see important developments, but throughout this fast-moving year the Earth Horse should keep alert for opportunities.

Progress at work may lead to an improvement in income and this will help with deposits the Earth Horse may be required to put down and other plans and purchases he is considering. However, he does need to manage his spending well and be thorough when taking on new commitments.

Travel is favourably aspected and even if the Earth Horse is not able to travel too far in distance, he should try to make provision for a holiday. A rest and change of scene can do him considerable good, especially in view of the busy lifestyle he tends to lead.

He should also not neglect his interests. These can be a good outlet for his ideas and skills as well as give him the chance to socialize or take additional exercise. He would also do well to give some consideration to his well-being and, should he have concerns or decide on a new diet or fitness regime, seek advice.

With all his various activities, the Earth Horse is set to see his social circle increase over the year and his geniality and conversational talents will make him popular company. Earth Horses who are unattached and/ or lonely can enjoy a transformation in their situation. With the Horse year capable of surprises, romance can come unexpectedly, but March, June, late July, August and December could see the most social opportunities.

The Earth Horse's domestic life will also see a great deal happen this year. Some flexibility could help, as could putting off non-urgent plans and projects to less busy times. With organization, prioritizing and good liaison between everyone involved, however, a surprising amount can be accomplished. The Earth Horse will also give valuable support to his loved ones and his care and involvement can again be significant. Over the year he could be especially proud of the achievements of someone close, and his encouragement and empathy will have been an important factor in their success.

Overall, the Year of the Horse will allow the Earth Horse to make good progress and make more of his strengths. He does need to act quickly when opportunities arise and, if currently dissatisfied, seize the initiative and look for new possibilities, but he does have much to offer and the Horse year will be an encouraging one for him. The support he receives (and gives) will be important, and by keeping his lifestyle in balance, he can make this a constructive and rewarding year.

Tip for the Year

Build on your strengths. Some good opportunities can arise this year and with a willing and flexible outlook, you can make valuable progress. Also, give yourself some 'me time' and value your relations with those who are special to you.

Famous Horses

Roman Abramovich, Neil Armstrong, Rowan Atkinson, Samuel Beckett, Ingmar Bergman, Leonard Bernstein, Halle Berry, Joe Biden, James Blunt, Helena Bonham Carter, David Cameron, James Cameron, Jackie Chan, Ray Charles, Chopin, Nick Clegg, Sir Sean Connery, Billy Connolly, Catherine Cookson, Elvis Costello, Kevin Costner, James Dean, Clint Eastwood, Thomas Alva Edison, Harrison Ford, Aretha Franklin, Bob Geldof, Samuel Goldwyn, Billy Graham, Rita Hayworth, Jimi Hendrix, François Hollande, Janet Jackson, R. Kelly, Calvin Klein, Jennifer Lawrence, Lenin, Annie Lennox, Pixie Lott, Sir Paul McCartney, Nelson Mandela, Angela Merkel, Ben Murphy, Sir Isaac Newton, Louis Pasteur, Katie Price (Jordan), Dennis Quaid, Gordon Ramsay, Lou Reed, Rembrandt, Ruth Rendell, Jean Renoir, Theodore Roosevelt, Helena Rubenstein, Adam Sandler, David Schwimmer, Martin Scorsese, Kristen Stewart, Barbra Streisand, Kiefer Sutherland, Patrick Swayze, John Travolta, Usher, Vivaldi, Robert Wagner, Emma Watson, Billy Wilder, Brian Wilson, the Duke of Windsor, Caroline Wozniacki, Jacob Zuma.

1 February 1919 to 19 February 1920 — *Earth Goat*

17 February 1931 to 5 February 1932 — *Metal Goat*

5 February 1943 to 24 January 1944 — *Water Goat*

24 January 1955 to 11 February 1956 — *Wood Goat*

9 February 1967 to 29 January 1968 — *Fire Goat*

28 January 1979 to 15 February 1980 — *Earth Goat*

15 February 1991 to 3 February 1992 — *Metal Goat*

1 February 2003 to 21 January 2004 — *Water Goat*

The Goat

The Personality of the Goat

Amid the complexities of life,
it is the ability to appreciate that is so special.

The Goat is born under the sign of art. He is imaginative, creative and has a good appreciation of the finer things in life. He has an easy-going nature and prefers to live in a relaxed and pressure-free environment. He hates any sort of discord or unpleasantness and does not like to be bound by a strict routine or rigid timetable. He is not one to be hurried against his will, but despite his seemingly relaxed approach to life, he is something of a perfectionist and when he starts work on a project he is certain to give his best.

The Goat usually prefers to work in a team rather than on his own. He likes to have the support and encouragement of others and if left to deal with matters on his own he can get very worried and tend to view things rather pessimistically. Wherever possible he will leave major decision-making to others while he concentrates on his own pursuits. If, however, he feels particularly strongly about a certain matter or has to defend his position in any way, he will act with great fortitude and precision.

The Goat has a very persuasive nature and often uses his considerable charm to get his own way. He can, however, be rather hesitant about letting his true feelings be known and if he were prepared to be more forthright he would do much better as a result.

The Goat tends to have a quiet, somewhat reserved nature, but when he is in company he likes he can often become the centre of attention. He can be highly amusing, a marvellous host at parties and a superb entertainer. Whenever the spotlight falls on him, his adrenaline starts to flow and he can be assured of giving a sparkling performance, particularly if he is allowed to use his creative skills in any way.

Of all the signs in the Chinese zodiac, the Goat is probably the most gifted artistically. Whether it is in the theatre, literature, music or art, he is certain to make a lasting impression. He is a born creator and is rarely happier than when occupied in some artistic pursuit. But even in this he does well to work with others rather than on his own. He needs inspiration and a guiding influence, but when he has found his true *métier*, he can often receive widespread acclaim and recognition.

In addition to his liking for the arts, the Goat is usually quite religious and often has a deep interest in nature, animals and the countryside. He is also fairly athletic and there are many Goats who have excelled in some form of sporting activity or who have a great interest in sport.

Although the Goat is not particularly materialistic or concerned about finance, he will find that he will usually be lucky in financial matters and will rarely be short of the necessary funds to tide himself over. He is, however, rather self-indulgent and tends to spend his money as soon as he receives it rather than make provision for the future.

The Goat usually leaves home when he is young but he will always maintain strong links with his parents and the other members of his family. He is also rather nostalgic and is well known for keeping mementoes of his childhood and souvenirs of places that he has visited. His home will not be particularly tidy, but he knows where everything is and it will be scrupulously clean.

Affairs of the heart are particularly important to the Goat and he will often have many romances before he finally settles down. Although he is fairly adaptable, he prefers to live in a secure and stable environment and he will find that he is best suited to those born under the signs of the Tiger, Horse, Monkey, Pig and Rabbit. He can also establish a good relationship with the Dragon, Snake, Rooster and another Goat, but he may find the Ox and Dog a little too serious for his liking. Neither will he care particularly for the Rat's rather thrifty ways.

The female Goat devotes all her time and energy to the needs of her family. She has excellent taste in home furnishings and often uses her considerable artistic skills to make clothes for herself and her children. She takes great care over her appearance and can be most attractive to others. Although she is not the most organized of people, her engaging manner and delightful sense of humour create a favourable impression wherever she goes. She is also a good cook and usually derives much pleasure from gardening and outdoor pursuits.

The Goat can win friends easily and people generally feel relaxed in his company. He has a kind and understanding nature and although he can occasionally be stubborn, he can, with the right support and encouragement, live a very satisfying life. And the more he can use his creative skills, the happier he will be.

The Five Different Types of Goat

In addition to the 12 signs of the Chinese zodiac there are five elements and these have a strengthening or moderating influence on the signs. The effects of the five elements on the Goat are described below, together with the years in which they were exercising their influence. Therefore Goats born in 1931 and 1991 are Metal Goats, Goats born in 1943 and 2003 are Water Goats, and so on.

Metal Goat: 1931, 1991

This Goat is thorough and conscientious in all that he does and is capable of doing very well in his chosen profession. Despite his confident manner, he can be a great worrier and he would find it helpful to discuss his concerns with others rather than keep them to himself. He is loyal to his family and employers and will have a small group of particularly close friends. He has good taste and is usually highly skilled in some of aspect of the arts. He is often a collector of antiques and his home will be very tastefully furnished.

Water Goat: 1943, 2003

The Water Goat is very popular and makes friends with remarkable ease. He is good at spotting opportunities but does not always have the necessary confidence to follow them through. He likes to have security both in his home life and work and does not take kindly to change. He is articulate, has a good sense of humour and is usually very good with children.

Wood Goat: 1955

This Goat is generous, kind-hearted and always eager to please. He usually has a large circle of friends and involves himself in a wide variety of activities. He has a very trusting nature but can sometimes give in to the demands of others a little too easily and it would be in his interests if he were to stand his ground more often. He is usually lucky in financial matters and, like the Water Goat, is very good with children.

Fire Goat: 1967

This Goat usually knows what he wants in life and often uses his considerable charm and persuasive personality to achieve his aims. He can sometimes let his imagination run away with him and has a tendency to ignore matters that are not to his liking. He is rather extravagant in his spending and would do well to exercise a little more care when dealing with financial matters. He has a lively personality, many friends, and loves attending parties and social occasions.

Earth Goat: 1919, 1979

This Goat has a considerate and caring nature. He is particularly loyal to his family and friends and invariably creates a favourable impression wherever he goes. He is reliable and conscientious in his work but sometimes finds it difficult to save and never likes to deprive himself of any little luxury he might fancy. He has numerous interests and is often very well read. He usually derives much pleasure from following the activities of the various members of his family.

Prospects for the Goat in 2014

The Year of the Snake (10 February 2013–30 January 2014) is an encouraging one for the Goat and by setting about his activities in determined fashion, he can accomplish a great deal. He will benefit from the support of those around him throughout the year and the aspects are especially promising for the closing months.

One of the features of Snake years is that they favour creativity and innovation, and as the Goat is a natural creator, he should make the most of his strengths. Whether in his work (particularly if in a creative environment) or personal interests, he should follow through his ideas and seize his opportunities. Many Goats will make headway at this time. To benefit fully, though, the Goat will need to be active and put himself forward, but September and November could see encouraging developments.

With the closing months of the year likely to be an active time *and* to include travel, the Goat's spending will increase and he will need to keep a close watch on outgoings and take his time when considering major purchases.

On a personal level, many a Goat will find himself in demand, with an interesting mix of domestic and social occasions to look forward to. With an already busy schedule, he will need to remain well organized and draw on the support available to him. For the unattached, as well as those enjoying newfound romance, the latter part of the Snake year could see exciting times.

Overall, the Goat can emerge from the Snake year with some satisfying achievements to his credit.

The Year of the Horse starts on 31 January and has great potential for the Goat. He will delight in the opportunities it offers as well as enjoy an often pleasing personal life.

One of the major strengths of the Goat is his ability to forge good connections with people. He has a good understanding of human nature, empathizes with others and has an engaging manner. Over the year he should make the most of his chances to meet others, as he will find much truth in the saying that the more people you know, the more possibilities open up for you. Some of the people he meets this year could be especially helpful and if there are particular activities the Goat would like assistance with, he should ask. He does a lot for others and over the year quite a few will be pleased to reciprocate.

The aspects are also encouraging for any Goat who, possibly because of a change in personal circumstances, has been feeling lonely or a bit lacklustre. To help their situation, these Goats should consider joining social groups in their area. Positive action on their part could introduce them to some purposeful new pursuits. April, June, July and October could have good social opportunities.

Romance is favourably aspected and quite a few Goats who are in a relatively new relationship will decide to settle down together or marry, while some who start the year unattached could meet someone who will quickly become special. The Goat can be on great personal form this year.

He can also look forward to pleasing developments in his home life, although to fit in all he wants, he will need to be well organized and plan ahead. With co-operation with those around him, however, he can make some useful enhancements to the home and enjoy some family occasions. While a lot will go well, should any difference of opinion arise or interests (and schedules) clash, the Goat does need to talk matters through and find an acceptable solution. If not, sometimes niggling matters can escalate and the Goat does need to be aware of this. With this proviso, this will be a full and rewarding year domestically.

At work, many Goats will find their background and experience helping their prospects. Those in large organizations in particular could have chances to move their career to a new level. For those who feel opportunities are limited where they are, as well as those seeking work, the Horse year can open up interesting possibilities. By considering different ways in which they could use their strengths and keeping alert for vacancies, many could secure a position that offers a new career challenge and has the potential for development. Chances need to be seized quickly, however – this is no time for reticence. March, June, September and October could see encouraging work developments.

The Goat can also derive a lot of satisfaction from his personal interests over the year. The many Goats who enjoy creative pursuits will often be inspired. Goats are rarely short of ideas and the Horse year will give them plenty more. Some may be tempted by a completely new activity, enrol on a course or decide to contribute to their community in some way. Whatever the Goat decides, his actions can help make this a fulfilling time.

The Goat can fare reasonably well in financial matters, although should he take risks or be lax in certain undertakings he could find himself ruing his actions. In addition, if he is considering large purchases or is involved in considerable expenditure, he needs to allow time to make comparisons, check terms and, where necessary, obtain professional advice. This is a year for vigilance and good financial control.

Overall, the Year of the Horse can be a lively one for the Goat. It encourages growth and development and he can make good progress in his work and interests and add considerably to his skills. Ideas and opportunities can take him in new directions and this is a time to be open to possibility, although to benefit fully the Goat will need to be more assertive than usual and make his talents count. He will benefit from the support of those around him, however, and his personal life can be rewarding, with new friends and, for the unattached, possible romance.

The Metal Goat

This will be a year of significant decisions for the Metal Goat. Although a lot will go well, certain activities could take an unexpected course and the Metal Goat will need to be adaptable and make the most of situations *as they arise*. With an open mind and a willing 'can do' approach, however, he can make this a successful year.

Many of the Metal Goats in education will be reaching the final stages of their courses and a lot will rest on the exams they take and the work they submit. By focusing on what needs to be done and putting in the effort, many will obtain the qualifications they have been working towards and will mark the successful culmination of several years' hard work.

The aspects are also encouraging for Metal Goats in work or seeking a position. Those already established in a particular type of work will often be encouraged by senior colleagues to make more of their strengths and take on increased responsibilities. By showing willingness and rising to the challenge, these Metal Goats can not only strengthen their reputation but also underline their potential. The Horse year does require effort and hard work, but the committed Metal Goat can lay an important foundation on which to build in the future.

For Metal Goats seeking work, the Horse year can also have interesting developments. Although the job-seeking process will be difficult and at times disheartening, by keeping alert for openings and not being too restrictive in the type of work they consider, many will be offered a new position. Sometimes this may be in a different capacity, or industry, from what they were originally intending, but once on the employment ladder, these Metal Goats will have the chance to prove themselves. March, June and September to early November could see good opportunities, although in this year of swift-moving developments, whenever the Metal Goat sees an opening that appeals to him, he should act quickly.

Progress at work can also help financially and many Metal Goats will increase their income over the year. However, with possible deposits to save for, an active social life, interests to pursue and the likelihood of travel, the Metal Goat will need to be disciplined and budget carefully. To succumb to too many temptations could mean he has to cut back on other activities. Also, with any major transaction or new commitment, he does need to check the terms and obligations. This is a time to be thorough.

The Metal Goat often has specific interests and during the year these can continue to bring him great pleasure. Here again he does need to be receptive to new ideas, but if he is open to exploring possibilities, this can be a successful and inspiring time. Some of his interests can also have a good social element and he will be encouraged by friends and other enthusiasts.

On a personal level, the Metal Goat will find himself in demand. If he changes his location this year he will find that by immersing himself in activities in his new area, a new social circle can open up for him. For the more withdrawn Metal Goat (and there are some) as well as those who would like a more active social life, the Horse year can reignite the sparkle that may have been missing in recent times. April, June to early August and October could see the most social opportunities.

The Metal Goat's romantic prospects are also encouraging and while the path of true love may not always run smooth, this can be a time of excitement, passion and great happiness. Quite a few unattached Metal Goats will meet their future partner, sometimes in chance circumstances, marry or settle down over the course of the year.

For those already with a partner, the Horse year will see many plans come to fruition. Where accommodation is concerned, the Metal Goat's decorative flair will be evident and he will delight in some acquisitions he makes for his home, as well as the other plans he is able to carry out. Sometimes initial thoughts will need to be modified as new possibilities arise, but domestically this can be a busy and exciting year.

With so much happening, it is important that the Metal Goat is open about his thoughts and ideas, including with senior relations. This way he will give others a better chance to assist. Also, while he will often be involved in his own activities, the support he can give family members may be greatly appreciated.

Overall, the Year of the Horse is a good one for the Metal Goat. It will give him the chance to show his potential as well as gain what can be important skills and qualifications. He can benefit from emerging opportunities and, by keeping alert and showing willingness, enhance his prospects for the future. His relations with others are favourably aspected and the Horse year will contain some special and potentially significant times.

Tip for the Year
Show commitment and seize your chances to develop your skills, strengths and interests. You have many talents and now you can take them further. Use this year well, for its legacy can be far-reaching.

The Water Goat

One of the hallmarks of the Water Goat's character is his alert and inquisitive nature and he has a great talent for filling his time with worthwhile and satisfying pursuits. This will be especially the case in this year of interesting possibilities.

For Water Goats born in 1943 this can be a particularly rewarding year, although to get the most from it the Water Goat does need to involve others in his undertakings. With their input, he could see some of his hopes enjoying an unexpected fillip.

To help get this Horse year off to a positive start the Water Goat would find it helpful to draw up some ideas of what he would like to do over the next 12 months and then discuss them with others. This way he will not only have something to work towards but may also find that certain plans can quickly get underway. Chance developments may also help on several occasions.

Some plans the Water Goat will be keen to implement will concern his home and, if he has one, garden. It could be he decides to replace old furnishings with something more stylish, rearrange certain rooms or sort through old belongings and make storage areas neater and less cluttered. No matter what he decides, he will take great pleasure in his activities as tasks get done and benefits follow. His creative talents will often be to the fore and, particularly when choosing items for the home, he will delight in selecting things that not only satisfy requirements but also look good. For the keen gardener, time spent tending plants can be especially satisfying and many Water Goats will be tempted to try out new varieties. Horse years are ones for action and the Water Goat will frequently be inspired.

In addition to the practical activity, there will also be family occasions for the Water Goat to look forward to. Younger family members could have good news to celebrate and achievements which will make many a Water Goat proud. Also, while the Water Goat may not wish to interfere, his talent for imparting advice may be particularly appreciated and of more value than he may realize.

The Horse year has good travel possibilities and if there is a particular destination or special event the Water Goat is especially keen to see, he would do well to make early enquiries and see what is possible. Sometimes chance or attractive offers can help.

With Water as his element, the Water Goat is creative and expresses himself well, and he should again make the most of his talents. New ideas and information can inspire him this year. Some Water Goats may be persuaded to take an existing interest in a new direction or even take up something completely different. For personal interests, the Horse year can be both satisfying and encouraging.

The Water Goat will also appreciate the social opportunities the year brings and some of his friends could be especially helpful as well as instrumental in some of the opportunities that open up. Any Water Goats who are feeling lonely or would welcome a more active social life would find it well worth considering participating in their community. April, June, July and October could be active and interesting months.

With all his various activities, and some sizeable purchases likely, the Water Goat will need to keep a close watch on his financial situation and make advance provision for more expensive plans. Over the year he does need to be wary of too many indulgences or impulse buys. Although not a bad year financially, it does require good management and self-control.

The Water Goat would also do well to give some consideration to his well-being this year, including the quality of his diet and his general level of exercise. To be lax or neglectful could leave him lacking his usual energy. If he feels modifications would help or has any concerns, he should seek medical advice. In some cases he could be introduced to a beneficial new form of exercise. Much good can follow on from positive action taken this year.

For Water Goats born in 2003, this will be a busy and eventful time. Quite a few will not only change school but also be introduced to new activities. Although a lot that happens may initially seem daunting, by being willing to make the most of his opportunities, the young Water Goat can not only benefit from what he does but also have fun in the process. The key is being willing to try rather than being reticent or holding back.

The young Water Goat will also appreciate the camaraderie of his friends as well as the fun that shared interests can bring. As he changes schools or starts new activities, he will also have the chance to meet new people and some important and long-standing friendships can be made.

Overall, this is a positive year for the Water Goat. Whether born in 1943 or 2003, he can benefit from some good opportunities and make this a satisfying time.

Tip for the Year

Act upon your ideas. This is a year for making things happen. Also, draw on the support and encouragement of those around you. With their backing, a great deal can open up for you.

The Wood Goat

One of the strengths of the Wood Goat is his versatility. He has widespread interests and is adept at using his skills in different ways. Over the year his talents will serve him well, although with a lot happening quickly, he will need to keep alert and be prepared to act. If he does so, he can make pleasing headway.

One area which is likely to see change is his work situation. Although many Wood Goats will be well established where they are and proficient in their line of work, the winds of change will blow strongly during parts of the Horse year. More senior colleagues could leave and create promotion opportunities and, with many workplaces being affected by change this year, there could also be new objectives and technologies to deal with. As a result the Wood Goat will be required to adapt and learn, but the changes can bring opportunities and in many instances the Wood Goat's reputation and in-house knowledge will make him a strong candidate to take on new responsibilities.

Most Wood Goats will make headway with their present employer, but for those who desire more substantial change, as well as those seeking work, the Horse year can have surprising developments in store. Although the job-seeking process will be difficult and at times disheartening, some enquiries the enterprising Wood Goat makes can often lead to an opening being found. Horse years favour initiative and this one could see quite a few Wood Goats taking on a completely new type of work. Possibilities can arise at almost any time, but March, June and September to early November could be significant months.

However, it is not just the Wood Goat's work situation which can see important developments. The Horse year favours learning and personal development, and over the year many Wood Goats will be encouraged to take their interests further or be tempted by a new pursuit. For those who lead busy lifestyles in particular, it is important that they allow themselves time for their own interests – and for relaxation. Driving themselves relentlessly could take its toll. In this active year, all Wood Goats should aim for a more balanced lifestyle.

The Wood Goat would also find it helpful to give some consideration to his well-being this year, including the quality of his diet and the amount of exercise he tends to take. If he feels improvements are needed, he should seek advice.

With his amiable nature, the Wood Goat enjoys good relations with many people and will find himself in demand during the year. Not only will he enjoy meeting up with his friends, but also, in view of some of the decisions he may face, be glad of their opinion and sometimes specialist knowledge. A long-standing friend could be particularly important this year. The Wood Goat will also enjoy the social occasions he attends, with locally held events often of particular interest. Travel or new interests could bring additional social opportunities.

For Wood Goats who are hoping for a more active social life, the Horse year can offer improvement. Immersing themselves in local activities or joining an interest group could help, but with their broad interests and genial nature, whatever they choose to do these Wood Goats will have good opportunities to make some important new friends in this lively and fast-moving year. Significant romance is also possible. April, June, July and October could see the most social activity.

Domestic life will also be busy, with the Wood Goat giving much time and assistance to family members. Being such a good listener and adviser, he will find many seeking his views and appreciating his opinions. During the year he will play a significant role in the lives of several people. There could also be key family events to arrange. However, while willing, the Wood Goat should not feel certain tasks are just his preserve and, if busy or under pressure, should ask for assistance. More practical undertakings or home purchases should also be carried out jointly and may benefit from an unexpected opportunity or offer.

In view of his obligations and varied activities, the Wood Goat will need to keep a careful watch on outgoings and, where possible, make advance provision for more substantial plans and purchases. With good budgeting, however, he will be able to proceed with many of his plans. Attention is required where paperwork is concerned – this is not a year to be lax.

Overall, the Wood Goat will see a lot happen this year and although this can give rise to moments of uncertainty (which the Wood Goat will not welcome), the changes that take place can open up some good possibilities. In the Wood Goat's work and personal interests there will be chances to use his talents in new ways and throughout the year he will enjoy a busy social life and value the support of those around him. The Horse year may bring its pressures, but it is an encouraging one.

Tip for the Year
Be open to chance and prepared to adapt as situations require. There can be some excellent opportunities for you to develop yourself, your skills and your interests. Make the most of them and you will be well rewarded.

The Fire Goat

The Fire Goat has a keen and engaging nature and is set to do well this year. To help make the most of this encouraging time, as the year starts he would do well to give some thought to what he wants to see happen over the next 12 months. His thinking can concern his work situation, personal interests, hopes, travel plans and/or projects he would like to carry out in his home, but whatever he chooses, having some objectives in mind will give him something to work towards and the year more direction. He would also find it helpful to talk his thoughts through with his loved ones, as their enthusiasm and support can help his ideas along.

Any Fire Goat who has had recent personal difficulties to contend with will also find it helpful to draw a line under what has happened and regard this Horse year as the dawning of a new day. If these Fire Goats focus on the present and are determined to move on, important possibilities can start to open up.

Although almost all areas of the Fire Goat's life will see interesting developments this year, this will be particularly the case in his work situation. With the skills he has recently demonstrated and the knowledge he has built up, he could well have the offer of increased responsibilities, the chance to put in for promotion or the opportunity to transfer to another section. New initiatives can also create some specialist openings.

For Fire Goats who feel their prospects are limited where they are, including those who want to take their career in a new direction, the Horse year can again hold interesting possibilities. Although the Fire Goat may know the sort of position he would like, by not being too restrictive in his search, he could secure a position that is different from what he has done before but allows him to use his strengths in new ways. This also applies to Fire Goats seeking a position. Sometimes what they are offered could entail a lot of learning but also give them the chance they have been wanting for some time. March, June, September and October could be important months for work activities, and with this being a swift-moving year, chances need to be seized without delay.

Progress at work can also help the Fire Goat's financial situation. However, he will need to keep a careful watch on spending and budget ahead for specific requirements. The more control he has, the more he can ultimately do. Also, when considering large purchases, he should give himself the time to investigate different possibilities. That way his decisions will not only be better but often obtained on more advantageous terms as well.

Some Fire Goats could also be tempted by the travel opportunities that the Horse year can so suddenly open up.

Another encouraging feature of the year will be the way in which the Fire Goat can develop his personal interests. Some Fire Goats may set themselves a project or task for the year, while others may decide to start something new. Creative pursuits are particularly well aspected. Fire Goats who have let their personal interests lapse or do not allow themselves much time for recreation, would do well to redress this early on in the year and aim to get their lifestyle into better balance. This can make an appreciable difference to how they fare.

The Fire Goat's active and genial nature makes him popular company and throughout the year he will value the support of his friends and enjoy the social occasions he attends. His various interests can also introduce him to new people and, if applicable, any networking he does related to his work can add to his circle of contacts. For the unattached, the Horse year also has romantic possibilities. April, June to early August and October could see the most social activity.

The Fire Goat's domestic situation will also keep him busy and at times he may despair of all that is being asked of him. However, rather than spread his energies too widely, if he focuses on priorities and, if necessary, postpones certain projects to less busy times, he can accomplish a lot this year, including some pleasing home improvements. It is also important that he spends some quality time with his loved ones. That way, some of the special times, including the personal and family successes, can become more meaningful.

Overall, the Year of the Horse can be a good one for the Fire Goat. By looking to build on his situation, he can benefit from some good opportunities and have the chance to prove himself in new ways. In 2014 he can make his talents and personal abilities count. He will also be encouraged by the support he receives from others in this favourable year.

Tip for the Year
Seek to advance and do not limit yourself by being too restrictive in outlook. You are by nature versatile and by making the most of your ideas and strengths, you can make this a rewarding and potentially successful year.

The Earth Goat

With his conscientious nature, the Earth Goat puts a lot of effort into his activities. He is determined and ambitious and may regard his recent progress as mixed. However, in 2014 he can look forward to making important headway.

One important feature of the Horse year is that it is one for building. The Earth Goat will have already laid some important foundations and now is a time to build on them. With purpose and resolve, he will find that a lot can now become possible.

This is especially the case with his work situation. With the skills and reputation he has built up, the Earth Goat can be a particularly strong candidate when promotion opportunities occur or new positions become available. In the Horse year, opportunities can arise with little warning, so if he sees something of interest, the Earth Goat should seize the chance. Delay or hesitation can be costly.

Throughout this fast-moving year the Earth Goat will also need to keep himself informed about what is going on in his workplace rather than restricting himself to just his own sphere. This can not only alert him to emerging trends but also raise his profile and strengthen his prospects. Similarly, by taking advantage of networking opportunities, he can do his reputation a lot of good. The Earth Goat has already proved himself in many capacities, but this year it is worth him putting in that extra effort and looking to progress.

Many Earth Goats can make important advances with their present employer, but for those who feel ready for a new challenge or are seeking a position, the Horse year can bring some interesting possibilities. Although the job-seeking process will be demanding, by talking to advisers and contacts, obtaining information and making enquiries, the Earth Goat may come across some good openings which will allow him to both use and extend his skills. March, June and September to early November could see important developments, but the key to progress this year is to act swiftly and look to adapt and develop skills. What is achieved now can often shape the Earth Goat's prospects for the next few years.

The progress the Earth Goat makes at work will often bring an increase in income and financially this can be an improved year. However, it can also be an expensive one, and the Earth Goat will need to remain disciplined and watch his spending. Also, when entering into agreements or making large purchases, he does need to study the terms and implications and seek advice when necessary. Where finance is involved, he needs to be thorough. Where possible, he should also make early provision for specific requirements, including deposits he may need to put down and travel plans. The more control he exercises, the better.

Although the Earth Goat will often be kept busy with his commitments, it is also important that he allows time for his own interests. These can not only help him relax but often be an outlet for his talents and help him in other ways. Earth Goats who enjoy outdoor pursuits may get the chance to exercise more or enjoy watching some exciting activities, while more creative Earth Goats can derive much satisfaction from carrying out particular projects. The Horse year may often be an active one, but 'me time' can be a source of considerable benefit to the Earth Goat.

Also, to keep himself on good form, he should pay attention to the quality of his diet and ensure he takes appropriate exercise. To be neglectful could sometimes leave him lacking his usual zest and energy.

The Earth Goat's interests, work situation and existing group of friends can all lead to some interesting social opportunities this year. There will also be excellent chances to meet others and Earth Goats who move or find themselves in a new environment can look forward to making important new friends and contacts. April, June, July and October could see the most social activity. Also, several times this year friends will seek the Earth Goat's views on personal matters and his ability to empathize and convey shrewd insights will once more be valued. For the unattached, even though they may not be necessarily seeking it, romance is possible and could come in a sometimes unexpected way. Horse years have the ability to surprise.

The Earth Goat's domestic life will also see much activity, with the Earth Goat playing a significant role in the lives of several family members. Whether offering advice or support or attending to domestic matters, he will do much to assist others and his ability to keep tabs on a great many activities will be appreciated. However, while willing, the Earth Goat should be careful not to assume responsibility for just too much and should make sure everyone does their fair share. Also, should a particular matter concern him at any time, he does need to be open rather than let it linger in the background or go unaddressed. The better the communication and co-operation in his household, the better for all.

There will also be some special family occasions that will be a source of considerable joy, and for Earth Goats who are parents, the time and encouragement they give their children will be important and meaningful.

Overall, the Horse year is one of considerable activity for the Earth Goat and throughout he needs to keep well organized and use his time well. He will be encouraged to make more of his strengths and in his work situation he may well have the chance to move his career forward. However, to fully benefit he will need to be active and involved. This is no year to sit on the sidelines and wait for opportunity. It is those who participate and show initiative who will benefit most. The Earth Goat also needs to set time aside to enjoy with those who are special to him as well as to pursue his personal interests. In this active and promising year he will benefit from keeping his lifestyle in balance.

Tip for the Year
Make the most of your abilities. With resolve and self-belief, you can make good progress this year. Also, value your relations with those around you. Their support and goodwill can help in a lot of what you set out to do.

Famous Goats

Pamela Anderson, Jane Austen, Jenson Button, Lord Byron, Vince Cable, Coco Chanel, Mary Higgins Clark, Nat 'King' Cole, Jamie Cullum, Robert de Niro, Catherine Deneuve, Charles Dickens, Ken Dodd, Sir Arthur Conan Doyle, Douglas Fairbanks, Will Ferrell, Dame Margot Fonteyn, Jamie Foxx, Noel Gallagher, Bill Gates, Robert Gates, Mel Gibson, Whoopi Goldberg, Mikhail Gorbachev, John Grisham, Oscar Hammerstein, George Harrison, Billy Idol, Julio Iglesias, Sir Mick Jagger, Steve Jobs, Norah Jones, John Kerry, Nicole Kidman, Sir Ben Kingsley, Christine Lagarde, John le Carré, Matt LeBlanc, Franz Liszt, James McAvoy, Sir John Major, Michelangelo, Joni Mitchell, Rupert Murdoch, Randy Newman, Sinead O'Connor, Michael Palin, Eva Peron,

Pink, Marcel Proust, Keith Richards, Julia Roberts, Philip Seymour Hoffman, William Shatner, Gary Sinise, Jerry Springer, Lana Turner, Mark Twain, Rudolph Valentino, Vangelis, Barbara Walters, John Wayne, Fay Weldon, Bruce Willis.

20 February 1920 to 7 February 1921 — *Metal Monkey*

6 February 1932 to 25 January 1933 — *Water Monkey*

25 January 1944 to 12 February 1945 — *Wood Monkey*

12 February 1956 to 30 January 1957 — *Fire Monkey*

30 January 1968 to 16 February 1969 — *Earth Monkey*

16 February 1980 to 4 February 1981 — *Metal Monkey*

4 February 1992 to 22 January 1993 — *Water Monkey*

22 January 2004 to 8 February 2005 — *Wood Monkey*

The Monkey

The Personality of the Monkey

The more open to possibility,
the more possibilities open.

The Monkey is born under the sign of fantasy. He is imaginative, inquisitive and loves to keep an eye on everything that is going on around him. He is never backward in offering an opinion or trying to sort out the problems of others. He likes to be helpful and his advice is invariably sensible and reliable.

The Monkey is intelligent, well read and always eager to learn. He has an extremely good memory and there are many Monkeys who have made particularly good linguists. The Monkey is also a convincing talker and enjoys taking part in discussions and debates. His friendly, self-assured manner can be very persuasive and he usually has little trouble in winning people round to his way of thinking. It is for this reason that he often excels in politics and public speaking. He is also particularly adept in PR work, teaching and any job that involves selling.

The Monkey can, however, be crafty, cunning and occasionally dishonest, and he will seize any opportunity to make a quick profit or outsmart his opponents. He has so much charm and guile that people often don't realize what he is up to until it is too late. But despite his resourceful nature, he does run the risk of outsmarting even himself. He has so much confidence in his abilities that he rarely listens to advice or is prepared to accept help from anyone. He likes to help others, but prefers to rely on his own judgement when dealing with his own affairs.

Another characteristic of the Monkey is that he is extremely good at solving problems and has a happy knack of extricating himself (and others) from the most hopeless of positions. He is the master of self-preservation.

With so many diverse talents, the Monkey is usually able to make considerable sums of money, but he does like to enjoy life and will think nothing of spending his money on some exotic holiday or luxury he has had his eye on. He can, however, become very envious if someone else has what he wants.

The Monkey is an original thinker and despite his love of company, he cherishes his independence. He has to have the freedom to act as he wants and any Monkey who feels hemmed in or bound by too many restrictions will soon become unhappy. Likewise, if anything becomes too boring or monotonous, the Monkey will soon lose interest and turn his attention to something else. He lacks persistence and this can often hamper his progress. He is also easily distracted, a tendency that he should try to overcome. By concentrating on one thing at a time, he will almost certainly achieve more in the long run.

The Monkey is a good organizer and even though he may behave slightly erratically at times, he will invariably have a plan at the back of his mind. On the odd occasion when his plans do not work out, he is usually quite happy to shrug his shoulders and put it down to experience. He will rarely make the same mistake twice and throughout his life he will try his hand at many different things.

The Monkey likes to impress and is rarely without followers or admirers. Many are attracted by his good looks, his sense of humour, or simply because he instils so much confidence in those around him.

Monkeys usually marry young and for it to be a success their partner must allow them time to pursue their many interests and indulge their love of travel. The Monkey has to have variety in his life and is especially well suited to those born under the sociable and outgoing signs of the Rat, Dragon, Pig and Goat. The Ox, Rabbit, Snake and Dog will also be enchanted by his resourceful and outgoing nature, but he is likely to exasperate the Rooster and Horse, and the Tiger will have little patience with his tricks. A relationship between two Monkeys will work well – they will understand each other and be able to assist each other in their various enterprises.

The female Monkey is intelligent, extremely observant and a shrewd judge of character. Her opinions are often highly valued and, having such a persuasive nature, she invariably gets her own way. She has many interests and involves herself in a wide variety of activities. She pays great attention to her appearance, is an elegant dresser and likes to take particular care over her hair. She can be a doting parent and will have many good and loyal friends.

Provided the Monkey can curb his desire to take part in everything that is going on around him and concentrate on one thing at a time, he can usually achieve what he wants in life. Should he suffer any disappointment, he is bound to bounce back. He is a survivor and his life is usually both colourful and eventful.

The Five Different Types of Monkey

In addition to the 12 signs of the Chinese zodiac there are five elements and these have a strengthening or moderating influence on the signs. The effects of the five elements on the Monkey are described below, together with the years in which they were exercising their influence. Therefore Monkeys born in 1920 and 1980 are Metal Monkeys, Monkeys born in 1932 and 1992 are Water Monkeys, and so on.

Metal Monkey: 1920, 1980

The Metal Monkey is very strong-willed. He sets about everything he does with dogged determination and often prefers to work independently rather than with others. He is ambitious, wise and confident, and is certainly not afraid of hard work. He is very astute in financial matters and usually chooses his investments well. Despite his somewhat independent nature, he enjoys attending parties and social occasions and is particularly warm and caring towards his loved ones.

Water Monkey: 1932, 1992

The Water Monkey is versatile, determined and perceptive. He also has more discipline than some of the other Monkeys and is prepared to work towards a particular goal rather than be distracted by something else. He is not always open about his true intentions and when questioned can be particularly evasive. He can be sensitive to criticism but also very persuasive and usually has little trouble in getting others to fall in with his plans. He has a very good understanding of human nature and relates well to others.

Wood Monkey: 1944, 2004

This Monkey is efficient, methodical and extremely conscientious. He is also highly imaginative and is always trying to capitalize on new ideas or learn new skills. Occasionally his enthusiasm can get the better of him and he can get very agitated when things do not quite work out as he had hoped. He does, however, have a very adventurous streak and is not afraid of taking risks. He also loves travel. He is usually held in great esteem by his friends and colleagues.

Fire Monkey: 1956

The Fire Monkey is intelligent, full of vitality and has no trouble in commanding the respect of others. He is imaginative and has wide interests, although sometimes these can distract him from more useful and profitable work. He is very competitive and always likes to be involved in everything that is going on. He can be stubborn if he does not get his own way and he sometimes tries to indoctrinate those who are less strong-willed than himself. He is a lively character, attractive to others and loyal to his partner.

Earth Monkey: 1968

The Earth Monkey tends to be studious and well read, and can become quite distinguished in his chosen line of work. He is less outgoing than some of the other types of Monkey and prefers quieter and more solid pursuits. He has high principles, a very caring nature and can be most generous to those less fortunate than himself. He is usually successful in handling financial matters and can become wealthy in old age. He has a calming influence on those around him and is respected and well liked. He is, however, especially careful about whom he lets into his confidence.

Prospects for the Monkey in 2014

The Monkey has considerable drive and involves himself in a great many activities. However, he could have found the Snake year (10 February 2013–30 January 2014) having a tempering influence on him. His progress may not have been as easy or swift as he would have liked and he could also have faced some difficulties.

In the remaining Snake months the Monkey will need to keep his wits about him. While he can look forward to some fine social opportunities, he does need to remain mindful when in company. To appear preoccupied, misread a situation or make an uncharacteristic *faux pas* could lead to problems. Although usually masterful in his relations with others, he should remember that Snake years require care and discretion.

The Monkey could also have concerns relating to his work, especially as he could now face increased pressures or have complex issues to deal with. In the closing months of the Snake year his skills and patience may be tested. However, by remaining focused and using his time and energy wisely, the Monkey can not only cope with a great deal but also do his standing considerable good. September could be an important month and for Monkeys who are looking for work, a chance offered now, even if only temporary, could turn out to be a useful platform to build on.

The Monkey is fairly adroit in financial matters and could be pleased with some purchases made towards the end of the year. However, he does need to guard against rush or risk and should not be dilatory when dealing with important correspondence.

Overall, parts of the Snake year will have exasperated the Monkey. Keen for results, he could have found pressures, delays and niggling problems all getting in his way. However, the Monkey is resourceful, and with effort and his customary good skill, he can still emerge from the year with some positive gains to his credit and some personal highlights to look back on.

The Monkey will welcome the vitality and energy that characterize the Horse year. As it starts, on 31 January, he may sense that this is a time of opportunity. However, while he is set to do well, he does need to be careful not to overreach himself or push his luck too far. The Monkey may not be averse to risk or making the utmost of opportunities, but the proverbial banana skin could cause the careless to slip up. Monkeys, take note. This is a potentially good year for you, but it is still one for care and realism.

The aspects are particularly encouraging for work prospects. With a lot of organizations undergoing change, many a Monkey will detect chances they could benefit from. Sometimes what opens up could mean a substantial change in duties, but by indicating a willingness to adapt, many Monkeys will be able to make important headway.

Any Monkey who has felt himself becoming staid of late, or who would welcome a new challenge or fresh start, will also find that the Horse year can bring the chance he has been waiting for. Such is the significance of this year that for quite a few Monkeys it could mark the start of a whole new chapter in their working life.

For Monkeys seeking work, again interesting possibilities can arise. Although these may involve considerable adjustment, once in a position these Monkeys will find themselves quickly settling into their new role and, in the process, gaining skills which can strengthen their future prospects. Opportunities can arise fairly quickly and these Monkeys do need to keep alert and act swiftly. While the job-seeking process can bring its disappointments, with self-belief and persistence, they will find doors opening for them. Events can often take a sudden and unexpected course this year, but March, May, July and September could see encouraging developments.

However, while the Monkey's efforts at work will serve him well, he does need to be realistic in expectations. To be impulsive, overreach himself or be lax in certain situations could undermine his position. In

2014 he needs to keep his feet on the ground and proceed determinedly – but thoughtfully too.

His financial prospects are encouraging and as well as enjoying an increase in earnings and possibly an extra sum or gift, he may, with his entrepreneurial skills, be able to put a personal interest or specialist knowledge to profitable use. The extra funds will enable many Monkeys to proceed with plans and purchases they have been considering as well as take advantage of chances to travel. With good planning and care, the Monkey will be pleased with most of what he does, although he does need to be wary about spending or making decisions too hurriedly. To be swept up in the fervour of some situations or be inclined to extravagance or risk could lead to regret. Again, while a good year, it does require care.

The Monkey would also do well to give some consideration to his lifestyle, including giving himself the chance to unwind and spend time on pursuits he enjoys. Monkeys who lead pressured lifestyles in particular, do take note and give yourself some time off this year. It *will* make a difference.

With his genial nature, the Monkey will welcome the social opportunities of the year and April, June, August and December will see a lot of activity. However, while in general the Monkey's relations with others will be positive, he does need to be open and forthcoming. Without care, the tendency of some Monkeys to be evasive or secretive could cause resentment and difficulty. Monkeys, take note.

This need for openness is especially important in the Monkey's home life. With a lot happening, he does need to regularly consult others and talk his thoughts and hopes through. This way he can not only gain from the advice and support of those around him but also find some plans quickly being advanced. This is a time favouring a joint approach. Should any difference of opinion arise, often caused by pressure and tiredness, this needs to be talked through and solutions found.

If possible, the Monkey should also try to take a holiday with his loved ones during the year. Spending time together away from busy schedules can do everyone good.

Overall, the Monkey can accomplish a great deal this year and will have the chance to extend his skills and experience. To benefit fully, he will need to act swiftly and be prepared to adapt. However, the Monkey is usually canny and as long as he does not overreach himself or try for too much too soon, he can make this a good and constructive year.

The Metal Monkey

The Metal Monkey has qualities that can take him far and while he may have considered his progress mixed in recent times, this Horse year is encouragingly aspected and he may welcome an improvement in his situation.

The Metal Monkey will generally enjoy good support from those around him and when he has decisions to take, or has a problem, it is important that he seeks their views. Although he may possess an independent streak, Horse years encourage openness and the more he is prepared to consult others, the more he can benefit from their assistance.

In addition, the Metal Monkey will enjoy great rapport with some of the people he meets this year. For Metal Monkeys who start the year alone, the Horse year has good romantic opportunities and some Metal Monkeys may meet their future partner in what could be rather unusual circumstances. April, June, late July, August and December could see the most social activity, although at most times of the year the Metal Monkey will have things to look forward to.

His domestic life will also see considerable activity. With changes in work routines likely, there will need to be good co-operation, and here the Metal Monkey's attentiveness will be particularly valued, as will his ability to support those who may be facing daunting situations. The Metal Monkey will be very much at the heart of family life and yet again both younger and more senior relations will be grateful for some of the practical ways in which he can help. It is also important that more pleasurable family activities are not lost due to general busyness. If family life is balanced rather than conducted in a whirl, this can make it far more rewarding.

With travel favourably aspected, the Metal Monkey should try to take a holiday with his loved ones during the year. Time spent relaxing together, as well as visiting some interesting attractions, can do everyone a lot of good.

The Metal Monkey can also derive considerable pleasure from his interests this year. For sport enthusiasts, there can be exciting matches or other occasions to enjoy, while the music-lover will enjoy concerts, and all kinds of enthusiasts can benefit from joining societies and organizations. The Horse year is rich in possibility and any Metal Monkey who has been feeling uninspired lately should take the time to find out about new pursuits they may enjoy. Their efforts can make an important difference to their outlook.

With this being a busy year, the Metal Monkey should also be aware that skimping on exercise or ignoring the quality of his diet could leave him lacking his usual energy and sparkle. It could be to his benefit to consider some modifications and seek appropriate advice.

Work prospects are favourably aspected this year and in view of the skills many Metal Monkeys have recently been able to demonstrate, they will now feel ready to move their career forward. As they will find, once they start to make enquiries, events can quickly gain momentum. Some Metal Monkeys could be offered greater responsibilities in their present place of work while others could be successful in finding a position elsewhere, but in either event this is a year to seize the initiative. March, May, July and September could see important developments, but opportunities could arise at any time and need to be acted upon without delay.

For Metal Monkeys who start the year looking for work, the Horse year will again reward effort. While the job-seeking process will be far from easy, by actively making enquiries, many Metal Monkeys will be successful in securing a position that is very different from what they have done before. This may involve considerable adjustment, but these Metal Monkeys will welcome the challenge and set out to prove themselves (often very successfully) in their new role.

Progress made at work will allow many Metal Monkeys to increase their income over the year and some will also benefit from the receipt of extra funds. While this will be welcome, the Metal Monkey will still need to budget for specific requirements and watch his everyday spending. With discipline, he will be able to go ahead with many of his plans, possibly including some ambitious accommodation ones, but outgoings do need to be carefully controlled.

Overall, the Year of the Horse can be a successful one for the Metal Monkey. Some good opportunities will arise, and the year favours initiative and resourcefulness, which will suit the Metal Monkey's personality. He does, however, need to consult others and be aware of their views. To be too independent or narrow-minded could work to his disadvantage. Also, he should keep his lifestyle in balance and preserve time for his interests as well as for his loved ones. This year has considerable potential for him and, if he uses it wisely, he can make substantial headway.

Tip for the Year
Value your relations with others and watch your independent tendencies. Also, seize any opportunities to develop your skills and interests. This year encourages personal growth, and a 'can do' attitude can lead to a lot happening.

The Water Monkey

There is a Chinese proverb that has great relevance for the Water Monkey this year: 'There is no limit to learning.' This can be an instructive and encouraging time, and by making the most of his opportunities, the Water Monkey can enjoy some well-deserved success.

Another significant feature of the year will be the decisions the Water Monkey has to take. These could be of a personal and relationship nature, connected with his work or education, or to do with accommodation. Sometimes the choices facing him could have far-reaching implications and even cause some anguish, and the Water Monkey needs to be guided by instinct and what feels right for him. He would also find it helpful to talk his options over with family members, close friends and, if applicable, professionals. Although keen to take responsibility, he will find that relatives in particular can often assist and advise in important ways. With advice and proper consideration, he will be satisfied with the choices he makes.

Water Monkeys in education could find pressures mounting as they have coursework to submit and important exams to take. The conscientious Water Monkey may find the amount of material he has to study daunting, but by remaining focused and working consistently, he will often be pleased with the results and qualifications he gains.

During the course of their studying, some Water Monkeys could be alerted to possible subjects or specialisms they will be keen to find out more about, or advised of vocations worth considering. The Horse year can be positive and encouraging and provide opportunities that can in time be significant.

The Horse year also holds good prospects for the Water Monkey's work situation. For Water Monkeys already established in a position, this can be a year of interesting but unexpected developments. Often, having proved themselves in one capacity, they will be encouraged to further their career by taking on new responsibilities or offered a different role. In addition, with many companies implementing change, there could be interesting new openings to pursue. Such is the nature of the year that by the end of it, few Water Monkeys will find themselves in the same position as at the start.

For Water Monkeys seeking work and those keen to move on from their current position, the year has interesting possibilities. Although the job-seeking process will be competitive, the Water Monkey's strengths, keenness and personal qualities will be very much to his advantage. By keeping alert for vacancies and actively making enquiries, he can uncover possibilities worth pursuing. Even if some applications do not go his way, he should not lose heart. He has a lot to offer and in time he will prevail. March, May, late June to early August and September could see important work developments.

The Water Monkey's financial prospects can be helped by an increase in earnings, but in view of his many outgoings he will need to watch his spending and be careful not to yield to too much indulgence or too many impulse buys. This year requires careful control of the purse-strings. Also, if the Water Monkey has plans to travel, he would do well to make early allowance for this.

The Water Monkey will derive considerable pleasure from his interests this year and new possibilities can also arise. Here again the Horse year is encouraging and offers considerable scope.

The Water Monkey attaches a lot of importance to his social life and yet again it will be full of interest and variety. There will be parties and other occasions to look forward to and the Water Monkey will appreciate the contact he has with his friends. On a personal level, he will be much in demand, with April, late May, June, August and December seeing the most activity. However, while a keen socializer, the Water Monkey does need to keep a sensible balance in his lifestyle and when studying for exams or busy at work, he must be careful not to exhaust himself. Too many late and exuberant nights could take their toll and start to affect his abilities. Water Monkeys, take note.

For the unattached, the Horse year has interesting romantic prospects, although it would be better to let any new romance develop and strengthen over time rather than get carried away.

Overall, the Year of the Horse can be a highly significant one for the Water Monkey. Whether in his education, work or personal interests, there will be excellent chances to develop, to learn and to prove himself. With commitment and self-belief, he can make this both an interesting and a valuable time. His relations with others can also be special and encouraging and he will benefit from the support of those around him in this important and rewarding year.

Tip for the Year
'There is no limit to learning.' By adding to your skills and capabilities, you can increase your options for the future. As a Water Monkey you have great potential and can make the Horse year a valuable, instructive and often personally enjoyable one.

The Wood Monkey

The element of Wood adds to the versatility and confidence of a sign and this certainly applies to the Wood Monkey. With his wide interests, he likes to engage in a variety of pursuits and can look forward to a full, interesting and sometimes surprising year.

For the Wood Monkey born in 1944, this marks his seventieth year, and his loved ones will not only often be keen to commemorate his birthday in style but could also have several surprises lined up. Any party or celebration may also help the Wood Monkey re-establish contact with friends or relations he may not have seen or heard from for some time. In addition, some of the messages and gifts he receives during the year will be especially meaningful and underline the affection others have for him. Parts of this year will be particularly special.

The Wood Monkey can also look forward to many positive developments in his home life, including some modifications to his accommodation which may make certain tasks easier and more efficient. Such is the nature of the year that one idea will often lead on to another and some projects will become more extensive than first anticipated. Where home purchases are concerned, the Wood Monkey could enjoy some good fortune, either identifying what he wants fairly easily and/or obtaining it on favourable terms. When plans are set in motion this year, an element of luck can often help them along.

The Wood Monkey will take great interest in family developments over the year and the achievements of younger relations could be a source of much pride. There could be a graduation or other academic success to mark, or a wedding, and some Wood Monkeys will become great grandparents. The Wood Monkey will often be glad to help out when he can, giving advice, time and support. Domestically, this can be a full and rewarding year.

The Wood Monkey also has a special group of friends and will value the contact he has with them. Not only will there be news to share but the Wood Monkey will also be glad to talk over certain ideas and concerns and seek advice. As with all years, 2014 will not be entirely problem-free, and when he is anxious or in a dilemma, a long-standing friend could be of especial help.

For Wood Monkeys who are, possibly because of personal circumstances, feeling lonely and who would welcome new friends or a fresh activity to do, the Horse year can offer support and encouragement. Horse years favour activity, and by going out, becoming more involved in their community and perhaps joining a local interest group, these Wood Monkeys can meet others as well as gain a rewarding new interest. The aspects are on the Wood Monkey's side this year, but to benefit, he does need to act. April, June, August and December could see the greatest amount of social activity.

The Wood Monkey's personal interests can also bring him considerable satisfaction and the Horse year may well inspire him to develop his ideas and make more of his personal strengths. Some Wood Monkeys will decide to share their knowledge by writing or exchanging thoughts with fellow enthusiasts.

With home, family expenses and travel opportunities, however, the Wood Monkey will have quite a few large outgoings. As a result he will need to make early provision for these and keep a close watch on spending. He also needs to be thorough when dealing with forms and important correspondence. A delay or oversight could take some time to rectify. Wood Monkeys, do be thorough and vigilant.

For the Wood Monkey born in 2004, the Horse year can again be an exciting one, especially as there will be new activities and experiences to enjoy. By nature, the young Wood Monkey is inquisitive and the Horse year will encourage him to develop his interests. With a game attitude, he can benefit considerably from the opportunities it will bring.

Throughout the year the young Wood Monkey will also be helped by the support of those close to him and at all times needs to be open and forthcoming. If he has ideas and hopes, he should let these be known, and if he has doubts or concerns, he should voice them. This is no time to keep his thoughts to himself, particularly as others will be able to assist if necessary.

For the young Wood Monkey, the Year of the Horse can be an exciting and wondrous time as he enjoys new activities and develops his capabilities. For the more senior Wood Monkey, it can also be special. Not only will many of them celebrate their seventieth year in style but also enjoy the way many of their hopes and plans proceed. The Wood Monkey can fare well this year and his enthusiasm and actions can help to make this a satisfying and rewarding time.

Tip for the Year

Act upon your hopes and ideas and share them with others. This year favours joint activity, and positive developments can quickly follow on. A year to act and to enjoy what you do.

The Fire Monkey

The Fire Monkey likes to keep active and busies himself in a great many things, but this year even he may sometimes despair of the amount he has to do! This will be a year of great activity for him, but with help, good organization and resolve, he will not only accomplish a lot but also reap many rewards as a result.

Almost all areas of the Fire Monkey's life will be busy, but this will be especially the case in his work. Although the many Fire Monkeys who are well established in a career may be content to concentrate on the duties they know and do so well, Horse years are times of change. Staff movements can lead to restructuring, new procedures and objectives may bring a change in duties, and sometimes the experience the Fire Monkey has behind him will involve him in training others. Many Fire Monkeys will see their working role change over the year and may feel uncomfortable with the suddenness of developments. However, despite misgivings and pressures, by making the best of their situation, these Fire Monkeys will not only have the chance to use their skills to advantage but will also find the changes in their role leading them to refocus and apply themselves in new ways. Particularly for any who have become staid or in a rut recently, the Horse year can give them new incentive and purpose.

Although the majority of Fire Monkeys will remain with their existing employer over the year, there will be some who will take advantage of early retirement options or choose to seek work elsewhere. For Fire Monkeys who do look for work, the job-seeking process will require effort and initiative. Competition for positions will be keen, but throughout the process the Fire Monkey should have self-belief and be alert for opportunity. This not only includes being quick in following up any vacancies he may hear about (and making sure his applications emphasize relevant strengths), but also investigating possible training and re-employment initiatives. One of the talents of the Fire Monkey is his resourcefulness, and through sheer determination many will secure a position this year and be keen to make the most of the opportunity. March, May, July and September could see important developments.

Whether in his work or his personal interests, the Fire Monkey would do well to take any chances to extend his knowledge and skills over the year, whether through local or online study programmes or research he can carry out himself. By using his time well, he can make this a satisfying year. Any Fire Monkeys who have let their interests lapse or would welcome the chance to do something new should explore possibilities, including activities available in their area.

Another feature of the year will be the travel opportunities that arise, sometimes at short notice. It may be that a last-minute offer appeals or the Fire Monkey suggests going away on a whim. By making the most of such chances, he can look forward to some pleasing times which are often made all the more exciting by their spontaneity.

The Fire Monkey will fare reasonably well in financial matters and may receive an extra sum or payment over the year. However, he will need to remain disciplined. With many outgoings, family expenses and travel costs, he should set funds aside in advance and take control of his budget. Also, when dealing with potentially important matters, including pensions, taxes or benefits, he needs to attend to paperwork carefully and seek advice if necessary. This is not a time to make assumptions or take risks concerning what could be potentially important matters.

The Fire Monkey will welcome the contact he has with his friends this year and their support can be particularly significant. He will also appreciate the social opportunities that come his way, and if a special event or other attraction appeals to him, he should do his best to attend. The Horse year can bring some very satisfying and special occasions.

Fire Monkeys who are feeling lonely will find that interests and activities pursued this year can often introduce them to others, and some important friendships and connections can be forged. Such is the nature of the year that for a few unattached Fire Monkeys sudden and unexpected romance may also blossom. April, June, August and December could see the most social activity.

This will also be a busy year domestically, with many Fire Monkeys involved in an important family event, possibly a wedding or another major celebration. The Fire Monkey will often play a valued role in the organization. In many a Fire Monkey household this can be a memorable year.

In addition to any key event, the Fire Monkey will be kept busy assisting family members and running his household in his usual efficient and attentive way. However, with possible work pressures and changes, some of the year will be demanding and, to help, the Fire Monkey should make sure decisions and tasks are shared rather than try to do too much single-handed. Similarly, if he has any concerns or is toying with ideas, he needs to be forthcoming rather than keep them to himself. The more that can be shared, the better.

In general, the Horse year will bring its pressures and busy times, especially as work changes have an impact and decisions need taking, but while there may be uncomfortable moments, benefits can often result and the Fire Monkey's determined nature and versatility will allow him to get a lot out of the year. He will value his relations with others and may well enjoy an important personal and family occasion. However, he will need to remain organized as well as draw on the support available to him. This will be a demanding year, although it will allow the Fire Monkey to enjoy some pleasing accomplishments.

Tip for the Year

Pay attention to what is going on around you. There may be uncertainty and confusion, but new possibilities can emerge. This is a year to show your strengths. With a positive 'can do' attitude, *you can do* what is needed to move your situation forward. Also, enjoy your relations with others and seek support at busy times.

The Earth Monkey

The Earth Monkey reads situations well. Observant and aware, he notices a great many things and is adept at gauging the best times to act. Almost as soon as the Horse year begins, if not shortly before, he will sense this will be a good year for him and a time to take action. His assessment will not let him down – this has the potential for being a full and exciting year.

For any Earth Monkey who starts the year dissatisfied with their situation, this is a time to focus on the present rather than feel hindered by what has gone before. With drive and self-belief, many Earth Monkeys will be able to turn the corner and move ahead.

Another feature of the Earth Monkey's character is his ability to delve deeply into certain matters. Often well read, he is always keen to add to his knowledge and skills and this can have a significant impact on his progress this year. If he feels an additional skill could be helpful or he would like to develop greater proficiency in a certain activity, he should investigate ways in which he could to do this. It could be through an online study course, reading he could do by himself, training of some kind or just by practice, but by looking to further his skills in some way, he could soon see benefits following on. This is very much a year for investing in himself and his future.

This emphasis on development will be particularly evident in his work situation. Earth Monkeys who are well established in a career will find their in-depth knowledge can make them strong candidates for promotion. In some cases, the position offered will be a considerable step up the career ladder, but the Earth Monkey will feel ready for the challenge.

Many Earth Monkeys will make important headway with their present employer, but for those who feel opportunities are limited where they are or are seeking work, the Horse year can again provide interest-ing openings. Although the job-seeking process will involve great effort, by keeping alert for chances, investigating possibilities and talking to employment officials, the Earth Monkey can find his initiative and personality shining through and leading to a new position with potential for the future. March, May, July, September and early October could see encouraging developments.

Progress at work can lead to an increase in income and some Earth Monkeys will also benefit from the receipt of extra funds. However, with accommodation, travel and some expensive purchases, the Earth Monkey will need to keep a close watch on outgoings and make early provision for larger obligations and plans. To do all he wants will require discipline and good financial management.

This can, however, be a time of good social opportunities and the Earth Monkey should make the most of his invitations. He could also be helped by the experience and advice of a close friend. While sometimes he keeps his thoughts to himself (a typical Monkey trait), he would benefit from being receptive to the advice he is offered. It may be more pertinent than he may realize.

For Earth Monkeys who change their location or work this year, as well as those currently feeling lonely, the Horse year can bring some excellent chances to meet new people. Some of these can be especially helpful and for a few Earth Monkeys who are unattached, romance could come unexpectedly and transform their lives. The Horse year is supportive and not without its surprises. April, June, August and December could be important months for social activity.

The Earth Monkey's domestic life will also be eventful. A few Earth Monkeys may move, but whatever happens, this will be a year of considerable activity and some important decision-making. Accordingly, there will need to be good liaison and it is important that the Earth Monkey preserves some quality time with his loved ones. Without care, a few disagreements could arise. Fortunately the Earth Monkey's attentive nature will help, but this is something he needs to be aware of.

Where possible, he should try to take a holiday with his loved ones this year as well as some occasional trips and other family treats. There could be additional travel opportunities late in 2014 or early 2015 as well as a possible family surprise at this time.

Overall, the Year of the Horse will be a busy and eventful one for the Earth Monkey. He will be keen to make more of himself this year and his talents will take him forward. His prospects are good and his actions can help make this a successful and progressive time.

Tip for the Year
Allow some time for yourself, your loved ones, your own interests – and recreation. This will be a busy and rewarding year, but to be at your best you need to maintain a good lifestyle balance.

Famous Monkeys

Christina Aguilera, Gillian Anderson, Jennifer Aniston, Patricia Arquette, Lady Ashton, J. M. Barrie, José Manuel Barroso, Joe Cocker, Colette, John Constable, David Copperfield, Patricia Cornwell, Daniel Craig, Joan Crawford, Miley Cyrus, Leonardo da Vinci, Timothy Dalton, Bette Davis, Danny De Vito, Celine Dion, Michael Douglas, Mia Farrow, Carrie Fisher, F. Scott Fitzgerald, Ian Fleming, Paul Gauguin, Ryan Gosling, Jake Gyllenhaal, Jerry Hall, Tom Hanks, Harry Houdini, Hugh Jackman, P. D. James, Katherine Jenkins, Julius Caesar, Buster Keaton, Alicia Keys, Gladys Knight, Taylor Lautner, George Lucas, Bob Marley, Kylie Minogue, V. S. Naipaul, Lisa Marie Presley, Debbie Reynolds, Little Richard, Mickey Rooney, Diana Ross, Tom Selleck, Wilbur Smith, Rod Stewart, Jacques Tati, Dame Kiri Te Kanawa, Justin Timberlake, Harry Truman, Venus Williams.

8 February 1921 to 27 January 1922 — *Metal Rooster*

26 January 1933 to 13 February 1934 — *Water Rooster*

13 February 1945 to 1 February 1946 — *Wood Rooster*

31 January 1957 to 17 February 1958 — *Fire Rooster*

17 February 1969 to 5 February 1970 — *Earth Rooster*

5 February 1981 to 24 January 1982 — *Metal Rooster*

23 January 1993 to 9 February 1994 — *Water Rooster*

9 February 2005 to 28 January 2006 — *Wood Rooster*

The Rooster

The Personality of the Rooster

With a clear destination
and firm will,
I raise my sails
to the winds of fortune.

The Rooster is born under the sign of candour. He has a flamboyant and colourful personality and is meticulous in all that he does. He is an excellent organizer and wherever possible likes to plan his various activities well in advance.

The Rooster is usually highly intelligent and very well read. He has a good sense of humour and is an effective and persuasive speaker. He loves discussion and enjoys taking part in any sort of debate. He has no hesitation in speaking his mind and is forthright in his views. He does, however, lack tact and can easily damage his reputation or cause offence by some thoughtless remark or action. He has a very volatile nature and should always try to avoid acting on the spur of the moment.

He is usually very dignified in his manner and conducts himself with an air of confidence and authority. He is adept at handling financial matters and organizes his financial affairs with considerable skill. He chooses his investments well and is capable of achieving great wealth. Most Roosters use their money wisely, but there are a few who are the reverse and are notorious spendthrifts. Fortunately, the Rooster has great earning capacity and is rarely without sufficient funds to tide himself over.

Another characteristic of the Rooster is that he invariably carries a notebook or scraps of paper around with him. He is constantly writing himself reminders or noting down important facts lest he forgets – the Rooster cannot abide inefficiency and conducts all his activities in an orderly, precise and methodical manner.

The Rooster is usually very ambitious, but can be unrealistic in some of what he hopes to achieve. He occasionally lets his imagination run away with him and while he does not like any interference from others, it would be in his own interests to listen to their views a little more often. He also does not like criticism, and if he feels anybody is doubting his judgement or prying too closely into his affairs, he is certain to let his feelings be known. He can also be rather self-centred and stubborn over relatively trivial matters, but to compensate for this he is reliable, honest and trustworthy, and this is appreciated by all who come into contact with him.

Roosters born between the hours of five and seven, both at dawn and sundown, tend to be the most extrovert of their sign, but all Roosters like to lead an active social life and enjoy attending parties and big functions. The Rooster usually has a wide circle of friends and is able to build up influential contacts with remarkable ease. He often belongs to several clubs and societies and involves himself in a variety of different activities. He is particularly interested in the environment, humanitarian affairs and anything affecting the welfare of others. He has a very caring nature and will do much to help those less fortunate than himself.

He also gets much pleasure from gardening, and while he may not spend as much time in the garden as he would like, his garden is invariably well kept and productive.

The Rooster is generally very distinguished in his appearance and if his job permits he will wear an official uniform with great pride and dignity. He is not averse to publicity and takes great delight in being the centre of attention. He often does well at PR work or any job which brings him into contact with the media. He also makes a very good teacher.

The female Rooster leads a varied and interesting life. She involves herself in many different activities and there are some who wonder how she can achieve so much. She often holds very strong views and, like her male counterpart, has no hesitation in speaking her mind or telling others how she thinks things should be done. She is supremely efficient and well organized and her home is usually very neat and tidy. She has good taste in clothes and usually wears smart but very practical outfits.

The Rooster usually has a large family and takes a particularly active interest in the education of his children. He is very loyal to his partner and will find that he is especially well suited to those born under the

signs of the Snake, Horse, Ox and Dragon. Provided they do not interfere too much in his various activities, the Rat, Tiger, Goat and Pig can
also establish a good relationship with him, but two Roosters together
are likely to squabble and irritate each other. The rather sensitive Rabbit
will find the Rooster a bit too blunt for his liking, and the Rooster will
quickly become exasperated by the ever-inquisitive and artful Monkey.
He will also find it difficult to get on with the anxious Dog.

If the Rooster can overcome his volatile nature and exercise tact, he
will go far in life. He is capable and talented and will make a lasting –
and usually favourable – impression almost everywhere he goes.

The Five Different Types of Rooster

In addition to the 12 signs of the Chinese zodiac there are five elements
and these have a strengthening or moderating influence on the signs. The
effects of the five elements on the Rooster are described below, together
with the years in which they were exercising their influence. Therefore
Roosters born in 1921 and 1981 are Metal Roosters, Roosters born in
1933 and 1993 are Water Roosters, and so on.

Metal Rooster: 1921, 1981

The Metal Rooster is a hard and conscientious worker. He knows
exactly what he wants in life and sets about everything in a positive and
determined manner. He can at times appear abrasive and he would
almost certainly do better if he were willing to reach a compromise with
others rather than hold so rigidly to his beliefs. He is very articulate and
most astute when dealing with financial matters. He is loyal to his
friends and often devotes much energy to working for the common
good.

Water Rooster: 1933, 1993

This Rooster has a very persuasive manner and can easily gain the co-operation of others. He is intelligent, well read and enjoys taking part in discussions and debates. He has a seemingly inexhaustible amount of energy and is prepared to work long hours in order to secure what he wants. He can, however, waste a lot of valuable time worrying over minor and inconsequential details. He is approachable, has a good sense of humour and is highly regarded by others.

Wood Rooster: 1945, 2005

The Wood Rooster is honest, reliable and often sets himself high standards. He is ambitious, but also more prepared to work in a team than some of the other types of Rooster. He usually succeeds in life but does have a tendency to get caught up in bureaucratic matters and attempt too many things at the same time. He has wide interests, likes to travel and is very caring and considerate towards his family and friends.

Fire Rooster: 1957

This Rooster is extremely strong-willed. He has many leadership qualities, is an excellent organizer and is most efficient in his work. Through sheer force of character he often secures his objectives, but he does have a tendency to be very forthright and not always consider the feelings of others. If he can learn to be more tactful he can often succeed beyond his wildest dreams.

Earth Rooster: 1969

This Rooster has a deep and penetrating mind. He is efficient, perceptive and particularly astute in business and financial matters. He is also persistent and once he has set himself an objective, he will rarely allow himself to be deflected from achieving his aim. He works hard and is held in great esteem by his friends and colleagues. He usually enjoys the arts and takes a keen interest in the activities of the various members of his family.

Prospects for the Rooster in 2014

The Rooster has considerable style and energy and in the Snake year (10 February 2013–30 January 2014) he will generally have fared well. In the remaining Snake months he will be kept busy and will see some interesting opportunities arising.

In his work in particular, the Rooster should keep alert for developments, and if he has the chance to put forward ideas, make suggestions or contribute in another way, he should do so. With his knowledge and insights, he can do his prospects considerable good. Roosters who are seeking a position should keep alert for openings, even in a different type of work. The closing months of the year can see quite a few Roosters proving themselves in new ways.

With many activities, travel possibilities and an increasing number of purchases, the Rooster will, however, need to be disciplined in his spending and, if possible, try to spread his spending out rather than doing all at once.

He will find himself in demand as the year draws to a close, with friends to meet, family and social occasions to enjoy and domestic arrangements to make. Although kept busy, he will delight in many of his activities and, thanks to his organizational skills, manage to fit in a great deal. For the unattached, romance can add extra meaning to the year's end. However, one word of warning: the straight-talking Rooster does need to be aware of the sensitivities of others. An inadvertent remark could cause difficulty and take some time to put right. With this in mind, the closing Snake months can be an active and personally rewarding time.

Of all the signs in the Chinese zodiac, the Rooster is one of the best organized. As the Horse year starts, on 31 January, many Roosters will already have thought about what they would like to accomplish over the next 12 months. If not, now would be an excellent time to decide on plans and, to give them more weight, *write them down*. With something to work towards, the Rooster will find that far more will happen. As with the hard-working Horse, whose year it is, the Rooster puts a lot of effort into his activities and this can be a time of important and encouraging developments for him.

At work, Roosters who are well established in a particular career will find their expertise can lead to them being excellently placed for promotion. Sometimes this may involve a considerable change in duties as well as learning new procedures, but the Horse year encourages growth and these Roosters will delight in making more of their potential.

The speed with which some offers may be made could surprise the Rooster. He does, after all, like to plan and be prepared, but there is an element of spontaneity to the Horse year and opportunities need to be seized quickly before they are lost or withdrawn.

Most Roosters will make considerable headway where they are, but there will be some who will be keen to move elsewhere. For these Roosters, as well as those seeking a position, the job-seeking process will be challenging, but by emphasizing their experience, qualities and achievements, many will be successful in their quest. Initiative and drive will be important, and March, April, June and November will be key months for employment matters.

However, while work prospects are encouraging, throughout the year the Rooster does need to be aware of the views of his colleagues *and listen to them*. He does have a dominant personality and not being sufficiently mindful of those around him could cause problems. Office politics can sometimes be tricky and the candid and upfront Rooster will need to tread carefully this year. Roosters, take note. Moments of outspokenness could undermine your prospects. Do not let this happen.

This need for care also extends to finance. Although the Rooster's progress at work may increase his income, he does need to keep a tight rein on outgoings and check the terms of any agreement he takes on. This is no year to be lax or take risks. Roosters involved in property transactions, do seek sound professional advice.

With the active nature of the year, the Rooster will, though, often feel inspired to take certain interests further. Whether starting new projects, acquiring equipment which will allow him to do more, joining groups or going to events, he will find his personal interests can bring him considerable pleasure this year. Roosters like adding to their knowledge and the Horse year is an encouraging time for this. For Roosters who would like to add new meaning to any free time they may have, taking up a new interest, possibly something quite different from what they have done before, is particularly recommended.

The Rooster will often have opportunities to go out and May, July, September and October could see the most social activity. However, the Horse year may not be problem free. Jealousy, disagreements and a clash of personality could all surface and cause anxiety. Similarly, romances will need careful nurturing if they are to develop and strengthen. The Rooster needs to be particularly careful in his handling of personal relationships and to ensure, if possible, that minor disagreements do not escalate.

The Rooster's home life will keep him busy and will often be conducted at a fast pace. However, despite his willingness, he should make sure he does not take on too much by himself and that household tasks are shared. He should also encourage discussion. With good communication and co-operation, family life can proceed well, and the Rooster's input will be both valued and significant. However, if more pleasurable activities and quality time are pushed aside amidst all the activity, in some Rooster households tensions could arise which, with more time and forethought, could have been be avoided. In the Horse year the Rooster does need to keep alert for any possible signs of discord. Fortunately, due to his perceptive nature, it is likely that he will.

Overall, the Year of the Horse will be a busy one for the Rooster. In both his work and personal interests he will have the opportunity to add to his skills. For one so determined and forward-thinking, this year offers considerable scope. The Rooster can also look forward to a full and rewarding personal life. However, where his relations with others are concerned, be they colleagues, friends or family, he will need to remain his attentive self and proceed carefully and tactfully. In this otherwise good year, relationships do need careful handling. Overall, a progressive and satisfying year.

The Metal Rooster

The Metal Rooster has great determination and when he sets himself a task, he likes to see it through. He also possesses considerable self-belief. While sometimes this can take some knocks, he knows he is capable of great things. And his resolve can make this both a successful *and* personally rewarding year.

Many Metal Roosters will have some ambitious plans for their home, including, for some, a move to accommodation that is more suitable. In addition, as Horse years encourage practical activity, many will spend time making improvements, buying new equipment and making alterations to living areas. With the latter, the Metal Rooster's good taste will be particularly evident. With so much happening, however, it is important that decisions are talked through and any problems fully discussed.

Many Metal Roosters will also assist more senior relations this year and their advice on accommodation, technical or practical matters will be especially valued. Yet again the Metal Rooster is set to play a significant part in the lives of quite a few people.

With the busy nature of the year he should also pay some attention to his well-being. This includes having a healthy and nutritious diet, taking regular exercise and resting after especially demanding times. To be neglectful of his well-being or drive himself too hard could leave him under par. In this active and potentially rewarding year, he needs to keep on good form.

In view of his various commitments, the Metal Rooster may decide to cut back on his socializing this year. However, it is important that he does not lose contact with good and important friends. Even if meeting up is not always possible, an e-mail or phone call can help maintain contact. Also, the Metal Rooster should not deny himself (and others) the pleasure that going out can bring, and if a particular event appeals to him, he should consider attending. Sometimes his interests can have a social element too and this should not be ignored this year. Socializing, conversing with others and pursuing his personal interests can all do the Metal Rooster good as well as bring important balance to his lifestyle. Late April, May, July, September and October could see the most social opportunities.

Affairs of the heart, however, will need careful nurturing. Sometimes existing commitments and pressures will not make courtship easy, and if a relationship is to thrive and endure, care will be needed. In his relations with others, the Metal Rooster needs to be particularly attentive and aware this year.

At work, this can be an important year. In view of the expertise and reputation many Metal Roosters have built up, not only will they feel ready in themselves to advance their career, but they can often benefit from the changes that take place over the year. As more senior staff move on, promotion possibilities will become available, and Metal Roosters in large organizations will also find opportunities arising in other sections and locations. This is a good time for the Metal Rooster to build on his achievements.

For Metal Roosters who feel unfulfilled in their present position, as well as those looking for work, the Horse year can develop in an often unexpected fashion. By making enquiries and keeping alert for possibilities (including perhaps companies looking to recruit in their area), they may be alerted to a significant new opportunity. Here the Metal Rooster's determination and initiative can make a considerable difference, impressing prospective employers and often securing a new position, or even career. March, April, June and November could be key months.

Although the aspects are encouraging in work matters, personal relations do need care, and the Metal Rooster will need to be mindful of the views of his colleagues. Sometimes jealousy, rivalry or office politics could raise their head and the Metal Rooster should not allow himself to be distracted from his work or objectives. The Horse year does have its problem areas, and work relations and petty annoyances could be troublesome. Metal Roosters, take note, be aware and remain focused.

Money matters also need care. Although the Metal Rooster's income may improve over the year and he may receive an additional sum, outgoings do need to be watched. The greater control, the better. Also, if entering into a long-term agreement, the Metal Rooster should seek professional advice and be aware of the terms and obligations. Finances require good management this year and the avoidance of risk and rush.

In general, although the Horse year will require the Metal Rooster to be alert and careful, it is still one of considerable possibility. In his home and personal life, he will often set about his plans with gusto and will be pleased with what he accomplishes. In his work, too, he will have the chance to move forward and to prove himself in new ways. This is a year which suits the active and determined Metal Rooster, and it can reward him well.

Tip for the Year
Pay close attention to your relations with others. Extra care may not only prevent possible misunderstandings but also lead to more happening. Also, keep your lifestyle in balance and preserve some time for enjoying the rewards you work so hard for.

The Water Rooster

The Water Rooster is blessed with many capabilities. He is not only a good and effective communicator but is also determined and prepared to work hard for what he wants. Admittedly, circumstances may not always make things easy, but the Water Rooster, with his persistence and self-belief, invariably wins through. His steadfast qualities will be very much to his advantage in this significant and fast-moving year.

For Water Roosters in education, the demands can be considerable. With often complex subject matter to study and possible presentations to prepare for, many a Water Rooster will find himself being stretched and occasionally forced out of his comfort zone. However, while the Horse year can be exacting, it is by being challenged that skills will be refined and knowledge gained. What the Water Rooster achieves over the year will be to his benefit both now and in the future.

The Horse year can also be highly instructive for Water Roosters in work. Again the pressures can be considerable and some of the tasks and objectives challenging. However, yet again, this will allow the Water Rooster to learn and apply himself in new ways and give him excellent experience.

The Horse year encourages growth and learning, but while important headway can be made, the Water Rooster does need to exercise care. Office politics, jealousy or a clash of personality may cause problems, and this needs to be kept in perspective and not distract him from his work. This is a year to focus on what he has to do, develop his skills and widen his experience.

For Water Roosters seeking work, the Horse year can open up some important possibilities. However, these Water Roosters should not be too restrictive in the type of vacancies they pursue. By widening the scope of their search, they will not only have more chance of getting their foot on the employment ladder but also gain what can be useful work experience. It could also be worth these Water Roosters investigating apprenticeship schemes, work placements or government-sponsored initiatives. By keeping informed about what is available, they can benefit from some potentially significant opportunities. March to early May, June and November could see important developments.

In financial matters, the Water Rooster will need to be disciplined. With often ambitious ideas but limited means, he will need to keep strict control of his outgoings and be wary of succumbing to too many indulgences or extravagances. This is a year to avoid risk or hasty and ill-thought out purchases. Also, if entering into an agreement or borrowing funds, the Water Rooster does need to check the terms carefully.

With his friendly and outgoing nature, he can, however, look forward to an active social life. Often his situation will allow him to be with those of similar age, and shared interests and activities can lead to some good fun being had. Later in the year, as a result of changes in his situation or as his interests broaden, he will have the chance to meet new people and make some important new friends. May, July and mid-August to October could see considerable social activity, although at most times of the year there will be interesting things for the Water Rooster to do.

The Horse year can also be rich in romantic possibility and affairs of the heart will become especially important for some Water Roosters. However, while some romances can strengthen over the year, it will also become apparent that some are not meant to be. For Water Roosters who do suffer heartache during the year (and this will certainly not be all), an improvement in their situation could swiftly follow, with someone new quickly becoming significant. In the Horse year a lot can happen at an often bewildering pace.

Throughout the year the Water Rooster will be grateful for the support of his friends, and whenever facing pressures, in a dilemma or in a romantic quandary, he will value talking matters over with those he trusts. He need not feel alone this year. Also, when faced with significant decisions, particularly involving education or work, he should draw on the professional advice available to him as well as talk to senior family members. In view of their experience, the advice of certain relations can be particularly significant. In return, the Water Rooster may do a lot to assist those around him, perhaps with technical matters. The help he offers and interest he shows will mean more than he may realize.

In addition, many Water Roosters can look forward to an important family occasion this year. Whether this involves marking their own success, their twenty-first birthday or a milestone in the life of another family member, they can find the Horse year giving rise to some memorable moments.

The Water Rooster will also derive considerable pleasure from his personal interests, and while he will already have a lot to do, he should look at ways in which he can develop his skills and use his talents to good effect. It could be helpful for him to join an organization or society where he can be spurred on by the encouragement (and sometimes suggestions) other enthusiasts can give. For Water Roosters who are attracted to creative pursuits, this can be a particularly exciting time.

With his often demanding lifestyle, the Water Rooster should also give some consideration to his well-being. To keep his energy levels high, he needs to eat healthily and, with sometimes very long days, allow himself time to rest and catch up. Driving himself too hard could leave him susceptible to minor ailments. Those who travel this year should also go well prepared and follow the advice given.

Overall, this will be a busy year for the Water Rooster and while the pressures will sometimes be great, it will give him an excellent chance to gain experience and add to his skills and qualifications. It is definitely worth him making the effort and rising to the challenge. Sometimes the attitude of another person could cause him concern, but the Horse year is a fast-moving one and difficulties will often be short-lived. It will help if the Water Rooster concentrates on the positives in the situation and focuses on more beneficial pursuits. As a Water Rooster, he knows he has it within him to do well and the headway he makes now can be to his present *and* future advantage.

Tip for the Year

Value your relations with others. Also, if problems arise, keep them in perspective and concentrate on what you *can* do rather than cannot. This is a constructive year and the skills and knowledge you gain can often be of far-reaching value.

The Wood Rooster

The Wood Rooster has a practical and determined nature. When he does something, he does it well. In 2014 he can look forward to some particularly pleasing results.

During the year he will devote a lot of time to family and home matters. If a grandparent or great grandparent, he will often delight in finding out more about the activities of younger family members and offering time, support and advice. With his wide interests and his ability to empathize, he will especially enjoy the rapport he has with some members of his family.

However, while a lot will go well, as with any year, problems and pressures will arise. Whenever his loved ones are facing difficulties, the Wood Rooster will be keen to offer support. Whether by listening, assisting or – and this should not be overlooked – seeking the advice of a professional or expert, he can make a significant difference. The Wood

Rooster has never been one to hold back from expressing an opinion, and his sterling qualities will help many of those around him during the year.

The Horse year has a strongly practical nature and many Wood Roosters will enjoy setting about projects in their home (and garden, if they have one). Where purchases are concerned, whether equipment, furnishings or other items, the Wood Rooster will enjoy taking the time to make the most suitable choice and, where applicable, his sense of style will be evident. Whenever the Wood Rooster has something in mind, he likes to see it through to the best of his ability.

There will also be quite a few travel opportunities for the Wood Rooster this year. Not only could he be keen to take a family holiday, but he could also receive invitations to visit friends and relations as well as be tempted by shorter breaks, including perhaps some long weekends away. He could be particularly impressed by some of the places he visits this year.

The Wood Rooster will also derive considerable pleasure from his personal interests and will once again have ideas he is keen to pursue. Though he will often be content to proceed in his own way, talking to those around him or contacting enthusiasts could lead to useful assistance.

In addition, the Wood Rooster should keep informed about what is happening in his area. There could be an interest or activity group he could join or particular events that appeal to him. If he would like more company, he could consider involving himself more in his community or perhaps enrolling on a locally run course. The Wood Rooster likes to use his time well and the Horse year can open up some worthwhile possibilities.

The Wood Rooster will value his close circle of friends this year and, as with family matters, he could find himself giving advice and support to someone in need. Again his reassuring yet practical manner will be appreciated. In addition to the support he may give (and receive), he can look forward to some enjoyable social occasions during the year. There could be a spontaneous element to some of these which adds to the fun. May, July and late August to October could be active and interesting months.

Financially, with the various purchases the Wood Rooster is likely to make, as well as his other commitments, he will need to keep a careful watch on outgoings and budget accordingly. Should he be lax, he could find his expenditure exceeding what he has allowed for. Wood Roosters, take note. Also, be vigilant when completing financial forms and query anything that concerns you. Assumptions or delays could be to your disadvantage.

Overall, however, the Wood Rooster can fare well this year. His drive and initiative, together with often favourable circumstances, will allow many of his plans to proceed quickly and he can enjoy some good results. Home undertakings and personal interests can bring especial pleasure, as can travel and more local activities. The Wood Rooster will also value family occasions and during the year will give important support to some relations and possibly also a close friend. He has great personal strengths and can make this an interesting and personally rewarding year.

Tip for the Year

Enjoy carrying out your plans, because you can make a lot happen this year. Also, keep informed about social and other opportunities in your area. This is a time of considerable possibility for you.

The Fire Rooster

The Horse year is a time of opportunity and the Fire Rooster, with his resourcefulness and dynamism, can be very much in the driving seat and achieve some excellent results.

At work, many Fire Roosters will be well established where they are and able to use their experience to good effect. As a result of their seniority, they could often be asked to extend their duties, take on new initiatives or focus on more specialist areas. Although these Fire Roosters may sometimes have misgivings about what is happening, the new responsibilities they take on will often give them the chance to use their skills in new ways and turn out to be an interesting career challenge. Any Fire Roosters who have become staid or fallen into a rut recently will now have the change and incentive they need. Some Fire Roosters may also benefit from promotion opportunities as more senior colleagues move on or vacancies arise elsewhere.

Throughout the year the Fire Rooster will be helped by the support and co-operation of his colleagues, although if he finds himself in a tense or volatile situation, he should be wary of acting impulsively and should think his response through. Although the Fire Rooster is born under the sign of candour, outspokenness could cause problems this year. A minority of Fire Roosters could also be troubled by office politics or rivalry. These Fire Roosters should not allow themselves to be distracted by this, but concentrate on the tasks that need to be done.

For Fire Roosters who are keen to further their career elsewhere, as well as those seeking a position, the Horse year can have important developments in store. The job-seeking process will be difficult, but by talking to employment officials and keeping well informed of schemes and initiatives, these Fire Roosters can improve their prospects. In some cases they might be eligible for retraining courses or able to use their skills in new ways. By adapting, learning and showing persistence, quite a few will secure an interesting new opening this year. March, April, June and November could see important developments, but whenever an opportunity comes his way, the Fire Rooster needs to act swiftly.

In financial matters, he should be thorough, keep a close watch on outgoings and, where possible, make early provision for major outlay. With good management he will be able to proceed with many of his plans, including some pleasing acquisitions for himself and his home, but the year will require discipline. The Fire Rooster should also be careful and thorough when dealing with important paperwork and should keep it safe. A mistake or loss could inconvenience him.

In such a busy year, he should also allow some time for personal interests and recreational pursuits. These not only give him the chance to relax and take a break from everyday pressures, but in some instances can also enable him to pursue his ideas and enjoy some satisfying activities. If he is able to meet other enthusiasts or go to interest-related events, this can add to the fun. If, due to his present lifestyle, he has allowed his interests to lapse, he should consider restarting a former pursuit or taking up something new. Similarly, if he considers he does not get sufficient exercise or that the quality of his diet is lacking, he should seek advice on the improvements he could make. Horse years are constructive times.

During the year the Fire Rooster will particularly value his chances to socialize and any Fire Rooster who would welcome more company would do well to investigate what is available in his area. This is a year rewarding involvement and many Fire Roosters will be able to introduce new meaning – and friends – to their lives. May, July, September and October could see the most social opportunities.

This will also be a busy year in the Fire Rooster's home life, and his attentiveness and organizational abilities will be an asset, although he should not take on too much single-handed. This is a year for collective effort. Also, any strains caused by pressure at busy times should be talked through rather than left unaddressed. However, while many a Fire Rooster's home will buzz with activity, there will also be quite a few high points, with achievements and special occasions to celebrate as well as a possible family gathering. In addition, a holiday or short break will be much appreciated. It is important that the Fire Rooster and his family aim for a good lifestyle balance.

Overall, the Horse year offers considerable scope for the Fire Rooster, although it will bring its pressures and some anxious moments. At work there will be opportunities to move his career forward and use his talents in new ways. Personal interests can also be satisfying, while in his home and social life those around him will be grateful for his time, knowledge and judgement. However, with so much to do, the Fire Rooster does need to draw on the support available to him and to keep his lifestyle in balance. This can be a good year, but communication and good organization will be important.

Tip for the Year

Do not get distracted. In this busy year, there will be a lot going on and sometimes a few unhelpful influences. Concentrate on your objectives. With discipline and focus, you *can* make good headway.

The Earth Rooster

'He who comprehends the times is great', as the Chinese proverb reminds us. Observant, realistic and eminently practical, the Earth Rooster comprehends the times in which he lives and is under no illusion about the application required to reach certain objectives. He has commitment and a deep-rooted belief in his abilities and, as the Horse year begins, will resolve to make the most of the next 12 months.

In looking to improve his situation, it is important that the Earth Rooster does not rely solely on his own efforts. While he may be keen to realize his aims, he does need support. If he discusses his ideas with those close to him and speaks to friends and contacts who have relevant expertise, he will find that far more can be achieved.

One area which will see great activity will be his work situation. Although he may have made progress in recent times, he will be keen to build on this. As a result, if openings arise at his place of work or new initiatives are introduced, he should express interest and put himself forward. More senior personnel will be keen to help him make more of his potential.

The majority of Earth Roosters will make important headway with their present employer, but for those who are keen on more substantial change or looking for work, the Horse year can be significant. These Earth Roosters should widen the scope of positions they are prepared to consider and seek the advice of employment officials and agencies. By showing resolve and presenting themselves well, they will not only impress but could also benefit from a significant opportunity. March, April, June and November could be important months for work matters.

Although the aspects are encouraging, one word of warning does need to be sounded: at difficult times (and each year does have its share), the Earth Rooster needs to focus on what he has to do rather than become embroiled in unproductive matters or unhelpful office politics. Fortunately the Earth Rooster is usually adept at working round problems, but he does need to be on his guard this year.

This need for vigilance also applies to financial matters. If undertaking a large transaction or completing forms, the Earth Rooster should check the details and question anything that is unclear. This is not a year for risk. He would also do well to make early allowance for his more ambitious plans. Financially, this is a year for control.

With his active lifestyle the Earth Rooster should also make sure he allows time for recreation and pursuing his various interests. Not only can these give him a valuable break from other activities but may also give him the chance to take additional exercise or use his talents in other ways.

If possible, he should also try to take a holiday with his loved ones during the year. A break can benefit all and a carefully chosen location provide much to do and enjoy. Additional travel opportunities could arise late in the year.

The Horse year will see great activity in many an Earth Rooster household. Good communication will be essential and while family members will often be busy, time should regularly be set aside for shared activities, otherwise some strains could arise. Earth Roosters, take note, and do encourage everyone to spend some quality time together.

Many Earth Roosters will also have ambitious plans for their home and some practical projects may be more disruptive than envisaged, although the finished results will be much appreciated. Horse years favour practical activity, but Earth Roosters need to accept this may not be without difficulty or delay.

In view of the Earth Rooster's many commitments, he may decide to cut back on his socializing this year, but it is important he does not deny himself the pleasure of meeting his friends or enjoying special events. He does need to keep his lifestyle in balance. May, July, September and October could see the most social activity.

For unattached Earth Roosters who find love this year, as well as those enjoying the early stages of romance, relationships will need to be nurtured. Rushing into a commitment or building up expectations too early on could lead to disappointment. Earth Roosters, take your time, appreciate the moment and allow romance to develop in its own way.

The Year of the Horse encourages growth, and by putting himself forward and seizing his chances, the Earth Rooster can make important headway. However, the year will also bring its challenges and the Earth

Rooster will need to be focused and avoid distraction. He should also draw on the support of others rather than try to do everything himself. With awareness, commitment and determination, however, he can achieve a lot this year.

Tip for the Year
Keep your lifestyle in balance and do preserve quality time both for yourself and for those who are special to you. Their encouragement can make an important difference to the success you enjoy.

Famous Roosters

Fernando Alonso, Beyoncé, Cate Blanchett, Barbara Taylor Bradford, Gerard Butler, Sir Michael Caine, the Duchess of Cambridge, Enrico Caruso, Eric Clapton, Joan Collins, Rita Coolidge, Daniel Day Lewis, Minnie Driver, the Duke of Edinburgh, Gloria Estefan, Roger Federer, Errol Flynn, Benjamin Franklin, Dawn French, Stephen Fry, Joseph Gordon-Levitt, Melanie Griffith, Josh Groban, Goldie Hawn, Katharine Hepburn, Paris Hilton, Jay-Z, Catherine Zeta Jones, Quincy Jones, Diane Keaton, Søren Kierkegaard, D. H. Lawrence, David Livingstone, Jayne Mansfield, Steve Martin, James Mason, W. Somerset Maugham, Paul Merton, Bette Midler, Ed Miliband, Van Morrison, Willie Nelson, Kim Novak, Yoko Ono, Dolly Parton, Matthew Perry, Michelle Pfeiffer, Natalie Portman, Priscilla Presley, Joan Rivers, Kelly Rowland, Paul Ryan, Jenny Seagrove, George Segal, Carly Simon, Britney Spears, Johann Strauss, Verdi, Richard Wagner, Serena Williams, Neil Young, Renée Zellweger.

28 January 1922 to 15 February 1923 — *Water Dog*

14 February 1934 to 3 February 1935 — *Wood Dog*

2 February 1946 to 21 January 1947 — *Fire Dog*

18 February 1958 to 7 February 1959 — *Earth Dog*

6 February 1970 to 26 January 1971 — *Metal Dog*

25 January 1982 to 12 February 1983 — *Water Dog*

10 February 1994 to 30 January 1995 — *Wood Dog*

29 January 2006 to 17 February 2007 — *Fire Dog*

The Dog

The Personality of the Dog

I have my values
and beliefs.
These are my beacon
in an ever-changing world.

The Dog is born under the signs of loyalty and anxiety. He usually holds very firm views and beliefs and is the champion of good causes. He hates any sort of injustice or unfair treatment and will do all in his power to help those less fortunate than himself. He has a strong sense of fair play and will be honourable and open in all his dealings.

The Dog is very direct and straightforward. He is never one to skirt round issues and speaks frankly and to the point. He can be stubborn, but he is prepared to listen to the views of others and will try to be as fair as possible in coming to his decisions. He will readily give advice where it is needed and will be the first to offer assistance when things go wrong.

The Dog instils confidence wherever he goes and there are many who admire him for his integrity and resolute manner. He is a very good judge of character and can often form an accurate impression of someone very shortly after meeting them. He is also very intuitive and can frequently sense how things are going to work out long in advance.

Despite his friendly and amiable manner, the Dog is not a big socializer. He dislikes having to attend large functions or parties and much prefers a quiet meal with friends or a chat by the fire. He is an excellent conversationalist and is often a marvellous raconteur of amusing stories and anecdotes.

The Dog is also quick-witted and his mind is always alert. He can keep calm in a crisis and although he does have a temper, his outbursts tend to be short-lived. He is loyal and trustworthy, but if he ever feels badly let down or rejected by someone, he will rarely forgive or forget.

The Dog usually has very set interests. He prefers to specialize and become an expert in a chosen area rather than dabble in a variety of different activities. He usually does well in jobs where he feels that he is being of service to others and is often suited to careers in the social services, the medical and legal professions and teaching. He does, however, need to feel motivated in his work. He has to have a sense of purpose and if ever this is lacking he can quite often drift through life without ever achieving very much. Once he has the motivation, however, very little can prevent him from securing his objective.

Another characteristic of the Dog is his tendency to worry and to view things rather pessimistically. Quite often his worries are totally unnecessary and are of his own making. Although it may be difficult, worrying is a habit that all Dogs should try to overcome.

The Dog is not materialistic or particularly bothered about accumulating great wealth. As long as he has the money necessary to support his family and to spend on the occasional luxury, he is more than happy. However, when he does have any spare money he tends to be rather a spendthrift and does not always put it to its best use. He is also not a very good speculator and would be advised to get professional advice before entering into any major long-term investment.

The Dog will rarely be short of admirers, but he is not an easy person to live with. His moods are changeable and his standards high, but he will be loyal and protective to his partner and will do all in his power to provide a comfortable home. He can get on extremely well with those born under the signs of the Horse, Pig, Tiger and Monkey, and can also establish a sound and stable relationship with the Rat, Ox, Rabbit, Snake and another Dog, but will find the Dragon a bit too flamboyant for his liking. He will also find it difficult to understand the imaginative Goat and is likely to be highly irritated by the candid Rooster.

The female Dog is renowned for her beauty. She has a warm and caring nature, although until she knows someone well she can be both secretive and very guarded. She is highly intelligent and despite her calm and tranquil appearance can be extremely ambitious. She enjoys sport and other outdoor activities and has a happy knack of finding bargains in the most unlikely of places. She can also get rather impatient when things do not work out as she would like.

The Dog usually has a very good way with children and can be a doting parent. He will rarely be happier than when he is helping someone or doing something that will benefit others. Providing he can cure himself of his tendency to worry, he will lead a very full and active life, and in that life he will make many friends and do a tremendous amount of good.

The Five Different Types of Dog

In addition to the 12 signs of the Chinese zodiac there are five elements and these have a strengthening or moderating influence on the signs. The effects of the five elements on the Dog are described below, together with the years in which they were exercising their influence. Therefore Dogs born in 1970 are Metal Dogs, Dogs born in 1922 and 1982 are Water Dogs, and so on.

Metal Dog: 1970

The Metal Dog is bold, confident and forthright and sets about everything he does in a resolute and determined manner. He has a great belief in his abilities and no hesitation about speaking his mind or devoting himself to some just cause. He can be rather serious at times and can become anxious and irritable when things are not going according to plan. He tends to have very specific interests and it would certainly help him if he were to broaden his outlook and become more involved in group activities. He is loyal and faithful to his friends.

Water Dog: 1922, 1982

The Water Dog has a very direct and outgoing personality. He is an excellent communicator and has little trouble in persuading others to fall in with his plans. He does, however, have a somewhat carefree nature and is not as disciplined or as thorough as he should be in certain matters. Neither does he keep as much control over his finances as he should, but he can be most generous to his family and friends and will make sure that they want for nothing. He is usually very good with children and has a wide circle of friends.

Wood Dog: 1934, 1994

This Dog is a hard and conscientious worker and will usually make a favourable impression wherever he goes. He is less independent than some of the other types of Dog and prefers to work in a group rather than on his own. He is popular, has a good sense of humour and takes a keen interest in the activities of the various members of his family. He is often attracted to the finer things in life and can obtain much pleasure from collecting items of interest, beauty or antiquity. He prefers to live in the country rather than the town.

Fire Dog: 1946, 2006

This Dog has a lively, outgoing personality and is able to establish friendships with remarkable ease. He is an honest and conscientious worker and likes to take an active part in all that is going on around him. He also likes to explore new ideas and providing he can get the necessary support and advice, he can often succeed where others have failed. He does, however, have a tendency to be stubborn. Providing he can overcome this, he can often achieve considerable fame and fortune.

Earth Dog: 1958

The Earth Dog is very talented and astute. He is methodical and efficient and is capable of going far in his chosen profession. He tends to be rather quiet and reserved, but has a very persuasive manner and usually secures his objectives without too much opposition. He is generous and kind and always ready to lend a helping hand when it is needed. He is also held in very high esteem by his friends and colleagues and is usually most dignified in his appearance.

Prospects for the Dog in 2014

The Dog has considerable willpower and, when inspired, can achieve great things. In the Snake year (10 February 2013–30 January 2014) he will have generally fared well and the closing months will be a full and interesting time.

At work the Dog could have new pressures to deal with and find his workload increasing. However, by focusing on what needs to be done and using his skills to advantage, he is set to impress, and some Dogs will have the chance to take on a greater role. Late 2013 and early 2014 could be especially significant. For Dogs seeking work, opportunities can arise suddenly, and even if some positions are temporary, they may provide experience and useful insights into a particular industry.

The Dog can also enjoy some moments of good fortune in the closing months of the Snake year. These could be financial or involve a special gift or successfully tracking down a certain purchase. When shopping, the Dog's alert nature can serve him particularly well.

Although the Dog tends to be selective in his socializing, he should try to take up any invitations received at this time, especially as they may give him the opportunity to meet up with – or get back in contact with – some people he has not seen for some time. His home life, too, will see much activity and it would be helpful if certain occasions were spread out rather than having a lot happening in a short space of time. A loved one could have a surprise near the year's end.

The Year of the Horse begins on 31 January and will be an encouraging one for the Dog. Having learned a lot in recent years, he will be able to build on his experience and make important headway. To help get the year off to a positive start, he would do well to give some thought to his objectives for 2014. A few personal resolutions may also help, including perhaps looking to correct a weakness or bad habit. Whatever he decides, by determining to make this a year for positive action, the Dog will feel more motivated and ready to *make things happen*.

At work many Dogs will be excellently placed to benefit from the opportunities that will arise over the year. Staff movements can lead to vacancies and this is a year when commitment will be well-rewarded. Dogs who feel they have been held back in recent times will now have the opportunity to correct this and should be quick to put themselves forward. Horse years favour the industrious and many Dogs will now make excellent, and sometimes overdue, headway.

The majority will remain with their present employer over the year and build on their experience. However, for those keen for a new challenge or seeking work, the Horse year can bring important chances. These Dogs should not be too restrictive in the type of work they are prepared to consider. By widening their scope, many could successfully secure a position which will allow them to use their skills in other ways. Such are the workings of the year that some could be alerted to an opening by chance, perhaps through the recommendation of an ex-colleague or something they read about. February, April, June and November could be important months for work matters.

Progress at work can also help financially. As a result, the Dog will often be tempted to proceed with plans he has been considering for a while. By carefully considering choices and costs, he will be pleased with the decisions he makes. If possible, he should also take time over the year to look at his overall financial position. This includes looking to reduce any borrowings and making allowance for future requirements as well as checking that the accounts he holds are suitable. Good financial management can make an important difference this year. Also, the Dog should not be lax with personal security. A loss could be upsetting.

Travel is favourably aspected and the Dog should try to take a holiday during the year. Even if he decides not to travel too far, he will enjoy the chance to see new places. Many Dogs could have additional travel possibilities due to their work or personal interests. Travel will feature prominently on the agenda of many this year.

In his relations with others, the Dog is famed for his loyalty and thoughtfulness, and he will see an upturn in social activity over the year. For the unattached, there are also excellent romantic possibilities.

Indeed, some Dogs will find themselves the subject of a flurry of romantic interest. This can be an exciting time, with these Dogs enjoying the fun and attention. April to early June, September and December could be active months socially and the unattached could find Cupid's arrow aimed at them at almost any time, such is the nature of this splendid year.

Dogs who are feeling lonely or have had some recent personal upset will find the Horse year encouraging them to turn the corner. Both new and existing friends will be supportive and there may be interesting new activities to absorb them. For quite a few, the Horse year will mark the start of a new chapter in their life.

As always, the Dog will devote much time to his home life and this year he may be concerned about the difficulties loved ones are facing. As a natural worrier, he may have some anxious moments, but should try to keep things in perspective, encourage communication and, if appropriate, speak to professionals. Fortunately, problems can often quickly be resolved and the Dog is always adept at finding solutions. As he recognizes, all years have their difficult moments. This one will be no exception, but in the main, home life will proceed well, with domestic projects, shared activities, travel and some personal successes providing some key moments.

Overall, the Dog can fare well in the Horse year and by setting about his activities in determined fashion, he can accomplish a lot. Some particularly good opportunities can arise at work. The Dog always has a lot to offer and this year his talents will be recognized and rewarded. He will also have the chance to travel. On a domestic level, he will do a lot with his loved ones, while his social life will see an increase in activity and for the unattached there are exciting romantic prospects.

The Metal Dog

The Metal Dog is redoubtable and tenacious. He also has considerable faith in his abilities and, even when circumstances are not favourable, he knows he has it within him to overcome any difficulties and set situations right. His qualities will serve him well this year.

As it starts, he may feel the time is right to move forward and achieve some of his aims. And, determined and hopeful, he can make impressive headway. However, to get the best from the year, he should not be too independent in approach. Although he does like to make his own decisions, in this active year he needs to be willing to talk over his thoughts and ideas. The more he consults others, the more opportunities will open up for him.

In his home life in particular this will be a busy year, with some important events affecting those close to him. It could be a younger relation leaves home to further his education or for work purposes, or has major decisions to take concerning his future. Whatever happens, the Metal Dog will provide a lot of support, and his love, concern and dependability will be valued by those around him.

In addition, the Metal Dog will involve himself in various household projects over the year, including altering some living areas. This is very much a time for setting ideas in motion. However, it is also important that time is preserved for shared interests. These can bring particular pleasure this year, and with travel favourably aspected, the Metal Dog should try to arrange a holiday with family members too. It could also be worth making time for visits to nearby attractions.

The Metal Dog tends to be fairly selective about his socializing and in true Dog fashion he takes his time building friendships. However, this year could see an increase in social activity, with the chance for him to meet people with similar outlooks to his own, and he may find himself making new friends. For unattached Metal Dogs, the Horse year can also mark the start of a significant romance which can bring new joy to their lives. In some instances, a chance meeting will seem as if it was meant to be. April to early June, September and the last six weeks of the year could see a lot of social activity.

This is also an encouraging year for work prospects. Many Metal Dogs will be keen to build on their recent experience and seek a greater role. As is often the way this year, events can take a curious course, and once the Metal Dog starts to look at possibilities, he could be informed of an ideal opportunity. Often this will be with his present employer and will be a natural progression in his career. However, some Metal

Dogs will find their reputation making them strong candidates for an opening elsewhere. Some of their contacts could be particularly helpful, even putting in a recommendation on their behalf. This is a year when the talents and commitment of many Metal Dogs will be rewarded.

There will also be good opportunities for those currently seeking work. By keeping alert for openings, talking to employment officials and contacting relevant organizations, they can find their determination and background impressing others and often leading to the offer of a new position. Admittedly, this could involve considerable adjustment, but could also give the Metal Dog the challenge he has been wanting for a long time. February, April, June and November could see good possibilities, but throughout the year the Metal Dog should keep alert and be quick to follow up any possibilities.

Progress at work will lead to many Metal Dogs increasing their income over the year and some will also benefit from the receipt of additional funds. However, while the financial aspects indicate improvement, to benefit fully the Metal Dog does need to keep a close watch on outgoings and make early provision for expensive plans and purchases. If entering into any agreements, he should also check the terms and obligations, and he should not be lax with correspondence or personal possessions. A mistake, loss or theft could be upsetting and cause inconvenience. Metal Dogs, take note and do manage your finances carefully.

Although the Metal Dog will be kept busy over the year, he should not neglect his own interests or begrudge himself some 'me time'. In this active year he does need to give himself the chance to unwind. Also, if sedentary for much of the day, he will find that some suitable daily or weekly exercise can help keep him in good form.

The Metal Dog has many great skills and considerable personal presence and in the Horse year his qualities will be well rewarded. In his home life he will not only provide valuable support to his loved ones but also be the driving force behind many plans and activities. Socially, too, he will find himself in increasing demand, and for the unattached, new romance could be particularly important. There will also be opportunities for the Metal Dog to make deserved headway at work. This is a favourable and progressive year, with the Metal Dog's determined nature delivering some good results.

Tip for the Year

Have faith in yourself and act. With resolve, you can make a lot happen this year. Also, do involve others and watch your independent tendencies. With the support and goodwill of those around you, more will be accomplished.

The Water Dog

The Water Dog likes to proceed slowly but surely. He thinks things through and his achievements are often the result of much deliberation and effort. However, the Horse year will see the pace quicken and the Water Dog having to act swiftly. As he will find, the Horse year is not one for standing still, and the speed and course of events may sometimes take him by surprise.

However, while some parts of the year may be unsettling, a lot will be in the Water Dog's favour. Over the year he can benefit a lot from the support of others, and rather than keeping his thoughts and any anxieties to himself (as a Dog, he can be prone to worry), it is important that he talks to those around him.

In his home life this can be a particularly active year, especially as many Water Dogs will focus their attention on accommodation matters, including carrying out alterations and possibly moving. Throughout the year, thoughts and plans need to be fully discussed and sufficient time allowed for carrying them out. Water Dogs who move could find that once agreements are made, events move ahead rapidly. Some weeks in the Horse year can be particularly eventful.

While the Water Dog will often be kept busy with practical activities, he will also share many enjoyable times with his loved ones and, if a parent, do much to encourage his children. His care and attentive nature can make an important difference and the year can contain some proud moments.

Although the Water Dog may be selective in his socializing, the Horse year can also see an increase in social activity, in some cases due to the Water Dog's work situation or personal interests. Whenever he has invitations or other opportunities to go out, he should try to take these up. This can be an especially good year to become better known. April to early June, September and the last six weeks of the Horse year could see the most social activity.

For any Water Dog who is feeling lonely or has had some recent personal difficulty, the Horse year is also promising and may bring a new and meaningful romance. While the Water Dog may take his time in getting to know another person, in this Horse year love can quickly take hold.

It is also important that the Water Dog allows time for his personal interests and recreational pursuits rather than continually driving himself. These can give him a good chance to unwind as well as keep his lifestyle in balance. Water Dogs who like more creative pursuits can derive much satisfaction from developing their ideas and using their talents.

The Horse year can also bring some good travel possibilities, sometimes at short notice. During the year many Water Dogs can look forward to visiting some fascinating sites as well as going to events or places connected with their interests.

At work, the Water Dog is likely to see important developments taking place. With many companies and industries undergoing change this year, he could find his role suddenly changing or see vacancies arising elsewhere that offer him greater scope. To benefit, he will need to act swiftly, but any new position he takes on will give him the chance to extend his skills and, in the process, widen his options for the future. To help his prospects he should take any chances to network as well as be active in his work environment. The extra effort can repay him handsomely.

For Water Dogs seeking work, the Horse year can also open up important possibilities. However, such is the nature of the year that little may happen for months and then an ideal opportunity may suddenly arise and the Water Dog be surprised to find the position offered him quite quickly. Accordingly, during the year he will need to stay alert and be prepared to act swiftly when he sees something that interests him. Initiative can play a big part and some background research can also help. February, April, late May to early July and November could see important developments, but throughout 2014 the Water Dog needs to keep alert and be ready to act.

Progress at work can help financially and many Water Dogs will also benefit from a gift or some other good financial fortune over the year. However, with some large outlays (especially on accommodation) likely, together with existing commitments, the Water Dog will need to manage his situation carefully and, when appropriate, seek advice.

With travel well aspected, he would also do well to consider making provision for a holiday during the year.

In general, the Year of the Horse will be a busy one for the Water Dog, but while fast-moving (sometimes too fast for the Water Dog's liking), it will allow him to make progress and add to his skills. The changes that take place will require him to adjust and learn, but this can be an important stepping stone to future success. Throughout the year he should liaise with others and seek their opinions and advice – this is no year for being too independent. His home and social life can see increased activity, with some often special times to enjoy. Overall, a rewarding and constructive year.

Tip for the Year
Keep alert and seize your chances. This is no year for delay. Also, be mindful of others. You do a lot for those around you and in turn should let them help and advise you. Personal relationships can be important this year. Value and enjoy them.

The Wood Dog

This year marks the start of a new decade in the Wood Dog's life and will contain some personally happy times as well as give him an excellent chance to develop his skills.

On a personal level, the Wood Dog will find himself in demand. In addition to his existing circle of friends, changes in circumstances can often lead to him meeting new people and making new friends. Cupid's arrow is also set to strike, as the Horse year is rich in romantic possibility. Even more independent Wood Dogs will benefit from the social opportunities this year will offer, and the shy and reserved will gain in confidence. Horse years are encouraging in so many aspects. April to early June, September, December and early January could see the most social activity, although at most times of the year the Wood Dog will have a variety of activities to enjoy.

With the Wood Dog's relations with others being favourably aspected, he should also draw on the support available to him. If he feels in need of guidance, whether at home, in his place of education, at work or from a professional, he should ask. This is no year to hold back. He may well find that advice and assistance can add momentum to certain plans he has been considering.

This also extends to his personal interests. For Wood Dogs who have talents they are keen to make more of or projects to pursue, this is a year for action. In addition, by seizing any chances to practise and add to their skills (often with the help of others), many will find new possibilities opening up for them, as well as be encouraged to develop what they do. For Wood Dogs who enjoy active pursuits, this can also be a rewarding time. In addition, as some Wood Dogs change their location over the year or meet new people, there could be the opportunity to try different pursuits and some Wood Dogs may discover a new activity for which they have a natural aptitude. In the Horse year it is worth keeping an open mind, for what is started now can prove significant later.

Although the Wood Dog leads an active lifestyle, to neglect the quality of his diet or have a succession of late nights without giving himself the chance to catch up could leave him susceptible to colds or other minor ailments. To be at his best, he does need to look after himself. Wood Dogs, take note.

For the many Wood Dogs in education, this can be an interesting but demanding year. A lot will be expected of these Wood Dogs, but by applying themselves to what needs to be done and working consistently, they can make substantial progress and gain skills and knowledge they can subsequently build on. During the course of their studies, some could be alerted to new possibilities or career options or discover strengths they can develop in the future. Horse years are instructive and illuminating and reward commitment.

For Wood Dogs in work, this can be a time of important change. In many cases, in view of the skills they have recently acquired, these Wood Dogs will be encouraged to take on a greater role. By making the most of this, and any training they may receive, they can find that one small step can often lead to others. Many an employer will recognize the Wood Dog's potential this year and be keen to offer support.

There will also be many Wood Dogs seeking a position, and while the job-seeking process can be wearying, these Wood Dogs need to have faith in themselves and persevere. Talking with employment officials and getting advice and information from relevant organizations can be especially helpful. This can lead to many Wood Dogs being alerted to vacancies, including some just about to become available. By being quick to apply and emphasizing a willingness to learn, many will be successful in getting that all-important foot on the employment ladder. February, April, June and November could see encouraging developments.

Financially, the Wood Dog may only have limited means at his disposal, but by setting amounts aside for specific activities and doing his best to stay within his budget, he can still do a great deal. Whether socializing, following his personal interests or travelling (which is favourably aspected this year), he can make this a full and pleasing time.

The Year of the Horse not only marks the start of a new decade in the Wood Dog's life but is one favouring growth and personal development. The Wood Dog knows he is capable of a great many things and will be keen to get his twenties off to a good start. With support and commitment, he can learn a lot this year, including about his own strengths and capabilities. On a personal level this can be a full and exciting year, with an often lively social life and personal interests bringing pleasure. Overall, a year of growth and opportunity.

Tip for the Year

Have faith in yourself. This year will require effort and determination, but will bring the chance to prove yourself. Also, draw on the advice and support available to you. This can make an appreciable difference to how you fare. Your twentieth year can be a full, positive and often happy one. Use it well, for it can mark the start of an exciting and successful decade.

The Fire Dog

The Fire Dog has a lively mind and is rarely short of things to do. As a consequence, he will find the Year of the Horse a stimulating time.

In view of the active nature of the year, he would do well to keep an open mind and be willing to embrace the new. Whether trying out new technology, taking up a new interest or exploring new ideas, he will find that many interesting possibilities can open up for him this year. In addition, a lot will happen quickly. Developments may sometimes take the Fire Dog by surprise, but he needs to make the most of opportunities as they arise. To be slow or prevaricate could mean, in some cases, that he loses out. Horse years have an immediacy about them.

In view of his hopes for the year the Fire Dog will need to manage his financial situation well. This includes making advance provision for certain outgoings and purchases he is considering as well as monitoring his overall spending. He should also keep his financial paperwork in good order, including making sure that the accounts and policies he has are right for him. By investigating options and getting advice, he may be able to make improvements. Although he may find it irksome, it would also be in his interest to pay close attention to any forms he has to complete and query anything that is not sufficiently clear. Without care, he could find himself in some protracted correspondence. Fire Dogs, while this can be a good year, it is not one to be lax where paperwork is concerned.

Many Fire Dogs will have the chance to travel this year and would do well to make early provision for this. If there are specific places or events the Fire Dog is keen to see, he should make enquiries and find out what is possible. If he acts on his ideas, many of them can come to fruition.

The Fire Dog's personal interests can once more bring him considerable pleasure, but here again he needs to be open to possibility. In some cases, obtaining new equipment or trying new techniques or new software could make a huge difference to what he does. By being willing to experiment and learn, the Fire Dog will often be thrilled with his results.

If applicable, he can also benefit from getting in contact with fellow enthusiasts and, if he has not already done so already, finding out whether there is a relevant interest group or society in his local area. Again, by being proactive, he can make this a satisfying time. Any Fire Dog who would welcome the chance to get to know new people or would enjoy trying out a new pursuit should also investigate what is available in their area. Horse years can be times of exciting possibility. For Fire Dogs who start the year feeling lonely and unfulfilled in particular, it really would be worth making a special effort to go out more and find activities or groups to join.

The Fire Dog will welcome the social opportunities of the year and once again enjoy his chances to chat with his friends and exchange ideas. If he has any concerns, a friend may have some first-hand knowledge which could help. In this active and interesting year, the Fire Dog does need to be forthcoming so that he can benefit from the assistance and encouragement available to him. April to early June, September and December could see some interesting social occasions.

The active nature of the Horse year will also filter through to the Fire Dog's home life. Here again, a lot can happen quickly, and once certain plans and projects have been proposed, circumstances will often help them along. In fact, when one project is finished, it will often lead on to another. By the end of the year, many changes and improvements will have been made.

During the year the Fire Dog will also give valuable assistance to younger relations. When they are facing difficult decisions or are under pressure, his support will be particularly welcome. However, if any domestic or personal matter is of particular concern to the Fire Dog over the year, he should consider talking to a professional and remember that additional help is there should he require it.

Overall, the Year of the Horse will be a busy but interesting one for the Fire Dog. By following through his ideas and using his time well, he will be pleased with what he does. New possibilities will open up and the Fire Dog should make the most of them. His family and social life will, as always, be important to him, and with the support of others he can benefit all the more from the pleasing opportunities that will come his way.

Tip for the Year

Act with determination and make the most of your hopes and ideas. Also, be receptive to sudden opportunities. With a determined and willing attitude, you can make this a satisfying year.

The Earth Dog

There is a Chinese proverb that is especially apt for the Earth Dog this year: 'Perseverance will guarantee success.' This can be an auspicious year for him and by setting about his activities in his usual determined way, he can enjoy good results.

An encouraging aspect will be the way the Earth Dog will be able to build on recent developments. This is a year for moving forward, and for any Earth Dogs who start the year dissatisfied and unfulfilled, it is also a time to put the past behind them, focus their attention on the present and resolve to improve their situation. Horse years have energy and potential and in this one the Earth Dog's efforts can bring positive change.

At work this is a time of important developments. Change and innovation characterize Horse years, and new opportunities will arise as new systems and initiatives are introduced and requirements change. Many Earth Dogs will find themselves very much involved in what is happening and well placed to benefit. With the experience they have behind them, this may include taking on greater responsibilities and securing promotion.

For Earth Dogs who decide to move on from where they are, perhaps in search of a new challenge, as well as those seeking work, the Horse year can again open up interesting possibilities. To benefit fully, these Earth Dogs should widen the scope of what they are prepared to consider. In some instances, they will find that by adapting their skills and using their experience in new ways, they can gain entry into a different type of work and give their career fresh impetus. Some may also benefit from government initiatives or retraining opportunities. February, April, June to mid-July and November could see important developments, but in this fast-moving year opportunities could arise at almost any time and need to be acted upon without delay.

Progress at work can lead to a rise in income and many Earth Dogs will also benefit from a bonus or gift. However, the Earth Dog will need to keep a close watch on spending as well as make allowance for more major outgoings. Good financial management will make an important difference this year. The Earth Dog should also be thorough when dealing with financial correspondence and keep important documents and other possessions safe. A mistake or loss could inconvenience him. Earth Dogs, take note.

With travel favourably aspected, the Earth Dog should, if possible, try to budget for a holiday this year. A change of scene could bring him great pleasure. With opportunities arising quickly in the Horse year, he may decide to go away on the spur of the moment or take advantage of a last-minute travel offer. He may also find events in his local area of interest, but again, to benefit fully he does need to act.

Horse years encourage experimentation and there can also be excellent chances for the Earth Dog to develop his personal interests or even take up a new one and so introduce something new into his lifestyle.

His home life will see a lot happening during the year and there will need to be flexibility over arrangements and some latitude as changes take place. Here the Earth Dog's attentive and understanding nature can be a real asset. However, while a busy year, it will also contain some special moments. Not only will the Earth Dog's own progress delight his loved ones (particularly as they know how much it means to him), but there could also be a particular milestone to mark and some special

family news to enjoy, perhaps the academic success of a younger relation. Mutual interests, occasional treats and possible holiday will also
be appreciated and can help to bring balance to busy lifestyles.

The Earth Dog should also make the most of his social opportunities,
as these too can add balance to his life as well as bring him pleasure.
Any Earth Dog who is feeling lonely or dispirited will find that activities
in his local area can lead to new friendships being made. The Horse year
encourages a positive 'can do' spirit and if the Earth Dog shows willing,
it can reward him well. April to early June, September and December
could see the most social activity.

Overall the Horse year can be an active and promising one for the
Earth Dog and by persevering and making the most of himself, he can
enjoy some deserved success. He has much to offer and the Horse year
will open up some interesting possibilities for him.

Tip for the Year
Go forward and make the most of your ideas and opportunities. You
can accomplish a great deal this year. However, do keep your lifestyle in
balance and preserve some time for your personal interests and those
who are special to you.

Famous Dogs

King Albert II of Belgium, Brigitte Bardot, Gary Barlow, Candice Bergen,
Justin Bieber, Andrea Bocelli, David Bowie, George W. Bush, the Duke
of Cambridge, Naomi Campbell, Fabio Capello, Mariah Carey, King
Carl Gustaf XVI of Sweden, José Carreras, Paul Cézanne, Cher, Sir
Winston Churchill, Bill Clinton, Leonard Cohen, Matt Damon, Charles
Dance, Claude Debussy, Dame Judi Dench, Kirsten Dunst, Dakota
Fanning, Joseph Fiennes, Robert Frost, Ava Gardner, Judy Garland,
George Gershwin, Anne Hathaway, O. Henry, Victor Hugo, Barry
Humphries, Holly Hunter, Michael Jackson, Al Jolson, Jennifer Lopez,
Sophia Loren, Andie MacDowell, Shirley MacLaine, Madonna, Norman
Mailer, Barry Manilow, Freddie Mercury, Nicki Minaj, Liza Minnelli,

Simon Pegg, Sydney Pollack, Elvis Presley, Tim Robbins, Andy Roddick, Susan Sarandon, Claudia Schiffer, Dr Albert Schweitzer, Matt Smith, Sylvester Stallone, Robert Louis Stevenson, Sharon Stone, Donald Sutherland, Chris Tarrant, Mother Teresa, Uma Thurman, Donald Trump, Voltaire, Lil Wayne, Shelley Winters.

16 February 1923 to 4 February 1924 — *Water Pig*

4 February 1935 to 23 January 1936 — *Wood Pig*

22 January 1947 to 9 February 1948 — *Fire Pig*

8 February 1959 to 27 January 1960 — *Earth Pig*

27 January 1971 to 14 February 1972 — *Metal Pig*

13 February 1983 to 1 February 1984 — *Water Pig*

31 January 1995 to 18 February 1996 — *Wood Pig*

18 February 2007 to 6 February 2008 — *Fire Pig*

The Pig

The Personality of the Pig

It's the doing,
the giving,
the playing the part,
that makes life what it is.
And what it can be.

The Pig is born under the sign of honesty. He has a kind and understanding nature and is well known for his abilities as a peacemaker. He hates any sort of discord or unpleasantness and will do everything in his power to sort out differences of opinion or bring opposing factions together.

He is also an excellent conversationalist and speaks truthfully and to the point. He dislikes any form of falsehood or hypocrisy and is a firm believer in justice and the maintenance of law and order. In spite of these beliefs, however, he is reasonably tolerant and often prepared to forgive others for their wrongdoings. He rarely harbours grudges and is never vindictive.

The Pig is usually very popular. He enjoys other people's company and likes to be involved in joint or group activities. He will be a loyal member of any club or society and can be relied upon to lend a helping hand at functions. He is also an excellent fundraiser for charities and is often a great supporter of humanitarian causes.

The Pig is a hard and conscientious worker and is particularly respected for his reliability and integrity. In his early years he will try his hand at several different jobs, but he is usually happiest where he feels that he is being of service to others. He will unselfishly give up his time for the common good and is highly valued by his colleagues and employers.

The Pig has a good sense of humour and invariably has a smile, joke or some whimsical remark at the ready. He loves to entertain and to please others, and there are many Pigs who have been attracted to careers in show business or who enjoy following the careers of famous stars and personalities.

There are, unfortunately, some who take advantage of the Pig's good nature and impose upon his generosity. The Pig has great difficulty in saying 'no', and although he may dislike being firm, it would be in his own interests to say occasionally, 'Enough is enough.' He can also be rather naïve and gullible; however, if at any stage in his life he feels that he has been badly let down, he will try to become self-reliant. There are many Pigs who have become entrepreneurs or forged a successful career on their own after some early disappointment in life. Although the Pig tends to spend his money quite freely, he is usually very astute in financial matters and there are many Pigs who have become wealthy.

Another characteristic of the Pig is his ability to recover from setbacks reasonably quickly. His faith and his strength of character keep him going. If he thinks that there is a job he can do or there is something that he wants to achieve, he will pursue it with dogged determination. He can also be stubborn and no matter how many may plead with him, once he has made his mind up he will rarely change his views.

Although the Pig may work hard, he also knows how to enjoy himself. He is a great pleasure-seeker and will quite happily spend his hard-earned money on a lavish holiday or an expensive meal – for the Pig is a connoisseur of good food and wine – or a variety of recreational activities. He also enjoys small social gatherings and if he is in company he likes he can very easily become the life and soul of the party. He does, however, tend to become rather withdrawn at larger functions or when among strangers.

The Pig is a creature of comfort and his home will usually be fitted with the latest in luxury appliances. Where possible, he will prefer to live in the country rather than the town and will opt to have a big garden, for the Pig is usually a keen and successful gardener.

The Pig is very popular with others and will often have numerous romances before he settles down. Once settled, however, he will be loyal to his partner and he will find that he is especially well suited to those born under the signs of the Goat, Rabbit, Dog and Tiger and also to another Pig. Due to his affable and easy-going nature he can also establish a satisfactory relationship with all the remaining signs of the Chinese zodiac, with the exception of the Snake. The Snake tends to be wily, secretive and very guarded, and this can be intensely irritating to the honest and open-hearted Pig.

The female Pig will devote all her energies to the needs of her children and her partner. She will try to ensure that they want for nothing and their pleasure is very much her pleasure. She can be a caring and conscientious parent and has very good taste in clothes. Her home will either be very clean and orderly or hopelessly untidy. Strangely, there seems to be no in-between with Pigs – they either love housework or detest it! The female Pig does, however, have considerable talents as an organizer and this, combined with her friendly and open manner, enables her to secure many of her objectives.

The Pig is usually lucky in life and will rarely want for anything. Provided he does not let others take advantage of his good nature and is not afraid of asserting himself, he will go through life making friends, helping others and winning the admiration of many.

The Five Different Types of Pig

In addition to the 12 signs of the Chinese zodiac there are five elements and these have a strengthening or moderating influence on the signs. The effects of the five elements on the Pig are described below, together with the years in which they were exercising their influence. Therefore Pigs born in 1971 are Metal Pigs, Pigs born in 1923 and 1983 are Water Pigs, and so on.

Metal Pig: 1971

The Metal Pig is more ambitious and determined than some of the other types of Pig. He is strong, energetic and likes to be involved in a wide variety of different activities. He is very open and forthright in his views, although he can be a little too trusting at times and has a tendency to accept things at face value. He has a good sense of humour and loves to attend parties and other social gatherings. He has a warm, outgoing nature and usually has a large circle of friends.

Water Pig: 1923, 1983

The Water Pig has a heart of gold. He is generous and loyal and tries to remain on good terms with everyone. He will do his utmost to help others, but sadly there are some who will take advantage of his kind nature and he should, in his own interests, be a little more discriminating and be prepared to stand firm against anything that he does not like. Although he prefers the quieter things in life, he has a wide range of interests. He particularly enjoys outdoor pursuits and attending parties and social occasions. He is a hard and conscientious worker and invariably does well in his chosen profession. He is also gifted in the art of communication.

Wood Pig: 1935, 1995

This Pig has a friendly, persuasive manner and is easily able to gain the confidence of others. He likes to be involved in all that is going on around him but can sometimes take on more responsibility than he can properly handle. He is loyal to his family and friends and derives much pleasure from helping those less fortunate than himself. He is usually an optimist and leads a very full, enjoyable and satisfying life. He also has a good sense of humour.

Fire Pig: 1947, 2007

The Fire Pig is both energetic and adventurous and sets about everything he does in a confident and resolute manner. He is very forthright in his views and does not mind taking risks in order to achieve his objectives. He can, however, get carried away by the excitement of the moment and ought to exercise more caution in some of the enterprises in which he gets involved. He is usually lucky in money matters and is well known for his generosity. He is also very caring towards the members of his family.

Earth Pig: 1959

This Pig has a kindly nature. He is sensible and realistic and will go to great lengths in order to please his employers and to secure his aims and ambitions. He is an excellent organizer and is particularly astute in business and financial matters. He has a good sense of humour and a wide circle of friends. He also likes to lead an active social life, although he does sometimes have a tendency to eat and drink more than is good for him.

Prospects for the Pig in 2014

The Pig has great determination and resolve, but while his character and qualities can take him far, he may have met with difficulties in the Snake year. Despite his actions, his progress could have been disappointing and his relations with others could have caused him some anguish. The Snake year (10 February 2013–30 January 2014) is never the easiest for the Pig, and in what remains of it he will need to be alert and on his mettle.

In his home and personal life it is especially important that he liaises well with those around him and shows some flexibility. Pigs mean well and hate disharmony, but without increased mindfulness at this time, problems could arise. Similarly, in social situations a *faux pas* or lapse could cause difficulties and the Pig needs to be careful not to jeopardize his good standing. Snake years can cause problems for the unwary.

At work the pressures could be considerable and some Pigs will feel they have an unjustifiably high workload and/or will have to grapple with complex situations. However, it is situations like these that can give the Pig the chance to show his capabilities and gain the experience he can build on in the next Chinese year. All Pigs, whether in work or seeking it, should take advantage of training opportunities or look at other ways in which they could develop their skills. Any positive action they take now can prove significant in 2014.

Overall, the Year of the Snake will have been a demanding one, but the Pig is robust and although he may feel bruised by the Snake year's difficulties and pressures, he knows he has it in him to prevail. Pleasingly, the aspects are about to swing back in his favour.

'Fortune turns like a wheel' and in the Horse year the Pig's fortunes are set to greatly improve. Not only will many Pigs now feel more determined and optimistic about their prospects but they will also benefit from some of the opportunities the year will bring. Success often follows on from a time of struggle and this is what many Pigs will experience this year. The Snake year will have tested them, but the Horse year, which begins on 31 January, will deliver fresh opportunities and reward. It is a time for some deserved success.

To help get the year off to a positive start, the Pig would do well to think ahead and work out what he would like to see happen over the next 12 months. Having some aims to work towards will not only help him channel his energies more effectively but also underline the constructive nature of the year. This is a time for positive action.

The Pig's work prospects are particularly promising. Being astute (the Pig does have a good business brain) and a hard worker, he will be keen to seek out opportunities to better himself and move his career forward. Whether he decides to remain with his present employer or look elsewhere, by keeping alert for openings and considering possibilities, including using his experience in new ways or in a different industry, he could be surprised by how soon opportunities come his way. Horse years encourage progress and the Pig can be a main beneficiary.

For Pigs who decide on a career change or are seeking work, the Horse year can prove a significant juncture in their working life. While the employment situation may be difficult, the Pig's determination, self-belief and drive will often make him a strong candidate. It will take effort and initiative to secure a position, but once given a chance, even if on a temporary or trial basis, the Pig can quickly establish himself. February to early April, September and October could see encouraging developments, but generally this is a year for the Pig to keep alert, as chances could occur at almost any time.

Progress made at work will also help financially, but the Pig will need to be disciplined. Without care, any extra money could quickly be spent, and not always in the best way. To help, the Pig should closely monitor his spending and plan ahead for more major outgoings. In addition, he should be wary of risk or making informal agreements with others. He does have a trusting nature, but in 2014 he needs to be thorough and careful and manage his finances well.

In setting about his various activities, the Pig is usually conscientious and gives a lot of himself. However, while the aspects this year are encouraging, he needs to give himself some regular 'me time' too. As well as spending time on pursuits he enjoys, he should also give some thought to his general well-being, including paying attention to the quality and quantity of his diet. To ignore this, or perhaps overindulge, could leave him susceptible to minor ailments or feeling below his best. Some attention to his lifestyle could be very helpful this year.

The Pig's social life is well aspected and his genial nature will yet again make him popular company. He will have the chance to meet quite a few new people over the course of the year and, in the process, make new friends and build up some useful connections. April, May, August and December could see the most social opportunities.

For the unattached, this can be an exciting year with excellent chance of romance. For some, a chance encounter could sweep them off their feet and result in a sudden and glorious love affair. However, while some Pigs will find their soul mate and life partner, others may find that certain relationships were not meant to be. Yet in this fast-moving year, those who experience romantic disappointment can soon find love again. Horse years can be very eventful concerning affairs of the heart and many unattached Pigs will revel in the romantic opportunities that come their way.

The Pig attaches great importance to his home life and this again will see considerable activity. In view of some of the choices his loved ones will face this year, he will often be glad to advise, and his experience and wise counsel will do a lot to help. In addition, with his capacity for fun, the Pig will often be the instigator of some fine family occasions and his thoughtfulness will add to the quality and variety of home life. There will also be memorable moments to enjoy and successes to celebrate. However, the year will be a full one, and when undertaking practical projects or home maintenance tasks, the Pig does need to allow sufficient time for the work to be completed. Certain projects could be lengthier and more disruptive than anticipated. Pigs, take note.

Overall, the Year of the Horse holds good prospects for the Pig and if he acts with determination, he can make progress and enjoy his achievements. Throughout the year he should be open to opportunity, and while this can involve change, a lot that happens this year will work out as if it was meant to be. The Horse year can be a full one and, with personal relations and romance favourably aspected, an enjoyable one too.

The Metal Pig

There are lean years, good years and some that are middling. For the Metal Pig this will be one of the better ones. For Metal Pigs who have been disappointed with recent progress, it can herald a welcome improvement. However, to benefit fully the Metal Pig will need to be flexible in outlook and embrace change. Some of what happens this year may not be quite what he had in mind, but by being prepared to adapt, learn and make the most of his situation, he can do well. In addition, with 2015 being another good year, quite a few of his achievements now will lay the foundation for further success.

In recent times the Metal Pig will have seen a lot happen in his work. There will have been successes, but also some letdowns and disappointments. However, while the Metal Pig will have experienced some knocks, he will have added considerably to his experience and gained new insights into his strengths and capabilities. As the Horse year begins he should resolve to make more of himself. This is a time for growth and progress.

Throughout the year Metal Pigs in a large organization and/or pursuing a particular career will find it worth keeping alert for vacancies. Even if these are in a different section or involve duties that are substantially different from what they are doing now, by being prepared to extend their capabilities many of these Metal Pigs could succeed in giving their career new momentum. They will also be helped by their reputation and in-house contacts.

Metal Pigs seeking work will also find that by being prepared to adapt and learn, not only can they secure a new opening but also find the duties they take on widening their options for the future. February to early April and September to early November could see some interesting developments, but such is the nature of these times that many who take on a new position early in 2014 could find they have the chance to add to their responsibilities later on in the year or early in 2015.

Progress at work can also lead to an increase in income. However, the Metal Pig may have many outgoings and during the year he will need to be disciplined and make allowance for more major plans. Without careful budgeting, some may have to be reviewed or put back. He also needs to be careful if he lends money to another person as well as when dealing with financial paperwork. While his income may improve, his finances can benefit from good management.

With this being a year favouring development, the Metal Pig should also give some consideration to his personal interests. By setting himself some interesting goals, he can derive considerable satisfaction from what he does. Metal Pigs who feel their life has lacked sparkle in recent times would do well to consider taking up a new activity, possibly something very different from what they have done before. The Horse year can bring some good and sometimes unexpected possibilities.

Metal Pigs who tend to be sedentary for much of the day and lack regular exercise would also find it worth addressing this in the Horse year. A new and appropriate keep-fit activity could be of benefit as well as pleasurable to do.

The Metal Pig already knows a great many people and can enjoy a further increase in social activity this year. The Horse year can give him an interesting mix of things to do and late March to May, August and December could be the busiest months.

For unattached Metal Pigs, the Horse year is full of romantic possibilities. Those who have been feeling lonely or had some recent personal difficulty could find a chance meeting transforming their year, or even life. Horse years can have far-reaching significance.

The Metal Pig's home life will also be busy, with many calls on his time. Both younger and more senior relations could be particularly grateful for his assistance, especially concerning decisions they may have to make. With changes to routine likely, some domestic adjustments will be needed, and flexibility and understanding will be required while new arrangements take shape. It is also important that time is preserved for shared interests and there can also be good travel opportunities during the year.

Overall, a lot can happen in the Horse year and by looking to build on his current situation, the Metal Pig can often benefit. He is very much in the driving seat this year and can enjoy some overdue rewards. Relations with others are excellently aspected and for the unattached, the year is rich in romantic possibility.

Tip for the Year

Be open-minded and prepared to take on something new. This is a period of growth and you will have good opportunities to develop your strengths. Also, keep your lifestyle in balance and preserve time for those who are special to you. This can be a favourable year. Use it well.

The Water Pig

The Water Pig is conscientious and caring. As a result, when things are not going his way, he feels this deeply and can worry over his situation. However, in the Horse year his prospects are much improved and he will be able to put some of his problems and disappointments behind him. This is a year to focus on the present rather than feel hindered by what has gone before.

The Horse year is one of growth and will bring the Water Pig some excellent chances to develop his skills. Whether in his work or his interests, he should look to build on his strengths and invest in himself and his future. As he adds to his knowledge, new ideas can occur and new possibilities open up. A lot that the Water Pig does this year can have knock-on effects, and by furthering his skills, he will be helping create chances.

This emphasis on development will be especially evident in his work situation. Water Pigs who have been in the same position for some time will often find their in-depth knowledge leading to the offer of promotion. This may be something the Water Pig has been working towards for some time.

For Water Pigs who are dissatisfied in their present type of work, or seeking work, again the Horse year can bring interesting developments. To help their chances, these Water Pigs should widen the scope of positions they are prepared to consider as well as think of ways in which they can use and adapt their strengths. By showing determination and actively pursuing vacancies, quite a few will secure what can be a significant opportunity. Considerable learning may be involved, but with this being a year favouring development, skills and experience gained now can prove very helpful to longer-term prospects. February to early April, September and October could see encouraging developments, but throughout the Horse year when these Water Pigs see an opportunity they should act quickly.

Progress made at work can also help financially, but with existing commitments and expensive plans, the Water Pig will need to keep a close watch on outgoings. If he enters into an agreement he also needs to check the terms and be fully aware of the obligations and implications. This is a year when he needs to be thorough.

Personal interests are favourably aspected and the Water Pig will again have good opportunities to develop his skills and ideas. With the Pig being traditionally an enterprising sign, some Water Pigs may also find a way to turn a hobby or interest into a profitable sideline. Others could be attracted to a new interest this year or find an existing one opening up new possibilities. With a willing approach, the Water Pig can enjoy and often benefit from what he does over the year.

Being sociable and outgoing, he will also make the most of his chances to meet new people. These may come through changes in his work situation and, if appropriate, he should also make the most of any networking opportunities. With his ability to connect with others and put himself across well, he can do his prospects considerable good. His interests and existing group of friends can also introduce him to new people and the year will contain a good mix of social occasions. For the unattached, affairs of the heart can also add excitement. April, May, August and December could see the most social activity.

The Water Pig's home life will also be busy and he will need to be well-organized and concentrate on priorities. Rather than take on too much by himself, he does need to involve others. Joint effort will lead to far more happening as well as help ease certain pressures. In addition some family members may be able to assist the Water Pig in sometimes unexpected ways. Throughout the year, he does need to be open and forthcoming. If a parent, he will also be keen to support and guide his children and their achievements can strengthen the special family bonds the Water Pig enjoys.

Overall, the Horse year holds good prospects for the Water Pig. In view of the changes likely to take place and the plans he will be keen to realize, some parts of it will be demanding, but he will have excellent opportunities to further his skills and this will benefit him both now and in the near future. He will be helped by the support and encouragement of others and his home and social life will be busy but rewarding. A year of fine possibility and important personal growth.

Tip for the Year

Organize your time well and focus on what you want to achieve. Much is possible this year but it will require effort, commitment and dedication. Believe in yourself. You have considerable talents. Use them well.

The Wood Pig

The Chinese proverb reminds us, 'Learning is like a rapid journey – you can't pause for even a moment.' This will hold true for many a Wood Pig in this busy and potentially important year.

During it, a lot will be expected of the Wood Pig and he will need to use his time well. He also needs to focus on his objectives – should he slacken or drift, disappointments could loom. As far as his development – and future – are concerned, as the Chinese proverb suggests, 'You can't pause for even a moment.' Horse years are ones for effort and commitment.

For the many Wood Pigs in education this can be an especially important time. Quite a few will be starting new courses and studying subjects in greater depth. There will be a lot to take in and the Wood Pig will need to organize and structure his work. He will also need to be disciplined, especially as there could be many distractions around him. However, by working well and keeping in mind what his studies can lead to, he can make good headway and prepare himself for future opportunities.

The Horse year can have some curious twists and turns, however. There may be some Wood Pigs who start out on a particular course and then feel it is not right for them, while others could, by chance, discover they have a special talent for something they are now studying. In these and other instances, the Wood Pig should look to do what is right for him and then build on it over the year. Some of what occurs now can have far-reaching significance.

This also applies to the Wood Pig's personal interests. Some Wood Pigs may have the opportunity to try a new pursuit or decide to make more of a particular skill or idea, and by being eager and willing to learn, they can look forward to some encouraging results. In addition, it would be worth these Wood Pigs heeding any advice given by those with experience, especially if they are to take their interests further.

For those who enjoy more active pursuits, the Horse year can bring some exciting possibilities. Whether travelling, enjoying sporting and outdoor activities or setting themselves an interesting personal challenge, these Wood Pigs should take full advantage of what opens up for them.

The Wood Pig's social life will also see a lot of activity this year. Wood Pigs who change their location will have excellent opportunities to establish a new social circle and some friendships will quickly be made. For Wood Pigs who perhaps feel daunted by the year's changes, new friendships can be particularly reassuring. Horse years are very supportive of Wood Pigs, however, and many will enjoy a lively social life laced with romantic possibility. April, May, August and December could see the most social activity, although at most times of the year the Wood Pig will have parties and other occasions to look forward to.

For Wood Pigs in work or seeking work, the Horse year can see significant developments. Those already in a position will often be affected by change, including alterations to their workload and responsibilities. As a consequence, the pressure will increase and the Wood Pig may not always feel comfortable with what has taken place. By rising to the challenge, however, he will impress others, and the skills he gains can be something he can build on in the future. Horse years are demanding, but will enable many Wood Pigs to demonstrate their potential.

Wood Pigs seeking work will also be helped by their resolute nature. Not only should these determined Wood Pigs act quickly when they see a vacancy that appeals to them, but also take advantage of the support that is available. This can include assistance with applications and interview techniques and also employment or training initiatives. By drawing on this support and being active in the job-seeking process, many Wood Pigs will be successful in their quest. The main benefits of the year, however, will come through proving to themselves and others what they can do. February to early April, September and October could see encouraging developments.

Throughout the year the Wood Pig should also avail himself of the support that family members are able to give. Although he may have his own ideas, by talking over his choices and listening to advice, he could be alerted to other possibilities and be grateful of the help he receives. In return, some practical assistance he gives more senior relations could be particularly appreciated. The Wood Pig's family bonds are strong, and the support, affection and goodwill of those close to him will be an encouraging factor this year.

Financially, however, with an active social life, various interests, travel possibilities and the purchases he wants to make, the Wood Pig will need to budget wisely. With care, he will be able to carry out a lot of his plans, but it will require discipline. If entering into an agreement, he also needs to check the terms carefully. Financial matters cannot be left to chance this year.

Overall, the Year of the Horse will be a busy and eventful one for the Wood Pig. He will enjoy an often lively social life and some surprise opportunities could also come his way. Of paramount importance, however, will be the opportunity he will have to gain experience. With commitment and discipline, he can do his prospects a lot of good. A year of encouraging developments.

Tip for the Year
Use your time well and be disciplined and organized. Also, draw on the support available to you. With encouragement and good advice, you can learn a lot this year.

The Fire Pig

The Fire Pig likes to involve himself in a great many things. Whether pursuing his own interests, carrying out projects around the home or assisting others, he invariably has something worthwhile to do. This active and encouraging year will be no exception.

A particular feature of the year will be the way many of the Fire Pig's activities develop. Once he decides on a course of action, it will often get an early and unexpected boost. Luck can play a big part in his achievements this year.

As he considers his ideas, the Fire Pig should also talk them through with his loved ones. This way he can not only be given useful assistance but may also find that suggestions others make can make the activity easier or the outcome more assured.

His home life will be especially rewarding and he will be pleased by how his plans develop during the course of the year. These may include home projects and improvements made to living areas. Many Fire Pigs will also be keen to purchase new equipment and will spend a lot of time looking at different possibilities before making their final decisions. The Horse year is very much one for going ahead with plans.

The Fire Pig will also do much to assist his loved ones. He will take a keen interest in their activities and give much useful support, especially to younger relations. His ability to look at situations objectively will be appreciated and those around him will often value his words. The Fire Pig has a perceptive and caring nature and others do recognize this.

The Horse year has an element of spontaneity to it and on several occasions the Fire Pig could be invited to social occasions or to visit others at short notice. He could also be tempted by some last-minute travel opportunities. By being flexible and making the most of what arises, he will often delight in the variety of activities this year makes possible.

His personal interests can also be a source of great pleasure, and while he may already have considerable knowledge about a particular subject or pursuit, over the year he should look to extend this. Whether through reading, experimenting or meeting other enthusiasts, by taking his interests further, he can make this an especially interesting time. Fire Pigs who favour creative activities could be particularly encouraged by the response they receive, while Fire Pigs who enjoy gardening and/or like being out of doors will again find what they do bringing them pleasure and often other benefits too.

The Fire Pig's social life is favourably aspected and if he is a member of a group or society, he could find himself being invited to do more. Fire Pigs who would welcome a chance to meet others would find joining a local group or helping their community in some way well worth considering. The Horse year can give rise to quite a few pleasurable social occasions and the Fire Pig's genial manner will make him popular company. April, May, August and December could see the most social activity.

With all the activities the Fire Pig involves himself in and the plans he is eager to carry out, he will, however, need to keep careful control over his spending. Also, if he has any doubts or questions concerning possible purchases or new undertakings, he should get these resolved before proceeding. He does need to be thorough this year. This also applies to financial correspondence.

In most respects, this will be an active and agreeable year for the Fire Pig. In many of his activities he will not only be supported by others but also benefit from new opportunities. In 2014 he will have a lot working in his favour, including an element of luck. He will be pleased with how his domestic projects and personal interests develop and his relations with others can be particularly meaningful. The caring and considerate Fire Pig will be able to use his abilities to good effect in this fine and encouraging year.

Tip for the Year

This is a year for setting about your plans in earnest. Once you start, a lot can follow on. However, do be receptive to what others say and to ways in which they can help. This is a year favouring a joint approach and your relations with others can be special, both domestically and socially. Value them.

The Earth Pig

With his wide interests and an outgoing nature, the Earth Pig likes to keep himself active. He is also very alert and when he detects an opportunity, he is prepared to take it and see what happens. In 2014 his enterprising nature can reward him well. He will also be helped by the good relations he enjoys with many people.

In his work this can be an especially significant time. Many Earth Pigs will not only have demonstrated their skills in recent years but also built up valuable experience. As changes are introduced in this fast-moving year, opportunities can arise and these Earth Pigs find themselves excellently placed to benefit. Chances can also come from meeting other people connected to their industry.

Earth Pigs who decide to move on from where they are can also find other people particularly helpful, either in offering advice or alerting them to possibilities worth considering. With their background and reputation, many can successfully make the move and revel in the chance to develop their career in an often different way.

For Earth Pigs seeking work, the Horse year can also open up interesting possibilities. Although the employment situation may be difficult, by remaining alert and keeping in regular contact with employment agencies, they could find themselves in the right place at the right time when a new vacancy arises or a company decides to recruit. To benefit, the Earth Pig will need to act quickly and be prepared to adapt, but he may well be offered a fresh start and an interesting new challenge this year. February to early April and September to early November could see some interesting work developments.

The progress the Earth Pig makes at work, together with his enterprising ideas, can also lead to an increase in income. However, the Earth Pig will still need to manage his financial situation well and keep an eye on his outgoings. Without control, anything extra could quickly be spent, and not always in the best way. The Earth Pig also needs to be thorough with important correspondence and wary of entering into any new commitments without fully checking the terms and implications. This may be a financially improved year, but it is not one for carelessness, rush or risk.

Personal interests are favourably aspected this year and some Earth Pigs may find a skill or specialist knowledge allowing them to supplement their income. For the more enterprising, this is something worth exploring. However, no matter where the Earth Pig's interests lie, during the year he should allow himself time for activities he enjoys. Many Earth Pigs will find the Horse year an inspiring time and some may be attracted by a new interest or recreational activity and appreciate the chance to try something different.

Travel is also well aspected and if possible the Earth Pig should try to take a holiday with his loved ones over the year. He may be able to combine a holiday with a particular interest or a visit to a certain attraction and this could be among this year's highlights.

Many of the Earth Pig's activities can have a pleasing social element, and new interests and changes in his work situation can also introduce him to new people. His genial manner will bring him many new friends and acquaintances, and for the unattached, especially those who have had some recent personal difficulty, the Horse year can see a distinct brightening in their situation, with new friends, new activities and possibly new romance adding new meaning to their lives. April, May, August, December and January 2015 could see the most social activity.

The Earth Pig can also look forward to some special occasions in his home life, including the celebration of a family success or other event.

He will be very much at the heart of family life this year and his attentiveness and skill at bringing everyone together can make an important difference. Also, while he may not want to interfere, the support he may give a younger relation could be of more significance than he may realize.

In most respects, this will be a good year for the Earth Pig. In both his work and his personal interests, he will have opportunities to put his talents and ideas to greater use and his skills and enterprise will often reward him well. He will also be helped by the support he enjoys and his home and social life will bring him great pleasure this year. Overall, this is a fine year for him, but to fully benefit he does need to put himself forward, seize his opportunities and use his many abilities to good effect.

Tip for the Year
In this exciting and active year, do keep your lifestyle in balance. Also, value your relations with others. The help you receive can prove significant. You will also play an important part in the lives of those who are close to you, so take heart and move forward – your effort and enterprise can reap some well-deserved rewards this year.

Famous Pigs

Bryan Adams, Woody Allen, Julie Andrews, Marie Antoinette, Fred Astaire, Pam Ayres, Emily Blunt, Humphrey Bogart, James Cagney, Maria Callas, Samantha Cameron, Hillary Rodham Clinton, Glenn Close, Sacha Baron Cohen, Cheryl Cole, Alice Cooper, the Duchess of Cornwall, Noël Coward, Simon Cowell, Oliver Cromwell, Billy Crystal, the Dalai Lama, Ted Danson, Richard Dreyfuss, Ben Elton, Ralph Waldo Emerson, Henry Ford, Jonathan Franzen, Stephen Harper, Emmylou Harris, Ernest Hemingway, Chris Hemsworth, Henry VIII, Conrad Hilton, Alfred Hitchcock, Sir Elton John, Tommy Lee Jones, Carl Gustav Jung, Stephen King, Kevin Kline, Hugh Laurie, Nigella Lawson, David Letterman, Jerry Lee Lewis, Meat Loaf, Ewan McGregor, Ricky Martin, Johnny Mathis, Pippa Middleton, Dannii Minogue, Morrissey, Wolfgang

Amadeus Mozart, George Osborne, Sir Michael Parkinson, James Patterson, Luciano Pavarotti, Iggy Pop, Maurice Ravel, Ronald Reagan, Ginger Rogers, Winona Ryder, Françoise Sagan, Carlos Santana, Arnold Schwarzenegger, Steven Spielberg, Lord Sugar, David Tennant, Emma Thompson, Herman Van Rompuy, Jules Verne, David Walliams, the Duchess of York.

Appendix

The relationships between the 12 animal signs, both on a personal level and business level, are an important aspect of Chinese horoscopes and in this appendix the compatibility between the signs is shown in the two tables that follow.

Also included are the names of the signs ruling the hours of the day and from this it is possible to find your ascendant and discover yet another aspect of your personality.

Finally, to supplement the earlier chapters on the personality and horoscope of the signs, I have included a guide on how you can get the best out of your sign and the year.

Relationships between the Signs

Personal Relationships

Key

1. Excellent. Great rapport.
2. A successful relationship. Many interests in common.
3. Mutual respect and understanding. A good relationship.
4. Fair. Needs care and some willingness to compromise in order for the relationship to work.
5. Awkward. Possible difficulties in communication and few interests in common.
6. A clash of personalities. Very difficult.

	Rat	Ox	Tiger	Rabbit	Dragon	Snake	Horse	Goat	Monkey	Rooster	Dog	Pig
Rat	1											
Ox	1	3										
Tiger	4	6	5									
Rabbit	5	2	3	2								
Dragon	1	5	4	3	2							
Snake	3	1	6	2	1	5						
Horse	6	5	1	5	3	4	2					
Goat	5	5	3	1	4	3	2	2				
Monkey	1	3	6	3	1	3	5	3	1			
Rooster	5	1	5	6	2	1	2	5	5	5		
Dog	3	4	1	2	6	3	1	5	3	5	2	
Pig	2	3	2	2	2	6	3	2	2	3	1	2

Business Relationships

Key

1. Excellent. Marvellous understanding and rapport.
2. Very good. Complement each other well.
3. A good working relationship and understanding can be developed.
4. Fair, but compromise and a common objective are often needed to make this relationship work.
5. Awkward. Unlikely to work, either through lack of trust or understanding or the competitiveness of the signs.
6. Mistrust. Difficult. To be avoided.

	Rat	Ox	Tiger	Rabbit	Dragon	Snake	Horse	Goat	Monkey	Rooster	Dog	Pig
Rat	2											
Ox	1	3										
Tiger	3	6	5									
Rabbit	4	3	3	3								
Dragon	1	4	3	3	3							
Snake	3	2	6	4	1	5						
Horse	6	5	1	5	3	4	4					
Goat	5	5	3	1	4	3	3	2				
Monkey	2	3	4	5	1	5	4	4	3			
Rooster	5	1	5	5	2	1	2	5	5	6		
Dog	4	5	2	3	6	4	2	5	3	5	4	
Pig	3	3	3	2	3	5	4	2	3	4	3	1

Your Ascendant

The ascendant has a very strong influence on your personality and will help you gain an even greater insight into your true personality according to Chinese horoscopes.

The hours of the day are named after the 12 animal signs and the sign governing the time you were born is your ascendant. To find your ascendant, look up the time of your birth in the table below, bearing in mind any local time differences in the place you were born.

11 p.m.	to	1 a.m.	The hours of the Rat
1 a.m.	to	3 a.m.	The hours of the Ox
3 a.m.	to	5 a.m.	The hours of the Tiger
5 a.m.	to	7 a.m.	The hours of the Rabbit
7 a.m.	to	9 a.m.	The hours of the Dragon
9 a.m.	to	11 a.m.	The hours of the Snake
11 a.m.	to	1 p.m.	The hours of the Horse
1 p.m.	to	3 p.m.	The hours of the Goat
3 p.m.	to	5 p.m.	The hours of the Monkey
5 p.m.	to	7 p.m.	The hours of the Rooster
7 p.m.	to	9 p.m.	The hours of the Dog
9 p.m.	to	11 p.m.	The hours of the Pig

Rat

The Rat ascendant is likely to make the sign more outgoing, sociable and careful with money. A particularly beneficial influence for those born under the signs of the Rabbit, Horse, Monkey and Pig.

Ox

The Ox ascendant has a restraining, cautionary and steadying influence that many signs will benefit from. This ascendant also promotes self-confidence and willpower and is especially good for those born under the signs of the Tiger, Rabbit and Goat.

Tiger

The Tiger ascendant is a dynamic and stirring influence that makes the sign more outgoing, action-orientated and impulsive. A generally favourable ascendant for the Ox, Tiger, Snake and Horse.

Rabbit

The Rabbit ascendant has a moderating influence, making the sign more reflective, serene and discreet. A particularly beneficial influence for the Rat, Dragon, Monkey and Rooster.

Dragon

The Dragon ascendant gives strength, determination and ambition to the sign. A favourable influence for those born under the signs of the Rabbit, Goat, Monkey and Dog.

Snake

The Snake ascendant can make the sign more reflective, intuitive and self-reliant. A good influence for the Tiger, Goat and Pig.

Horse

The Horse ascendant will make the sign more adventurous, daring and on some occasions fickle. Generally a beneficial influence for the Rabbit, Snake, Dog and Pig.

Goat

The Goat ascendant will make the sign more tolerant, easy-going and receptive. It could also impart some creative and artistic qualities. An especially good influence for the Ox, Dragon, Snake and Rooster.

Monkey

The Monkey ascendant is likely to impart a delicious sense of humour and fun to the sign. It will make the sign more enterprising and outgoing – a particularly good influence for the Rat, Ox, Snake and Goat.

Rooster

The Rooster ascendant helps to give the sign a lively, outgoing and very methodical manner. Its influence will increase efficiency and is good for the Ox, Tiger, Rabbit and Horse.

Dog

The Dog ascendant makes the sign more reasonable and fair-minded and gives an added sense of loyalty. A very good ascendant for the Tiger, Dragon and Goat.

Pig

The Pig ascendant can make the sign more sociable and self-indulgent. It is also a caring influence and one that can make the sign want to help others. A good ascendant for the Dragon and Monkey.

How to Get the Best from your Chinese Sign and the Year

Each of the 12 Chinese signs possesses its own unique strengths and by identifying them you can use them to your advantage. Similarly, by becoming aware of possible weaknesses you can do much to rectify them and in this respect I hope the following sections will be useful. Also included are some tips on how you can get the best from the Year of the Horse.

The Rat

The Rat is blessed with many fine talents, but his undoubted strength lies in his ability to get on with people. He is sociable, charming and a good judge of character. He also possesses a shrewd mind and is good at spotting opportunities.

However, to make the most of his abilities, he does need to impose some discipline upon himself. He should resist the (sometimes very great) temptation of getting involved in too many activities all at the same time and should decide upon his priorities and objectives. By concentrating his energies on specific matters he will fare much better. Also, given his personable manner, he should seek out positions where he can use his personal relations skills to good effect. For a career, sales and marketing could prove ideal.

The Rat is astute in dealing with finance, but while often thrifty, he can sometimes give way to moments of indulgence. Although he deserves to enjoy the money he has so carefully earned, it would sometimes be in his interests to exercise restraint when tempted to satisfy too many expensive whims!

The Rat's family and friends are important to him and while he is loyal and protective towards them, he does tend to keep his worries and concerns to himself and would be helped if he were more willing to discuss his anxieties. Others think highly of him and are prepared to do a lot to help him, but for them to do so the Rat does need to be less guarded.

With his sharp mind, keen imagination and sociable manner, he does, however, have much in his favour. When he has commitment, he can be irrepressible and, given his considerable charm, often irresistible as well! Provided he channels his energies wisely, he can make much of his life.

ADVICE FOR THE RAT'S YEAR AHEAD

General Prospects

This is a year when the Rat will need to be on his mettle. Lapses, haste or risk can cause problems. However by remaining alert and putting in the effort, the Rat can prepare the way for the more successful times ahead, especially in 2015.

Career Prospects

Progress may not be easy, but the Rat will have an excellent chance to gain new skills and add to his experience. A demanding but constructive year.

Finance

The Rat needs to be thorough and keep a careful watch on spending. A year for discipline and good budgeting.

Relations with Others

Some memorable personal and family times can be enjoyed, but the Rat needs to be mindful of others – too much busyness and preoccupation could lead to problems. The more he is able to join with others, the more support will be forthcoming.

The Ox

Strong-willed and resolute, the Ox certainly has a mind of his own! He is persistent and sets about achieving his objectives with dogged determination. In addition he is reliable and tenacious and is often a source of inspiration to others. He is an achiever, and he often achieves a great deal. However, to really excel, he would do well to try and correct some of his weaknesses.

Being so resolute and having such a strong sense of purpose, the Ox can be inflexible and narrow-minded. He can be resistant to change and prefers to set about his activities in his own way rather than be dependent on others. His dislike of change can sometimes be to his detriment and if he were prepared to be more adaptable and adventurous he would find his progress easier.

The Ox would also be helped if he were to broaden his range of interests and become more relaxed in his approach. At times he can be so preoccupied with his own activities that he is not always as mindful of others as he should be, and his demeanour can sometimes be studious and serious. There are times when he would benefit from a lighter touch.

However, the Ox is true to his word and loyal to his family and friends. He is admired and respected by others and his tremendous will-power usually enables him to achieve a great deal in life.

ADVICE FOR THE OX'S YEAR AHEAD

General Prospects
The Ox may like to follow set patterns and procedures, but this year he will need to adapt to change. It will not always be an easy time, but his efforts can make it a personally rewarding one.

Career Prospects
An excellent year to be active and involved and to add to and adapt skills. What is accomplished now, often in the face of fast-moving developments, can pave the way for later progress.

Finance
With spending on accommodation and other expenses likely, the Ox will need to manage his outgoings with care. Large transactions should be carefully considered and risks avoided.

Relations with Others

This year the independent Ox does need to liaise closely with others. With their help and support, he can achieve – and enjoy – far more. He should also strive to keep his lifestyle in balance. Some attention to his own interests and well-being can make a difference to his year.

The Tiger

Lively, innovative and enterprising, the Tiger enjoys an active lifestyle. He has a wide range of interests, an alert mind and a genuine liking of other people. He loves to live life to the full. However, despite his enthusiastic and well-meaning ways, he does not always make the most of his considerable potential.

Being so versatile, the Tiger does have a tendency to jump from one activity to another or dissipate his energies by trying to do too much at the same time. To make the most of himself he should try to exercise a certain amount of self-discipline. Ideally, he should decide how best he can use his abilities, give himself some objectives and then stick to them. If he can overcome his restless tendencies, he will find he will accomplish far more.

Also, in spite of his sociable manner, the Tiger likes to retain a certain independence in his actions, and while few begrudge him this, he would sometimes find life easier if he were more prepared to work in conjunction with others. His reliance on his own judgement does sometimes mean that he excludes the views and advice of those around him, and this can be to his detriment. He may possess an independent spirit, but he must not let it go too far!

The Tiger does, however, have much in his favour. He is bold, original and quick-witted. If he can keep his restless nature in check, he can enjoy considerable success. In addition, with his engaging personality, he is well liked and much admired.

Advice for the Tiger's Year Ahead

General Prospects

The Tiger's enthusiasm and resourcefulness can lead to a lot happening this year, but he needs to be careful not to spread his energies too widely. With focus and application, he can make this a particularly rewarding time.

Career Prospects

A year to be alert and to seize opportunities. If frustrated, feeling held back or looking for a position, it would be worth the Tiger redoubling his efforts. With initiative and persistence, he can make significant progress.

Finance

The Tiger's enterprise and industry can be well rewarded this year and he could also enjoy an element of good fortune. Where possible, he does need to make early provision for expensive plans, but with care, good planning and control, he will be able to carry them through.

Relations with Others

An excellent year with good prospects of new friendships and romance. The Tiger will be on impressive form and his domestic life will be active and pleasurable. Occasionally consulting others, however, would be wise.

The Rabbit

The Rabbit is certainly one who appreciates the finer things in life. With his good taste, companionable nature and wide range of interests, he knows how to live well – and usually does!

However, for all his finesse and style, the Rabbit does possess traits he would do well to watch. His desire for a settled lifestyle makes him err on the side of caution. He dislikes change and as a consequence can miss out on opportunities. Also, there are many Rabbits who will go to great lengths to avoid difficult and fraught situations, and again, while few may relish these, sometimes in life it is necessary to take risks or stand your ground. At times it would certainly be in the Rabbit's interests to be bolder and more assertive in going after what he desires.

The Rabbit also attaches great importance to his relations with others and while he has a happy knack of getting on with most people, he can be sensitive to criticism. Difficult though it may be, he should really try to develop a thicker skin and recognize that criticism can provide valuable learning opportunities, as can some of the problems he strives so hard to avoid.

However, with his agreeable manner, keen intellect and shrewd judgement, the Rabbit does have a lot in his favour and invariably makes much of his life – and enjoys it too!

ADVICE FOR THE RABBIT'S YEAR AHEAD

General Prospects

An active and rewarding year, but with a lot happening quickly the Rabbit will need to remain alert and be swift to act. This is no time for delay or holding back. Fortune will favour the bold, enterprising and quick.

Career Prospects

A busy year with good opportunities for the Rabbit to make more of his skills. His ability to forge good working relations can also be useful and he should make the most of his networking opportunities. His efforts can reward him well and his accomplishments, including new skills, can enhance his future prospects. A progressive and often productive time.

Finance

The Rabbit can fare reasonably well, but needs to watch his outgoings. Expensive purchases should not be rushed and paperwork will require care and attention.

Relations with Others

An excellent year, with the Rabbit in demand and his domestic and social life both busy and pleasing. Romantic prospects are good and the support the Rabbit receives can make an important difference to his life and help him in many ways.

The Dragon

Enthusiastic, enterprising and honourable, the Dragon possesses many admirable qualities and his life is often full and varied. He always gives his best and even though not all his endeavours meet with success, he is nonetheless resilient and hardy, and is much admired and respected.

However, for all his qualities, the Dragon can be blunt and forthright and, through sheer strength of character, sometimes domineering. It would certainly be in his interests to listen more closely to others rather than be so self-reliant. Also, his enthusiasm can sometimes get the better of him and he can be impulsive. To make the most of his abilities, he should give himself priorities and set about his activities in a disciplined and systematic way. More tact and diplomacy might not come amiss either!

However, with his lively and outgoing manner, the Dragon is popular and well liked. With good fortune on his side (and the Dragon is often lucky), his life is almost certain to be eventful and fulfilling. He has many talents, and if he uses them wisely he will enjoy much success.

Advice for the Dragon's Year Ahead

General Prospects

Born under the sign of luck, the Dragon can do well this year. His efforts and resolve can certainly produce results, although he does need to keep alert, liaise with others and be thorough in his various undertakings. This may be a favourable year, but it is not one to push his luck too far.

Career Prospects

The Dragon will benefit from some excellent opportunities and may have the chance to take on a different type of work which can give his career a new lease of life. He does need to be receptive to what opens up and prepared to learn and adapt, but what he accomplishes now can be particularly helpful in the longer term.

Finance

The Dragon will have many plans for the year, especially accommodation-wise, and will need to be disciplined in his spending and budget ahead. His alert nature can lead to some shrewd purchasing decisions.

Relations with Others

The Dragon can gain a great deal from the support of those around him, but he does need to watch his independent tendencies. New friends and contacts can be helpful and romantic prospects are encouraging, but the Dragon does need to join forces with others rather than rely just on his own efforts.

The Snake

The Snake is blessed with a keen intellect. He has wide interests, an enquiring mind and good judgement. He tends to be quiet and thoughtful and plan his activities with considerable care. With his fine abilities he often does well in life, but he does possess traits which can undermine his progress.

The Snake is often guarded in his actions and sometimes loses out to those who are more action-oriented and assertive. He also likes to retain a certain independence in his actions and this too can hamper his progress. It would be in his interests to be more forthcoming and involve others more readily in his plans. The Snake has many talents and possesses a warm and rich personality, but there is a danger that this can remain concealed behind his often quiet and reserved manner. He would fare better if he were more outgoing and showed others his true worth.

However, the Snake is very much his own master. He invariably knows what he wants in life and is often prepared to journey long and hard to achieve his objectives. He does, though, have it in his power to make that journey easier. Lose some of that reticence, Snake, be more open and assertive, and do not be afraid of the occasional risk!

ADVICE FOR THE SNAKE'S YEAR AHEAD

General Prospects

The Snake may sometimes feel ill at ease with the pace of developments this year, but by making the most of emerging situations and furthering his skills and knowledge, he can benefit. This may be a challenging year, but it will bring some good opportunities.

Career Prospects

This can be an important year, with the Snake able to add to his skills and experience and further his position. The opportunities that arise may not always be what the Snake was anticipating and he may find his work developing in an unforeseen direction. To benefit fully, he needs to be adaptable and make the most of what happens.

Finance

Although a rise in income is likely, this can be an expensive year and the Snake needs to be disciplined in his spending and keep careful control of his budget. If possible, he should make allowance for a holiday – in this busy year, he deserves a break.

Relations with Others

The Snake can be greatly helped by the support of those around him, but does need to watch his independent Snake tendencies. This is no year to go it alone or to keep his ideas to himself – especially if they are to be realized. For the unattached, romance can be significant, but the Snake does need to be attentive and remain his honourable self. Lapses can cause problems. Generally, Horse years can be promising ones for personal relations, but the Snake needs to be alert and mindful.

The Horse

Versatile, hardworking and sociable, the Horse makes his mark wherever he goes. He has an eloquent and engaging manner and makes friends with ease. He is quick-witted, has an alert mind and is certainly not averse to taking risks or experimenting with new ideas.

He possesses a strong and likeable personality, but he does also have his weaknesses. With his wide interests he does not always finish everything he starts and he would do well to be more persevering. He has it within him to achieve considerable success, but to make the most of his talents he does need to overcome his restless tendencies. When he has made plans, he should stick with them.

The Horse loves company and values both his family and friends. However, there will have been many a time when he will have lost his temper or spoken in haste and regretted his words later. Throughout his life he needs to keep his temper in check and be diplomatic in tense situations, otherwise he could jeopardize the respect and good relations he so values.

However, the Horse has a multitude of talents and a lively and outgoing personality. If he can overcome his restless and volatile nature, he can lead a rich and highly fulfilling life.

ADVICE FOR THE HORSE'S YEAR AHEAD

General Prospects

With his drive, capabilities and personality, the Horse often sets his own agenda and in his own year he can benefit from a wide range of opportunities. However, he still needs to exercise care. Haste, risk or complacency could undermine his plans – and his reputation. This can be an excellent year, but it is still one to be aware and mindful of others.

Career Prospects

The Horse can make good headway this year and may take on different duties. He needs to keep alert for opportunities and grasp them when they come along. Fortune will favour the bold, active and enterprising.

Finance

Income may well increase this year, but for the Horse to do all he wants, he will need to be disciplined and control his budget wisely. Although he may be tempted, this is not a year for rush or risk.

Relations with Others

The Horse will benefit from the support of many people this year. He can also look forward to a busy home and social life and will see his social circle widening. Romantic prospects are also good. However, he does need to be attentive and watch his independent-mindedness. This can be a successful year and the support of others can make it even better.

The Goat

The Goat has a warm, friendly and understanding manner and gets on well with most people. He is generally easy-going, has a fond appreciation of the finer things in life and possesses a rich imagination. He is often artistic and enjoys the creative arts and outdoor activities.

However, despite his engaging manner, there lurks beneath his skin a sometimes tense and pessimistic nature. The Goat can be a worrier and without the support and encouragement of others can feel insecure and be hesitant in his actions.

To make the most of himself he should aim to become more assertive and decisive as well as more at ease with himself. He has much in his favour, but he really does need to promote himself more and be bolder. He would also be helped if he were to sort out his priorities and set about his activities in an organized and disciplined manner. There are some Goats who tend to be haphazard in the way they go about things and this can hamper their progress.

Although the Goat will always value the support of others, it would also be in his interest to become more independent and not be so reticent about striking out on his own. He does, after all, possess many talents, as well as a sincere and likeable personality, and by giving his best he can make his life rich, rewarding and enjoyable.

ADVICE FOR THE GOAT'S YEAR AHEAD

General Prospects

A successful year, but the Goat will need to be determined *and* act. This is no time to be reticent or hold back. With self-belief and resolve, and encouraged by the support of others, the Goat will be able to move forward and realize many of his ideas. A year of fine opportunity.

Career Prospects

Good progress can be made this year. Many Goats will make headway in their career and even take their work in a new direction. This can be an inspirational year, but the Goat will need to adapt as situations change, be bold, and make sure his ideas and talents count.

Finance

Income may improve, but with many plans and expenses likely, spending does need to be carefully watched. In all financial matters the Goat will need to be thorough and disciplined.

Relations with Others

The good relations the Goat enjoys with so many people will help and encourage him once more this year. However, he does need to be forthcoming and seek advice as situations change. He should also make the most of his chances to meet others socially and to network at work. New friends and contacts can be particularly helpful. For the unattached, romantic prospects are good and can make the year special.

The Monkey

Lively, enterprising and innovative, the Monkey certainly knows how to impress. He has wide interests, a good sense of fun and relates well to others. He also possesses a shrewd mind and often has a happy knack of turning events to his advantage.

However, despite his versatility and considerable gifts, he does have his weaknesses. He often lacks persistence, can get distracted easily and also places tremendous reliance upon his own judgement. While his belief in himself is a commendable asset, it would certainly be in his interests to be more mindful of the views of others. Also, while he likes to keep tabs on all that is going on around him, he can be evasive and secretive with regard to his own feelings and activities, and again a more forthcoming attitude would be to his advantage.

In his desire to succeed, the Monkey can also be tempted to cut corners or be crafty and he should recognize that such actions can rebound on him!

However, he is resourceful and his sheer strength of character will ensure that he has an interesting and varied life. If he can channel his considerable energies wisely and overcome his sometimes restless tendencies, his life can be crowned with success. And with his amiable personality, he will have many friends.

ADVICE FOR THE MONKEY'S YEAR AHEAD

General Prospects

The Monkey likes action and this year he will see plenty. Much is possible, but the Monkey does need to use his time well. With focus and determination, he can enjoy some deserved success. However, while the aspects are on his side, he does need to be careful not to overreach himself or push his good fortune too far.

Career Prospects

The Monkey can make important headway this year and by being prepared to adapt and extend his skills may be able to take on a new role and/or secure promotion. Importantly, what he achieves now can do a lot to strengthen his future prospects.

Finance

The Monkey's finances can improve this year, but with good travel possibilities, some expensive home plans and other commitments, he does need to manage his budget carefully. Making early provision for specific requirements will help.

Relations with Others

The Monkey will be kept busy and will enjoy the year's social occasions and make the most of his chances to meet others. New and existing friends can both be very helpful. There will also be good times domestically, but with an often busy lifestyle, the Monkey does need to strike a sensible balance in his many activities and preserve quality time for his loved ones, personal interests and himself. A good lifestyle balance is important in this busy but rewarding year.

The Rooster

With his considerable bearing and incisive and resolute manner, the Rooster cuts an impressive figure. He has a sharp mind, is well informed on many matters and expresses himself clearly and convincingly. He is meticulous and efficient in his undertakings and commands a great deal of respect. He also has a genuine and caring interest in others.

The Rooster has much in his favour, but there are some aspects of his character that can tell against him. He can be candid in his views and over-zealous in his actions, and sometimes he can say or do things he later regrets. His high standards also make him fussy, even pedantic, and he can get diverted into relatively minor matters when in truth he could be occupying his time more profitably. This is something all Roosters would do well to watch. Also, while the Rooster is a great planner, he can sometimes be unrealistic in his expectations. In making plans – indeed, in most of his activities – he would do well to consult others. He would benefit greatly from their input.

The Rooster has many talents as well as commendable drive and commitment, but to make the most of himself he does need to channel his energies wisely and watch his candid and sometimes volatile nature. With care, however, he can make a success of his life, and with his wide interests and outgoing personality, he will enjoy the friendship and respect of many.

ADVICE FOR THE ROOSTER'S YEAR AHEAD

General Prospects

Horse years are geared for action and hold great possibilities for the Rooster. Good progress can be made, although the Rooster does need to keep alert to potential problems and not be distracted by unhelpful matters. With focus, discipline *and* awareness, he can make this rewarding year even more successful.

Career Prospects

The Rooster will have some excellent opportunities to move his career forward and add considerably to his capabilities and skills. However, he may be troubled by jealousy, office politics or the awkward attitude of another person. If so, it will be a case of focusing on his objectives and doing his best. This year will have its challenges, but some important opportunities too.

Finance

With some ambitious home plans and a variety of commitments, the Rooster will need to be disciplined and control his budget carefully.

Relations with Others

This will be a very active year and there will be some particularly good times, with the Rooster enjoying great personal and family moments, but there will also be times of anxiety and pressure. If concerned by a particular matter, the Rooster does need to consult others, draw on their support and keep things in perspective. It is also important that he keeps his lifestyle in balance, preserves quality time for his loved ones and gives himself the chance to relax and enjoy his interests.

The Dog

Loyal, dependable and with a good understanding of human nature, the Dog is well placed to win respect and admiration. He is a no-nonsense sort of person and hates any sort of hypocrisy and falsehood. With the

Dog you know where you stand and, given his direct manner, where he stands on any issue. He also has a strong humanitarian nature and often champions good causes.

The Dog has many fine attributes, although there are certain traits that can prevent him from either enjoying or making the most of his life. He is a great worrier and can get anxious over all manner of things. Although it may not always be easy, he should try to rid himself of the 'worry habit'. Whenever he is tense or concerned, he should be prepared to speak to others rather than shoulder his worries all by himself. In some cases, they could even be of his own making! Also, he has a tendency to look on the pessimistic side and he would certainly be helped if he were to view his undertakings more optimistically. He does, after all, possess many skills and should have faith in his abilities. Another weakness is his tendency to be stubborn over certain issues. If he is not careful, at times this could undermine his position.

If the Dog can reduce the pessimistic side of his nature, he will not only enjoy life more but also find he is achieving more. He possesses a truly admirable character and his loyalty, reliability and sincerity are appreciated by all he meets. In his life he will do much good and befriend many people – and he owes it to himself to enjoy life too. Sometimes it might help him to recall the words of another Dog, Sir Winston Churchill: 'When I look back on all these worries, I remember the story of the old man who said on his deathbed that he had had a lot of trouble in his life, most of which never happened.'

ADVICE FOR THE DOG'S YEAR AHEAD

General Prospects

The Horse year encourages action and the Dog will find himself involved in a great many activities. With good opportunities emerging, he will have the chance to reap the benefits of his previous efforts and make good progress. Dogs who start the year dissatisfied will find that making an extra effort can bring a real improvement to their situation.

Career Prospects

With events happening quickly, some interesting opportunities can arise for the Dog. Sometimes considerable adjustment will be required, but the year encourages progress. The Dog can help his prospects by networking and raising his profile – his qualities will often be recognized and rewarded this year.

Finance

The Dog's efforts at work can lead to an increase in income and an improvement in his overall situation. However, he does need to budget ahead for more expensive plans. Carrying out a review of his financial situation could be helpful. He should also look after his personal possessions – a loss could be upsetting. With the year encouraging travel, if possible he should make provision for a holiday.

Relations with Others

Caring and understanding, the Dog will find himself much in demand and will do a lot to assist those close to him. However, he does need to be more forthcoming about his own activities and draw on the advice and knowledge of those around him. Their input and support can make a real difference this year. He should also make the most of his social opportunities – both existing contacts and new connections can be helpful. Romantic prospects are excellent.

The Pig

Genial, sincere and trusting, the Pig gets on well with most people. He has a kind and caring nature, a dislike of discord and often a good sense of humour. In addition, he has a fondness for socializing and enjoying the good life!

The Pig possesses a shrewd mind, is particularly adept at dealing with business and financial matters and has a robust and resilient nature. Although not all his plans may work out as he would like, he is tenacious and will often rise up and succeed after experiencing setbacks and difficulties. In his often active and varied life he can accomplish a great deal, although there are certain aspects of his character that can tell against him. If he can modify these or keep them in check then his life will certainly be easier and possibly even more successful.

In his activities the Pig can sometimes over-commit himself and while he does not want to disappoint, he would certainly be helped if he were to set about his activities in an organized and systematic manner and give himself priorities at busy times. He should also not allow others to take advantage of his good nature and it would be in his interests to be more discerning. There will have been times when he has been gullible and naïve; fortunately, though, he quickly learns from his mistakes. However, he possesses a stubborn streak and if new situations do not fit in with his line of thinking, he can be inflexible. Such an attitude may not always be to his advantage.

The Pig is a great pleasure-seeker and while he should enjoy the fruits of his labours, he can sometimes be self-indulgent and extravagant. This is also something he would do well to watch.

However, though the Pig may possess some faults, those who come into contact with him are invariably impressed by his integrity, amiable manner and intelligence. If he uses his talents wisely, his life can be crowned with considerable achievement and he will also be loved and respected by many.

ADVICE FOR THE PIG'S YEAR AHEAD

General Prospects

The Pig will respond well to the vibrancy and dynamism of the Horse year and be keen to make headway. If he puts in the effort he can be well rewarded and can also benefit from some unexpected opportunities. By keeping active and alert, he can enjoy much good fortune this year.

Career Prospects

The Pig is determined, enterprising and hard-working, and these qualities will stand him in excellent stead this year. By seizing his opportunities, he can advance his existing career or be successful in taking on something new. Experience and skills gained now can strengthen both his current situation and his future prospects.

Finance

Many Pigs can improve their income this year and some may also find personal interests helping to supplement their means. The enterprising can certainly do well this year, but the Pig *must* be disciplined in his spending and budget carefully. He also needs to be thorough in checking the terms of any new agreements he may enter into.

Relations with Others

The Pig's home and social life can be a source of great happiness this year and romantic prospects are also good. Others will respond well to the Pig's outgoing yet caring manner. By sharing his thoughts and seeking support for his plans and projects, he can fare very well this year.

A Closing Thought

I hope that having read *Your Chinese Horoscope 2014* you have found it of value and interest.

A great deal is set to happen in 2014 and if you have faith in your capabilities and work steadfastly towards your aims, your actions *will* make a difference.

Within you are the riches of your tomorrow. I wish you well and all good fortune.

Neil Somerville